'By far the best work on the EU's "rule of law crisis". Theuns puts the focus where it should be, on how to restore democracy rather than just on how to punish legal violations.'

— Kim Lane Scheppele, Laurance S. Rockefeller Professor of Sociology and International Affairs, Princeton University

'The cancer of far-right nationalism is destroying Europe. Theuns deliver a bracing diagnosis—current EU policies have not only failed to stop democratic decay but have allowed it to metastasize. His course of treatment is bold and bitter, but indispensable for the survival of democracy in Europe.'

— Paul Magnette, President of the Socialist Party, Belgium

'Theuns strikes a nerve when he qualifies the European institutions' approach to democracy as depoliticised, technocratic and legalistic. No quick fixes, but provoking food for thought for all who seek an effective approach to stop democratic backsliding in the EU.'

— Judith Sargentini, Alderman of the city of Gouda, and former member of the European Parliament (2009–2019)

'The erosion of democratic standards is a European drama. This important book distils key lessons from the decade-long struggle against autocratization in Hungary and Poland and lays out an ambitious programme for what the EU could and should do now. Theuns exposes the difficulties of tackling democratic backsliding and the EU's own complicity in the rule of law crisis. His point is not to find excuses but to outline more effective tools to contain autocra-tization and protect democracy in Europe.'

— László Andor, Secretary General, Foundation for European Progressive Studies, and former EU Commissioner for Employment, Social Affairs and Inclusion (2010–2014)

'Theuns makes a powerful case that the EU's timid, legalistic and depoliticised response to autocratic populism has allowed anti-democratic governments to become dangerously entrenched. He shows this has gravely weakened the European project and urges an explicitly political fight against autocrats.'

— Matt Steinglass, Europe correspondent, *The Economist*

'In the burgeoning literature on the role of the EU in policing democracy in its member states, Theuns' book stands out as one of the most valuable additions, for its impeccable methodology, breadth and critical-reflective analysis. No one who cares about democracy in Europe—and who does not?—can ignore this formidable work.'

— Wojciech Sadurski, Challis Professor of Jurisprudence, University of Sydney, and author of *Poland's Constitutional Breakdown*

'An utterly persuasive and highly original demonstration of the EU's often incoherent and contradictory responses to democratic backsliding. A lesson in applied democratic theory and immanent critique.'

— Colin Hay, Professor of Political Sciences, Sciences Po Paris

'No country should ever be expelled from the European Union, in my view, but Tom Theuns advances this controversial position with erudition and verve that make *Protecting Democracy in Europe* indispensable.'

— Stefan Auer, Professor of European Studies, University of Hong Kong, and author of *European Disunion*

'For all those concerned with the dangers of democratic back-sliding in Europe, Tom Theuns' book comes as a major contribution on the issue. It offers deep insights into the EU's failures to address member states' authoritarian drift. It also provides innovative ideas of potential solutions by using practice-dependent political theorizing to illuminate not only what the EU has done but also what it ought to do.'

— Vivien A. Schmidt, Jean Monnet Professor of European Integration, Professor Emerita, Boston University

'A bold and yet subtle addition to the literature on the question how the EU should react to Member States moving in an autocratic direction. The careful analysis of a possible expulsion mechanism is particularly welcome.'

— Jan-Werner Müller, Roger Williams Straus Professor of Social Sciences, Princeton University, and author of *What is Populism?*

'In *Protecting Democracy in Europe*, Theuns looks at how the EU can tackle democratic backslid-ing in its member states. Using political theory and real-world examples, he explores current challenges and calls for reforms to defend democracy in this pivotal moment for Europe.'

— Elena Sánchez Nicolás, Managing Editor, *EUobserver*

PROTECTING DEMOCRACY IN EUROPE

TOM THEUNS

Protecting Democracy in Europe

Pluralism, Autocracy and the Future of the EU

Oxford University Press is a department of the
University of Oxford. It furthers the University's objective
of excellence in research, scholarship, and education
by publishing worldwide.

Oxford   New York
Auckland   Cape Town   Dar es Salaam   Hong Kong   Karachi
Kuala Lumpur   Madrid   Melbourne   Mexico City   Nairobi
New Delhi   Shanghai   Taipei   Toronto

With offices in
Argentina   Austria   Brazil   Chile   Czech Republic   France   Greece
Guatemala   Hungary   Italy   Japan   Poland   Portugal   Singapore
South Korea   Switzerland   Thailand   Turkey   Ukraine   Vietnam

Oxford is a registered trade mark of Oxford University Press
in the UK and certain other countries.

Published in the United States of America by
Oxford University Press
198 Madison Avenue, New York, NY 10016

Copyright © Tom Theuns 2025

All rights reserved. No part of this publication may be reproduced,
stored in a retrieval system, or transmitted, in any form or by any means,
without the prior permission in writing of Oxford University Press,
or as expressly permitted by law, by license, or under terms agreed with
the appropriate reproduction rights organization. Inquiries concerning
reproduction outside the scope of the above should be sent to the
Rights Department, Oxford University Press, at the address above.

You must not circulate this work in any other form
and you must impose this same condition on any acquirer.

Library of Congress Cataloging-in-Publication Data is available
Tom Theuns.
Protecting Democracy in Europe: Pluralism, Autocracy
and theFuture of the EU.
ISBN: 9780197809358

Printed in the United Kingdom on acid-free paper
by Bell and Bain Ltd, Glasgow

CONTENTS

Acknowledgements ix

PART ONE

1. Introduction 3
2. Membership Fatalism and Depoliticization in EU Democracy Protection 19
3. 'Democracy without Politics': Unpacking Commission Speeches 45
4. An Immanent Critique of EU Tools Against Democratic Backsliding 65

PART TWO

Introduction to Part Two: Looking Forward—Protecting Pluralist Democracy 95
5. Correcting EU Complicity in Democratic Backsliding 101
6. Containing Autocracy in the EU 127
7. Cultivating Pluralist Democracy in Europe 151
8. *Quo Vadis?* Democracy Protection or Dissociation 179

Notes 199
Bibliography 223
Index 247

ACKNOWLEDGEMENTS

I am grateful to many people who have contributed in different ways to helping this book come about. People have been incredibly generous with me over the years, offering their most valuable commodity—focused time—to help me along the way. For their input and help with this project, I specifically want to acknowledge and thank the following people: Alexandre Afonso, Stefan Auer, Uğur Aytaç, Gabriele Badano, Christopher Bickerton, Jelena Belic, Richard Bellamy, Angela Bourne, Quinlan Bowman, Lydie Cabane, Ben Crum, Dimitrios Efthymiou, Franca Feisel, Afke Groen, Christophe Hillion, Adam Holesch, Adeel Hussain, Maurits de Jongh, Sandra Kröger, Adriaan Kroon, Matthew Longo, Tim Meijers, Glyn Morgan, Martijn Mos, Attila Mráz, Alasia Nuti, Gilles Pittoors, Rebecca Ploof, Karolina Pomorska, Janosch Prinz, Miriam Ronzoni, Orsolya Salát, Nicole Scicluna, Antoinette Scherz, Daniel Thomas, Lydia Tiede, Christina Toenshoff, Tiziana Torresi, Martijn van den Brink, Frank Vandenbroucke, Claire Vergerio, Amy Verdun, Wouter Wolfs, Fabio Wolkenstein, Bertjan Wolthuis, Nikoleta Yordanova, and Miklós Zala.

To offset the solitary nature of a sole-authored book project, I have leaned strongly on the community around me. I want to thank my colleagues in Leiden for their support with all aspects of academic life and for giving me such a rich and inspiring intellectual home. To add to those already mentioned above, I want to thank Adina Akbik, Nicolas Blarel, Arjen Boin, Corinna Jenzsch, Petr Kopecký, Tom Louwerse, Katharina Natter, Michael Sampson, Jonah Schulhofer-Wohl, Maria Spirova, Joop van Holsteijn, Wouter

ACKNOWLEDGEMENTS

Veenendaal, Marco Verschoor, and Cynthia van Vonno. In a similar spirit, there are some who, by their support and their example at key moments, have left a deep imprint. Some of these debts stretch back quite some time. I want to acknowledge Andrew Sewell at Pearson United World College, whose bold choice to teach whole books of political philosophy to teenagers first sparked my passion for the discipline. Teun Dekker and Sophie Vanhoonacker at Maastricht University inspired me to really start working, which made it possible, despite a rocky start to my studies, for me to go to the University of Oxford for my MPhil. I am grateful to Douglas Dupree at Balliol College for looking out for me. Astrid von Busekist and Carlo Invernizzi Accetti in Paris took my work and ideas seriously from the start. Justine Lacroix in Brussels stuck with my project despite changing circumstances. Bert van den Brink and Barbara Oomen at University College Roosevelt entrusted me with space and freedom when I needed both. I am also very grateful to Sciences Po's Centre d'études européennes et de politique comparée, which has accepted me as associate researcher for some years now. I owe special thanks to Colin Hay, who guided the HDR thesis that formed the basis of this book.

Over the years I have been working on this project, some people have been especially important to it taking shape. First, I would like to list and thank my co-authors on various writings on this topic: Jan Pieter Beetz, Merijn Chamon, Josette Daemen, Jakub Jaraczewski, Alvaro Oleart, Andrei Poama, and Samira Rafaela. There is nothing like writing together for enriching and challenging the thinking process—except perhaps having one's work taken seriously enough to warrant extended critical response. For that I want to particularly thank Tore Vincents Olsen and Antoinette Scherz. One of the pleasures of working on this book has been my ongoing collaboration with Natasha Wunsch, who has written alongside me from the start. Her insight and encouragement have been invaluable. For excellent research assistance in the final stretch of the project I want to thank Mateo Cohen and Natália Kubalová. Finally, I cannot overstate how much I owe to my partnership in all things with Alice Dejean de la Bâtie, whose innumerable qualities include sniffing out weak argumentation from across the living room.

ACKNOWLEDGEMENTS

Perhaps inspired by my three children, I increasingly 'throw mud at the wall and see what sticks' in my approach to trying out new ideas. When it is not one of my patient friends and colleagues listed above, the 'wall' is usually unsuspecting audiences in academic workshops and seminars. For comments and discussion, I would like to thank the participants of the workshop 'Normative and Conceptual Perspectives on Democratic Resilience' at the New Europe College in Bucharest; the ENROL workshop 'Theoretical Perspectives on Democratic Backsliding in the EU' at the Arena Centre in Oslo; the workshop 'Power and Counterpower in Democracy: Multidisciplinary Perspectives' at Leiden University; the OZSW workshop 'New Directions in Democratic Theory' in Utrecht; the populism seminar convened by Annika Werner, Andrej Zaslove, Robert Huber, and Maurits Meijers; the ECPR online seminar in political theory; the ECPR joint sessions workshop on militant democracy organized by Angela Bourne and Bastiaan Rijpkema; the 'Global Justice and Populism' workshop at the European University Institute in Florence; the ECPR online seminar on the European Union convened by Jonathan Zeitlin and Nathalie Brack; and the workshop 'Justice and Beliefs about Justice: Democracy, Stability and Reflective Equilibrium' at the Central European University. I have also thrown plenty of mud at walls at larger academic conferences, including conferences organized by the ECPR Standing Group on the European Union, the Council for European Studies and UACES. A final way my scholarship sometimes resembles the behaviour of my young children is in my stubbornness. In many instances in this book, I have stuck to an argument stubbornly, in the face of firm disagreement from peers and friends, many of whom are listed above.

Since I started researching this topic in 2018, I have published several journal articles which I draw on and build on throughout this book. They are listed below. Upon inquiry, I did not need permission to borrow from parts of them as they were all published open access either via agreements my university has with the publishers or in journals fully committed to open access—another reason why this publishing model is better than the paywall subscription system for journal articles. The editors and publishers of the below journals were

ACKNOWLEDGEMENTS

nevertheless all very helpful in figuring out these formalities, for which they have my thanks.

- Oleart, A., & Theuns, T. (2023). '"Democracy without politics" in the European Commission's response to democratic backsliding: From technocratic legalism to democratic pluralism'. *JCMS: Journal of Common Market Studies*, 61(4), 882–99.
- Theuns, T. (2020). 'Containing populism at the cost of democracy? Political vs. economic responses to democratic backsliding in the EU'. *Global Justice: Theory Practice Rhetoric*, 12(02), 141–60.
- Theuns, T. (2021). 'Pluralist democracy and non-ideal democratic legitimacy: Against functional and global solutions to the boundary problem in democratic theory'. *Democratic Theory*, 8(1), 23–49.
- Theuns, T. (2022). 'The need for an EU expulsion mechanism: Democratic backsliding and the failure of Article 7'. *Res Publica*, 28(4), 693–713.
- Theuns, T. (2024). 'Is the European Union a militant democracy? Democratic backsliding and EU disintegration'. *Global Constitutionalism*, 13(1), 104–25.

Finally, I would like to thank the staff at Hurst. I am particularly grateful to Michael Dwyer for his faith in the project, Mei Jayne Yew, my main editor, Daisy Leitch and her production team, and Kathleen May and her sales, marketing and publicity team.

The research that led to this book was financially supported by the Dutch Research Council (NWO) under Grant VI.Veni.201R.061, the Gratama Foundation, and the Institute for Political Science at Leiden University. I gratefully acknowledge their support.

PART ONE

1

INTRODUCTION

Until we are all free, we are none of us free.

Emma Lazarus, *An Epistle to the Hebrews*

The future of Europe as a community of democratic states is deeply uncertain. The idea that the European Union pursues the 'ever closer' integration of countries seeking peaceful, democratic cooperation beyond the paradigm of national competition has been battered by a series of bruising crises and now by war. In the area of democratic government—the subject of this book—there has been a marked deterioration. While European Union (EU) member states overall are still significantly more democratic than the global average, the trend is downward, and has been for some time. Indeed, Poland and Hungary have the dubious title of being world leaders in democratic decline in recent years, though the 2023 general elections in Poland give hope of democratic recovery there (Nord et al. 2024). And while Poland and Hungary have been the foremost examples of democratic regression, serious concerns about democratic health have been raised about many other EU member states in recent years.[1] In the Netherlands, where I live and work, the far-right Freedom Party, whose leader Geert Wilders has derided the Dutch Parliament as 'fake', won the 2023 general election and has formed a coalition government with right-wing partners.[2]

PROTECTING DEMOCRACY IN EUROPE

This book examines how, in this brave new world, actors in the European Union committed to democracy can protect democratic governance in EU member states. My goals are threefold. First, I show how European institutions have a depoliticized and even fatalistic attitude to democratic decline at the European level, something that I argue has its roots in political developments in the 1990s. I show how, particularly in the first decade of the recent episode of democratic erosion in Europe starting from around 2010, the European Commission has worked with a technocratic and legalistic understanding of democracy that has been all too easy for would-be autocrats to manipulate. Second, I examine recent and current policy and law that aim to respond to democratic backsliding in the EU, using tools of political theory.[3] In light of the failure of these policies, academics have been asking why they have been ineffective in preventing autocratization in EU member states. As a political theorist though, I am interested in a largely overlooked element—the coherence of existing legal tools with EU fundamental values. Studying the normative coherence of these tools reveals that key policies, such as the sanction mechanism in Article 7 of the Treaty on European Union (TEU), themselves undermine democratic values. Third, I review and assess proposals for reforms to the EU's response to democratic backsliding, setting out a three-pronged approach to protecting democratic pluralism that remains faithful to the values it seeks to protect. This strategy need not comprise only new tools—it is a mistake to seek to continually reinvent the wheel with new policy, wasting precious time (Kelemen 2023). While in some specific domains, new responses may be desirable, it is more urgent to use the possibilities of the existing legal and political framework fully to respond to democratic regression more decisively.

Why the European Union should care about member state democratic backsliding

For a long time, there was a deep reticence amongst EU actors to 'interfere' in the domestic politics of member states. The traditional view was that candidate countries wanting to join the EU could be transformed into consolidated democracies with open, robust econo-

INTRODUCTION

mies where human rights and minority rights were respected. The draw of membership was enough to motivate these transformations, and the wealth of the single market enough to finance them. There was little reflection on the eventuality that an EU member state could also relapse on these criteria. In hindsight, this was deeply naïve. Over the past decade and a half, some member states have had pervasive problems with corruption, upholding media and academic freedom, and judicial independence, alongside rising tensions regarding how to accommodate and integrate the most vulnerable minorities—ethnic minorities, sexual minorities, refugees, and migrants. In several cases, these problems have festered, giving rise to a harder, more populistic politics. Where such populists have gained power, they have frequently harnessed these divisions to try to cement their political control at great costs to democratic norms. It is clear that uniform progress on the standards stipulated as minima by the European treaties and the Copenhagen criteria has eluded both newer and older EU member states.

In spite of these developments, and with limited exceptions (notably in the activities of some Members of the European Parliament), the reticence against 'interfering' in domestic politics continues to shape the agendas and activities of many EU institutions facing the challenge of democratic backsliding (cf. Schlipphak and Treib 2017). Yet, this book makes the case that EU actors and pro-democratic member states have strong normative and political reasons to care about democratic backsliding in each member state. To date, failing to act decisively to protect democracy in Europe in the face of quite radical constitutional transformations in some member states has been a costly mistake. Whereas targeted, resolute action might have sufficed to deter would-be autocrats early on, autocratic politics has now become entrenched—at least in Hungary. The nature of democratic backsliding is that it becomes increasingly difficult over time for even well-organized and united opposition parties to mount an effective political challenge to incumbents. As such, restraint by EU actors and institutions to respond robustly early on means that responses must now be far more costly to be effective. The likely effect of earlier restraint is heavy collateral injustices to ordinary citizens caught in the crossfire later on.

Appeasing budding autocrats early on emboldens them, and gives them time to consolidate their position and continue to dismantle democratic checks and balances to their power. Only when pro-democratic actors in Europe take an explicitly partisan position in defence of democracy do their commitment to EU fundamental values go beyond empty rhetoric.[4] Lofty expressions of ideals are not enough when those ideals are dragged through the mud. Nor are timid expressions of concern. Allowing a member state to trash democracy and the rule of law without a strong response signals that commitment to these fundamental values is only skin deep. If a blind eye can be turned to electoral dirty tricks and slandering the opposition, perhaps ballot stuffing and the abusive criminal prosecution of critical voices will also be tolerated? Signalling weak commitment to democratic values also encourages would-be autocrats elsewhere. The unprovoked full-scale invasion of Ukraine by Russia in February 2022 again raised the stakes for marking the EU's commitment to democratic politics.

The tacit commitment of many EU political actors to the idea that European politics should rise above domestic pro-democratic partisanship is also deeply asymmetric. Authoritarian actors have not shown similar reserve when attempting to unite the anti-democratic European far-right. The cooperation of Poland's Law and Justice Party (Prawo i Sprawiedliwość, PiS) and Hungary's Fidesz was a powerful tool to resist EU sanctions for democratic backsliding while PiS was in power (Holesch and Kyriazi 2022). At the time of writing, it remains unclear to what extent other countries led by populists (e.g. Italy or Slovakia) will take over from Poland in sheltering Hungary from sanctions for undermining democracy and the rule of law. And while formal cooperation with other populist radical right (PRR) parties in European institutions remains limited (Chiru and Wunsch 2021), programmatic and discursive coherence is growing (Falkner and Plattner 2020; Bélanger and Wunsch 2022) and governments led by such parties have been quick to lend symbolic support for PRR opposition parties in other member states.[5] For example, in 2022, Polish and Hungarian government officials campaigned alongside the radical right-wing Vox party at a two-day summit in Madrid; in 2021, they joined far-right challengers from fourteen other member states

INTRODUCTION

at a conference in Rome in July; later that year, PiS hosted Vox's Santiago Abascal, Rassemblement National's Marine Le Pen and other European far-right leaders in Warsaw. Clearly, the principal agents of democratic backsliding in the EU do not themselves feel bound to an injunction against interfering in the domestic politics of other member states. If authoritarian diffusion is a project of Europe's antidemocratic political leadership, then protecting democracy in Europe through pro-democratic partisanship is needed to counterbalance their efforts.

Irrespective of the risks of autocratic politics spreading to other EU member states and institutions, there are two other key reasons why constraining democratic backsliding ought to be a priority for all pro-democratic actors in Europe. First, European legal and political integration means that if one member state becomes less democratic, the democratic legitimacy of all EU law and policy is tainted (Theuns 2022). All EU citizens are subject to EU law and policy. If these are (co-)decided by autocratic leaders, not only their citizens' lives but the lives of all EU citizens are affected. This idea can also be expressed through the Rousseauian notion that we are only free if we live under laws that we have an equal stake in creating. Where (some of) the laws we are subject to are co-decided by autocrats, the civic and political freedom of all EU citizens is undermined. Supranational legal and political integration with autocratic states is therefore incompatible with domestic democratic government. A consequence of this is that the frame of 'interfering' in the domestic politics of another EU member state is often misplaced. When pro-democratic member EU states act in a partisan manner to protect democracy in the EU, they also act to protect the democratic character of their own polity.

Second, EU actors have a share in the blame for democratic regression in member states, for instance by indirectly or directly funding autocratic actors or protecting them in the European Parliament (Bárd and Kochenov 2021; Kelemen 2020; Wolkenstein 2020, 2021). Arguably, the process of convergence with the EU *aquis communautaire* during the accession period was too fast, the shocks of economic liberalization too brusque, and the subsequent benefits of European integration too unequally distributed (Andor 2019; Raik 2004). Once democratic backsliding set in, the governments of

Poland and Hungary continued to enjoy net EU subsidies amounting to hundreds of millions of euros. The ability of the PiS and Fidesz governments to funnel such funds towards those supporting their activities—and even more broadly the contribution of such funds to the macroeconomic stability of Poland and Hungary—had a direct impact on the popularity of PiS and Fidesz over the past decade. While there was some progress towards budget conditionality since around 2022, the big picture is that the EU has continued to provide massive funding and subsidies to these countries in the face of widespread violations of democracy and the rule of law, and despite the existence of legal tools to cut the funds. In this sense, the EU is complicit in autocratic politics and has a responsibility to try to repair the damage that has been done.

Examples of direct complicity in democratic decay by nature concern the intricacies and specificities of particular cases, such as the 2019 decision by the Polish Prosecutor's office absolving Solidarna Polska (United Poland), a far-right Polish party led by former Polish Minister of Justice Zbigniew Ziobro, of breaking European Parliament funding rules (Jałoszewski and Szczygieł 2020), or the allegations Fidesz politicians in Hungary illegally used the disbursement of EU subsidies in political campaigning in the runup to the 2022 Hungarian general election (Tangentopoli 2022). But such details, while important, can obscure more widespread complicity. Transnational EU complicity with backsliding should be understood more broadly (Wolkenstein 2020), including not only blameworthy action, but also, crucially, omission. This suggests that EU actors are complicit at a much more massive scale than a focus on the particularities of cases of direct complicity suggest. And, as complicitous actors co-responsible for democratic erosion in EU member states, these actors should make reparations to those harmed by backsliding.

In sum, pro-democratic actors in the EU should be deeply concerned about democratic backsliding in EU member states. The nature of democratic backsliding means that the more member states deteriorate in their democratic governance, the more difficult it is for 'ordinary' domestic electoral competition to reverse these trends. Reticence about interfering in the domestic political affairs of EU member states is fanciful. Giving autocrats and would-be autocrats such protection without ensuring their own non-interference empowers these actors and their anti-democratic politics. Furthermore, given the supranational integration of EU law and policy, the democratic character of each and every member state is affected by the democratic character of each other member state. Democratic backsliding in one or more member states of the EU is thus an existential threat to the continued democratic character of the EU as a whole. And beyond this perspective of democratic self-defence, the EU now has a moral duty to rectify its own complicity in democratic backsliding and try to repair those harmed by it.

Methodology: Practice-dependence versus ideal theory

This book uses mostly practice-dependent political theory methodologies to study both the failures of EU responses to democratic backsliding in EU member states and to prescribe more normatively coherent alternatives. Practice dependence here means that evaluative standards are drawn from political practice rather than from universal presuppositions about what is valuable in politics (Sangiovanni 2007, 2015; cf. Erman and Möller 2015). The alternative methodological orientation in political theory is sometimes referred to as 'ideal theory' (Zala et al. 2020). The term ideal theory is used in diverse and sometimes contradictory ways, but the most pertinent contrast here is that ideal theory derives and applies normative standards externally. In contrast, practice-dependent methods lend themselves to this study because they can be more ecumenical; that is, one can support the evaluative and prescriptive conclusions of the practice-dependent arguments I make from a wide range of different philosophical and ideological positions. This makes such practice-dependent methodologies in political theory especially suitable for the study of democracy, given democracy's emphasis on the pluralist nature of the political sphere and therefore its reliance on 'incompletely theorized agreements' (Sunstein 1995; Theuns 2021).

Ideal theory would be a weaker methodological choice for the aims of this book for three further reasons: the ideal-theoretical commitments to compliance, 'end-state' analysis, and normative universalism. First, in a political arena characterized by noncompliance, ideal theory (which works out what political rights and duties are on the idealized assumption that each actor will comply) is ill equipped to figure out what second- or third-best choices need to be made in the context of real-world politics. Take democratic backsliding in Poland for instance. An ideal-theoretical approach, assuming compliance with the demands of justice and legitimacy, might argue that responsibility for resolving the rule of law crisis in Poland lies with the PiS Party—after all, it was the PiS-led government that caused this injustice (for example, by capturing the Polish Constitutional Tribunal and illicitly removing judges), so they ought to be the ones to try to remedy it. Non-ideal-theoretical approaches can take a more realistic line: PiS was unlikely to retreat from their project of dismantling rule of law checks while they were in power and will bear little practical responsibility now they are out of power. The urgent normative question is not what PiS ought to do now in an ideal world, but what European partners ought to do to support the opposition parties seeking to rebuild Polish democracy and the rule of law. Second, the ideal-theoretical focus on theorizing utopian 'end-states' (for instance, the question of what a perfectly democratic European Union would look like) seems cavalier in the context of the grossly unjust and illegitimate developments we see in some EU member states. Third, ideal theory is often cast in terms of universalist moral commitments. But such commitments come with controversial philosophical presuppositions. Non-ideal-theoretical approaches—including the practice-dependent methodologies I use—derive their normativity from actually existing political, legal and social practice instead of seeking agreement on (practice-independent) foundational moral claims (Sangiovanni 2007, 2015; cf. Erman and Möller 2015). To care about the conclusions of practice-dependent normative argumentation, one therefore only needs to care about those political, legal and social practices from which the normative standards are drawn.

Practice dependence is, properly speaking, not 'a methodology' of political theory as much as a methodological orientation—in other words, one can go about practice-dependent theory in various ways. Building on past methodological work (Theuns 2017, 2019, 2020, 2022; Poama and Theuns 2019), this book uses three specific practice-dependent methods: discourse analysis, the study of normative coherence, and tests of expressive (non-)contradiction. I use discourse analysis—generally a qualitative empirical method—in a way that combines philosophical and empirical analysis. The goal is to expose the tensions between the values professed in EU law and policy and the application of those laws and policies. In the first level of analysis, this facilitates an *internal* critique of EU law and policy, looking back at EU responses to democratic backsliding to date. One can ask, for example, how well the dialogue and monitoring mechanisms such as the Rule of Law Mechanism and the associated annual Rule of Law Reports live up to the standards of Article 10(3) of the TEU which stipulates that 'every citizen shall have the right to participate in the democratic life of the Union.' Or, to pre-empt the question I address in Chapter 3, how does the way European Commissioners conceptualize democracy shape and limit its responses to democratic backsliding in EU member states? Discourse analysis facilitates clarity over the content and meaning of a body of discourse and, in that regard, I focus mostly on EU law, policy and speeches by EU officials.

Whereas discourse analysis developed as a qualitative empirical method, the study of normative coherence and expressive (non-)contradiction are tools that originate in the discipline of political philosophy. I use these tools to uncover instances where EU law and policies fail to adequately express the EU's commitment to fundamental values. For EU law and policy responses to be normatively coherent, their goals and reasonably expected effects cannot be at cross-purposes. Normatively incoherent policy and law are not only a problem for political philosophers, but have concrete political consequences: if two policies pursued simultaneously by the same actors or institutions run at cross-purposes then they cannot both succeed on their own terms. Tests of expressive (non-)contradiction are similarly geared towards ascertaining whether a policy or law can undermine its own preconditions, but is focused on communicative or expressive aspects. To be expressively adequate in affirming specific political values (such as those listed in Article 2 TEU), EU policy and law geared towards protecting democracy in Europe must not involve sanctions that undermine the values that those policies and laws are intended to protect (Poama and Theuns 2019).

PROTECTING DEMOCRACY IN EUROPE

The organization of the book

This book is organized into two parts. The remainder of the first part (Chapters 2–4) analyses existing EU law and policy that has been developed and, to a more limited extent, used to respond to democratic backsliding in EU member states. I start with a historical perspective; we have to take seriously the EU's policy failures to avoid repeating past mistakes. What are the missed opportunities of pro-democratic actors to respond more effectively to democratic backsliding? In Chapter 2, I argue that there are two key flaws in the EU's handling of the democracy and rule of law crisis. The first flaw is a growing sense of membership fatalism—the idea that each member state has total and final sovereignty over their membership of the European Union despite repeated and deliberate violations of democratic standards. The second flaw is the depoliticization of responses to EU democratic backsliding—the idea that unanimity is a political prerequisite for robust action, and that the primary arena for responding to regressions on liberal democratic norms is the judicial one. I illustrate these two flaws through a study of the development of a sanctions mechanism in the 1990s, and the response to the inclusion of a far-right party in the Austrian government in 2000 (Sadurski 2009).

It is against this backdrop that we must understand the long delay of the European Commission to launch Article 7 TEU proceedings against Hungary. Path-dependency here is crucial. EU officials started on this path fearing that Article 7 proceedings against Poland and Hungary were doomed to fail given that the procedure requires, at a crucial step, unanimity of all EU member states besides the one under examination. But in the context of a culture of delay, crucial decisions were made that further stymied the possibility for effective action, such as the 2018 Council Legal Services opinion that responses to the violation of the EU fundamental values taken outside the framework of Article 7 fell outside of the competence of the European Commission (Council of the European Union 2018). The culture of delay has also taken the form of the proliferation of ever more complex and detailed mechanisms of dialogue and monitoring which, while seemingly innocuous, allow anti-democratic reforms to become entrenched.

INTRODUCTION

Where Chapter 2 analyses such missed opportunities in terms of failed policy, Chapter 3 focuses on the ideational aspects that help us understand why the Commission has been a reluctant actor in protecting democracy in the EU. I do this through a discourse and framing analysis of speeches by members of the European Commission. The aim is to grasp what the dominant conception of democracy has been in the Commission, especially in the crucial second decade of the twenty-first century, where trends towards democratic backsliding in EU member states have accelerated. This discourse and framing analysis reveals a fairly stable, impoverished conception of democracy that is overly technocratic, legalistic and depoliticized. And again, as was the case at the level of policy failures discussed in Chapter 2, I argue that this narrow legalistic conception was not a necessary constraint on Commission competence borne out by the treaties, but rather a self-imposed straightjacket. A richer, more political conception of democracy could have been used—and, crucially, *can* be used—by EU institutions seeking to protect democracy in Europe.

The final chapter of Part 1, Chapter 4, applies practice-dependent political theory methods to the study of the normative coherence of specific legal tools and policies that EU actors have at their disposal to respond to democratic backsliding. The ineffective Article 7 TEU mechanism, the Rule of Law Conditionality Regulation, a little known regulation that creates the possibility for sanctioning European political parties,[6] and the potential of using infringement actions under Articles 258–60 of the Treaty on the Functioning of the European Union (TFEU) to tackle the systemic degradation of democracy and the rule of law are tested on the standards of normative and expressive coherence. Article 7 suffers, I submit, from an incoherence in that the primary sanction it lays out—the disenfranchisement of a member state from voting in the Council of the European Union[7]—itself undermines the Article 2 TEU values of democracy and equality. EU Regulation 1141/2014, which governs the deregistration of EU political parties and foundations, suffers from the same paradoxical flaw: the penalties it prescribes contradict the values it aims to protect. On the other hand, the Rule of Law Conditionality Regulation and systemic infringement actions under Articles 258–60 TFEU stand on firmer ground, as they do not entail the same normative inconsistencies.

The second part of the book (Chapters 5–8) recommends an alternative path that EU responses could take to be more expressively and normatively coherent. These recommendations are organized initially into steps to correct policies that make EU actors complicit in backsliding (Chapter 5), to contain autocratic influences in EU policy and law-making (Chapter 6), and to cultivate pluralist democracy in EU member states (Chapter 7). Where such measures fail, Chapter 8 weighs the normative case for expelling frankly autocratic states from the EU.

A central difficulty of correcting policies that make EU actors complicit in democratic backsliding, such as those discussed in Chapter 4, is political. Votes of backsliding states are often needed for consensual decisions in the European Council and the Council of the European Union. As a result, legislative proposals and policies can be held 'hostage' by these actors. This was the case, for example, when Hungary and Poland successfully threatened to use their veto against the EU's Multiannual Financial Framework if significant concessions were not made on the Rule of Law Conditionality Regulation in 2020.[8] For this reason, correcting complicity may be most effective where European actors focus on tools that bypass voting in the European Council and the Council of the European Union. A good example of such an approach would be the use of infringement actions to address systemic deficiencies in the democratic character or EU member states (via Articles 258–60 TFEU), as has been suggested by legal scholars (Scheppele 2016; Kochenov 2015: 153; Scheppele, Kochenov and Grabowska-Moroz 2020: 3). However, this goes against the grain of the dominant European Commission culture and its conceptualization of democracy (explored in Chapter 3). Chapter 5 therefore calls on pro-democratic member states and other pro-democratic actors to step up their responses, for instance by taking direct action against backsliding states and by increasing discursive pressure against democratic and rule of law backsliding.

The challenge of containing autocratic influences in EU policy and law-making is taken up in Chapter 6. As will be discussed in Chapter 4, the core challenge for a normatively coherent approach is how to address the issue of containment without resorting to the sorts of anti-democratic action that are incompatible with democratic values

INTRODUCTION

like the Article 7 sanction and Regulation 1141/2014 (cf. Theuns 2023). While new containment mechanisms via treaty change can be considered as an exercise in ideal theory, such reforms are quite unrealistic at this point in time as they require unanimous adoption by member states; therefore, they are not in keeping with the non-ideal theoretic orientation of this book. Beyond economic containment through the use of financial conditionality, i.e. depriving authoritarian governments of EU funds (using tools covered in Chapter 4 and 5), non-ideal strategies of containment should therefore take two tracks. On the one hand, EU actors should maximally exclude authoritarian governments from European political procedures, insofar as that is compatible with EU law and coherent with fundamental values. Such 'hard legal containment' can be pursued, for example, by sidelining Hungary from leadership roles in the Council (Rafaela and Theuns 2023). Second, would-be autocrats should be deprived of political legitimacy and prestige by pro-democratic EU actors as much as possible. This can be done by starving them of political clout in the form of photo-ops, congratulations, hospitality and so forth. Sometimes, however, political containment will mean making difficult compromises to try to ensure divisions between different actors undermining democracy and the rule of law (Jaraczewski and Theuns 2022).

The last of the trio of chapters on coherent responses to democratic backsliding, Chapter 7, deals with cultivating pluralist democracy in EU member states. As I argue earlier in the book, responses to democratic backsliding have not only been generally characterized by deferral, dialogue and delay, but where they have been more substantive, they have mostly reflected a narrow, technocratic, legalistic, depoliticized understanding of democracy. This is normatively and politically impoverished. Chapter 7 further fleshes out the conception of pluralist democracy I first allude to in Chapter 3. Pluralist democracy focuses on a healthy public sphere and pluralist media/civil society landscape as vital and often overlooked elements of democratic governance. So, what are the constraints and possibilities for EU actors to cultivate pluralist democracy? In keeping with the call for pro-democratic partisanship I made in the opening of this introduction, this chapter makes the case for a much more involved and proactive approach to supporting pluralist civil society actors, pro-democratic opposition politicians, and media in EU member states showing deficiencies with regard to EU fundamental values. Such direct support can be quite plainly partisan, as long as it is tempered by the purpose of correcting democratic distortions.

The book ends with a radical reassessment of the stakes at play. While it is uncomfortable to contemplate, we must face up to the reality that several years of serious democratic backsliding in some EU member states has done damage that perhaps cannot be reversed. Even coordinated and coherent efforts to correct past policy failures, contain autocratic actors in the EU, and cultivate pluralist democracy in EU member states may fail. And more muscular intervention in the domestic affairs of a member state is proscribed given limits to EU political authority and legitimacy. Chapter 8 argues that dissociation with frankly autocratic members must therefore be the *ultima ratio* response to democratic backsliding.

Several proposals have been made in the literature for final expulsion mechanisms. Notably, Christophe Hillion (2020) has proposed that widespread violation of EU fundamental values *constitutes* notice to the European Council of the intention of the state in question to withdraw from the EU, as required by the withdrawal clause (Article 50 TEU). While I find this bold proposal a refreshing attempt to undermine a pervasive attitude of membership fatalism, the normative justification for this proposal is questionable from the perspective of democratic theory: if a backsliding member state government no longer adequately represents its citizens democratically then the condition of Article 50(1) TEU (that notification must take place in accordance with that state's constitutional principles) cannot be met. It would be more straightforward to propose that the European treaties are reformed to include an expulsion mechanism for violating fundamental values, such as the mechanism that exists in the Council of Europe (Article 9 of the Statute of the Council of Europe). But my commitment to non-ideal theory means I cannot rely on this track, given that backsliding states will never agree to treaty changes that would facilitate their expulsion. The proposal I develop in Chapter 8, then, is that an expulsion mechanism may take shape through the (threat of) the mass withdrawal of pro-democratic EU member states via a collective invocation of Article 50. For each member state com-

INTRODUCTION

mitted to democracy to withdraw from the current European Union and re-found a new Union without autocratic members. Such discussions may seem alien but, as the rest of this book endeavours to show, such is the price of protecting democracy in Europe.

2

MEMBERSHIP FATALISM AND DEPOLITICIZATION IN EU DEMOCRACY PROTECTION

All that is buried is not dead.

Olive Schreiner, *The Story of an African Farm*

Before we can grasp what is wrong with the current European response to democracy and rule of law backsliding in member states—let alone propose an alternative path to protecting democracy in Europe—we must first try to figure out how we came to be where we are. What are the critical junctures in recent European politics that have shaped the feeble and legalistic approach favoured by European Union (EU) institutions for over a decade? To grapple with this question, this chapter presents a sort of 'genealogy' of EU democracy protection since the early 1990s. The main argument I will make is that despite growing attention to values around the 'big bang' expansion of the EU, conflict over fundamental values steadily became depoliticized and membership came to be seen in an increasingly fatalistic manner.

First a note on method. The historical context for why democratic backsliding in the EU came to be seen through this depoliticized and fatalistic lens is complex. Neither the methodology I use here nor the purpose of my analysis are appropriate for trying to parse this history into necessary and sufficient causes. I am not, strictly speaking, trying to *explain* why EU actors have responded feebly to democratic backsliding in the 2010s and (to a lesser extent) the 2020s. For a start, I am not convinced that such a mechanistic reinterpretation of historical events is often convincing.[1] More importantly, the scope of this book and my training as a political theorist (rather than a historian) would make its attempt hubristic. Instead, I propose to evaluate recent developments in European integration that help us understand how these flaws emerged. In that way, rather than explaining past events, my goal in this chapter is to think through the past to understand the present.

My approach here shares some characteristics with the political theory method of genealogy.[2] Genealogical approaches to political ideas seek to understand concepts or ideologies in light of their evolution, to better grasp the tensions and contradictions of contemporary ways of understanding and interpreting the social and political world (Owen 2005; Bevir 2008). This contrasts to the approach which might be taken by a historian of ideas seeking to uncover truths about the meaning and understanding with which particular historical figures infused concepts and ideas. Similarly to the genealogical work by Michel Foucault, I am concerned here with examining the emergence and evolution of political-cum-ethical ideas. However, while Foucault's genealogies focused on questioning official histories by revealing alternative narratives, my purpose is slightly different; after all, there is no official narrative that tries to justify the inaction of EU actors in the face of democratic backsliding within it. In contrast, I reconstruct those errors and omissions that help us understand the logic of the current democratic malaise.

While backwards-facing (much like causal history), my purpose here is first and foremost pragmatic: to help us better understand the tensions and contingencies of the way that actors in the European political arena—from member states to EU institutions—have constructed their roles in responding to democratic backsliding. I will not try to isolate those necessary and sufficient conditions without which European institutions may have better responded to democratic backsliding in the past, but rather to look to the past to better understand where we are now with a view to exploring the possibilities for tearing up the singularly ineffective handbook currently in use for protecting democracy in Europe.

Specifically, I will assess two developments in European integration that are key, in my view, to understanding why, over the course of the past fifteen years or so, EU responses to democratic and rule of law backsliding have been weak. The first development is the emergence of sanctions mechanisms to respond to violations of democratic norms and fundamental rights. Prior to the mid-1990s, such mechanisms did not exist. But with the benefit of hindsight, we can see that their negotiation and eventual design proved more of a hindrance than a help to effective action. The second development is the early response to the rise of right-wing populism and Euroscepticism. In a specific key case, the inclusion of a far-right populist Eurosceptic party in the Austrian government coalition in 2000 led to a major ideational confrontation between a right-wing populism that sought to impose a sovereigntist vision and the traditional elite discourse of European integration. The resulting revisions to the sanctions mechanism and eventually the design of a procedure for withdrawing from the EU provided key opportunities to rethink membership norms in light of democratic backsliding. However, member states took care to protect their exclusive competence over the question of their own membership of the EU, naïvely supposing that states deviating from a common vision of European integration would voluntarily leave.

The conjunction of these two developments is somewhat disingenuous. Even while member states eventually rejected the possibility of expelling a member state from the EU for the violation of democratic norms and fundamental values, they created the possibility of withdrawing from the Union voluntarily. The argument on the supposed irreversibility of EU membership was taken to hold in the first but not in the second case. How can we make sense of this? In both cases, I think these choices reflect most fundamentally the unwillingness of member states to mutually surrender sovereignty over their membership. Yet, each defending their own sovereignty over EU membership had the correlative effect of impeding the collective control of member states on membership norms, including over core governance issues like democracy, the rule of law, and fundamental rights. While each state's own EU membership was thus protected from outside interference, this also resulted in a fatalistic attitude to the possibility of the eventual inclusion of member states violating EU fundamental values, something seen as largely outside of the control of EU institutions and other member state governments.

Through the development of a sanctions mechanism in the 1990s, and through the collective response to the reemergence of the populist radical right as a potentially governing force in the 2000s, we see two key flaws emerge. The first flaw is *membership fatalism*: the idea that each member state has total and final sovereignty over their membership of the EU in spite of governance failures and fundamental rights violations. The second flaw is the *depoliticization* of responses: the idea that the primary arena for responding to regressions on liberal democratic norms is the judicial one, and that unanimity is a political prerequisite for robust action.

As a result of membership fatalism, the procedures to contest and sanction the violation of fundamental values by member states became increasingly consensual, judicial or symbolic. And it is against the backdrop of this depoliticization of responses to extremism that we can most fruitfully interpret the culture of inaction and appeasement that has characterized the response of EU actors to the slow atrophying of some member state democracies. I also contend that membership fatalism and depoliticization help us to understand the proliferation of ever more complex mechanisms of dialogue and monitoring between EU institutions and recalcitrant member states. While seemingly innocuous, these mechanisms allow anti-democratic reforms to become entrenched.

The remainder of the chapter is structured as follows. First, I explore the early development of a 'value sanction' in the European treaties, which initially emerged in reaction to the planned expansion of the EU. The first challenge to this procedure came from an unexpected corner—Austria. The next section looks in detail at the context of that crisis and how ultimately it led to a weakening of EU sanctions for democracy and rule of law backsliding, and a fatalistic approach to membership that seemed to leave the question of inclusion in the European project entirely up to existing member states.[3] In the final section, I reflect on the concrete consequences of the emerging norms of depoliticization and membership fatalism: that

MEMBERSHIP FATALISM AND DEPOLITICIZATION

Hungary and Poland were able to erode democratic and rule of law standards for over a decade without robust sanctions, giving them the time to consolidate authoritarian reforms.

From a sanctions mechanism to membership fatalism

The first development in European integration that helps us understand the depoliticization of responses to political extremism in the domestic politics of EU member states and fatalism about EU membership is the emergence of a sanctions mechanism to enforce democratic norms and EU fundamental values. This started in the early 1990s and continued through to the Lisbon Treaty (2007/2009).[4] From the early 1990s, Western member states started to worry about the depth of the commitment to democracy and human rights in newer and prospective member states in South, Central and Eastern Europe. With this, democracy in Europe and the democratic character of the EU had become salient political issues. This helps us understand why a sanctions mechanism to try to enforce EU fundamental values was included in the Treaty of Amsterdam (Article F.1, 1997/1999). While exclusion from the Union was considered as a final sanction for violating fundamental values at this point, it was eventually rejected.

It has been noted that the inclusion of a sanctions mechanism for violations of fundamental values in the Treaty of Amsterdam (1997/1999) was motivated by concern with the 'big bang' expansion of the EU in 2004 (Sadurski 2009). While Austria, Finland and Sweden—the three states that joined the EU in 1995—were all considered stable liberal democracies, the fifth round of enlargement raised more question marks. Many of the countries joining in 2004 were post-communist states, and there was a concern that the commitment of political elites to democracy and human rights might only be skin-deep. Consequently, their accession negotiations took much longer,[5] and led to the inclusion of a mechanism for sanctioning violations of fundamental rights in the Treaty of Amsterdam.

There is of course something puzzling about the sudden urgency with assuring the protection of democratic values and fundamental rights in this period. Certainly, many of the applicant states in the 1990s had recent experience with authoritarian governments.

However, was that not also the case of many of the founding states and the first enlargements? The European Coal and Steel Community was proposed by Robert Schuman on 9 May 1950, five years and a day after the ultimate downfall of the Nazi regime in Germany. Yet it included West Germany and Italy amongst its first members. Greece joined the European Communities in 1981, seven years after the demise of the brutal regime of the Colonels. Spain and Portugal both joined in 1986, seven years after democratic elections marked the final end of the *Estado Novo* in Portugal and the Francoist dictatorship in Spain. If you compare that to the 2004 expansion, Hungary, Poland, the Czech Republic and Slovakia had to wait a full fifteen years after the breakup of the Soviet Union and the return to democracy to join the EU. The double standard is hard to miss.

Nevertheless, with the Eastern expansion of the EU on many minds, and with formal applications already submitted by Poland (on 8 April 1994) and Hungary (on 31 March 1994), the European Council formed a Reflection Group in June 1994 to prepare for the 1996 Intergovernmental Conference of the European Union, which would lead to the Treaty of Amsterdam (1997/1999).

However, it was not only the supposed fragility of prospective new members that put democracy on the agenda in the 1990s. The second development in EU integration that helps us to understand the emerging depoliticization of conflicts over fundamental values and membership fatalism was, somewhat paradoxically, the gradual questioning of the teleology and irreversibility of EU membership. This story is intertwined with the development of the sanctions mechanism since, besides the envisaged expansion of the EU, another reason that democracy and fundamental rights were hot-button issues in the early and mid-1990s was the growth of Euroscepticism in this period. This created real difficulties for the ratification of the Maastricht Treaty (1992/1993), which was initially rejected in a Danish referendum, and scraped through in the United Kingdom Parliament and in the French referendum (where the margin was just 2.1%—the so-called *petit oui*). Consequently, Denmark negotiated concessions to be released from certain obligations in the treaty to join a common European currency and to participate in European defence cooperation,[6] which were agreed in Edinburgh in December 1992. A second attempt to ratify Maastricht passed comfortably in Denmark in May 1993. The difficulties some member states had with the ratification of the Maastricht Treaty had led to spirited debates about the EU's democratic deficit (e.g. Boyce 1993; Featherstone 1994; Lodge 1994), and the logic of elite-driven European integration became increasingly contested.

There is something paradoxical in how these historical developments that increased the contestation over EU integration and membership—the end of a period marked by what is sometimes called the 'permissive consensus'—led to a fatalistic attitude to EU membership and the depoliticization of democratic standards. To see how this happened, we need to look more closely at some specific debates and projects for institutional reform. One of the ways contestation over the EU project was channelled was in the debate over the democratic character of EU institutions themselves. This was the so-called 'democratic deficit' or, in the words of Jacques Delors, the 'benign despotism' of elite-driven integration. The democratic deficit debate led in the treaties of Amsterdam (1997/1999) and Nice (2000/2001) to a far more expansive legislative role for the European Parliament and, overall, a moderate transfer of authority from the European Commission to the Parliament.

An even more fundamental renegotiation of membership norms came with the Constitutional Treaty, signed in 2004 but never ratified. Here, for the first time, the idea of the irreversibility of European integration was fundamentally questioned, which led to the inclusion of an article formalizing the possibility of withdrawal from the Union (European Convention 2003: Article I-60). At the same time, an expulsion mechanism was rejected by member states reluctant to give up control. This is pertinent, as an expulsion procedure could be considered a logical correlate to the 'voluntarist' understanding of Union membership captured by the withdrawal procedure (Athanassiou 2009). This link was explicitly raised by delegates negotiating the Constitutional Treaty at the so-called European Convention; the European Peoples' Party Convention Group proposed an amendment to I-59 which would have added the following clause:

> A Member State which continues a serious and persistent breach of the values mentioned in Article 2 for a period of 1 year following a

European Council decision in accordance with Article I-58 paragraph 2, or which has abused the right of withdrawal under the present Article, may be expelled from the Union by a decision of the European Council. Such expulsion shall require a qualified majority in the European Council and the consent of the European Parliament.

The representative of the Member State in question shall not participate in European Council discussions or decisions concerning it. It shall have a right to be heard prior to the final decision.[7]

In the written explanation of the proposal, the authors clarify that a withdrawal procedure, to which they remained in principle opposed, 'would have to be complemented by a *right of the Union to expel a Member State*' because 'a Union which every Member is free to leave must also be free to get rid of Members which violate persistently its values or which paralyse its functioning' (ibid., emphasis in original). The proposal failed, and sidelining exclusion from the Union as a possibility in the Constitutional Treaty resulted in a similar exclusion the Treaty of Lisbon, which copied the relevant elements almost verbatim (Article 50—the article which would become famous for its role in Brexit).

Conceiving membership as wholly a sovereign matter for each individual member state, rather than seeing supranational association as an open-ended and ultimately conditional agreement to integrate politically, has an element of utopianism but is also fatalistic. Taken from the utopian angle, this conception suggests EU membership rights enjoyed by member states are irreversible and, consequently, that EU citizenship is inalienable. What further accentuates the sovereigntist character of this way of looking at EU membership, and indeed exposes it to be fatalistic, is the rapid retreat of political responses to rising extremism at the turn of the century. We shall see that even the use of unilateral political responses and bilateral discursive pressure on domestic political developments that challenge liberal democratic norms was undermined, paving the way for the EU's typically technocratic and legalistic responses to democratic backsliding in the 2010s.

This period—the mid-1990s—was therefore one in which both the democratic character of the EU and the democratic commitment of its members were under scrutiny. On the one hand, this led to real changes to the Union's architecture, for instance with the European Parliament gaining veto rights over certain domains in the Maastricht Treaty (1992/1993) through the co-decision procedure. On the other hand, there were new concerns about securing baseline commitments to liberal democratic norms in what was perceived to be an increasingly heterogeneous union.

We can see this tension in the work of the Reflection Group, which concluded that the commitments to human rights and fundamental values in the Maastricht Treaty were inadequate. The Maastricht Treaty had declared that the member states' 'systems of government are founded on the principles of democracy' (Article F.1) and that 'the Union shall respect fundamental rights … as general principles of Community law' (Article F.2), but neither listed those rights nor considered sanctions were those rights to be violated. The Group argued that it was important to extend Article F.2 to include 'an obligation of the Member States to respect human rights and fundamental freedoms and add that noncompliance would prompt the Union to take suitable action' (European Council 1995: §32). The link was also explicitly made to enlargement, the Group's report noting that 'above all in the runup to enlargement, there is an urgent need to ensure full observance of fundamental rights' (ibid.: §33).

Regarding the proposed sanction for violating fundamental values, the Reflection Group' report noted that the majority of the Group's members supported sanctions up to and including the suspension of the rights derivative from the treaties, but that expulsion from the Union would both be 'unnecessary if suspension of rights achieved the desired effects' and that 'there might be a danger that this [expulsion] would call into question the irreversibility of membership of the Union' (ibid.: §34; cited in Sadurski 2009). These two rationales for sidelining an expulsion mechanism are interesting, not least because they are in tension. The first is conditional: *if* suspension of rights achieves the desired results, *then* an expulsion mechanism is unnecessary. The implication that if suspension of rights does not lead to the cessation of the violation of fundamental rights by the member state in question then an expulsion mechanism would be necessary is left hanging. The second logic is grounded on the putative problem with 'questioning the irreversibility' of Union membership. If such an unqualified commitment was ever justifiable from the perspective of democratic theory—and this seems doubtful[8]—it was certainly undermined by the inclusion of a procedure to leave the EU in Article 50 of the Lisbon Treaty (2007/2009).

The eventual sanction included in the Treaty of Amsterdam, and which would remain largely unchanged in the Nice (2001/2003), Constitutional (2004) and Lisbon (2007/2009) treaties, picks up the recommendation of the Reflection Group precisely. While expulsion is not an option, a sanctioned member state may be deprived of 'certain of the rights deriving from the application of the Treaties to the Member State in question, including the voting rights of the representative of the government of that Member State in the Council' (Article 7.3 Treaty on European Union [TEU]).[9] Importantly, the sanction remains open-ended: while only disenfranchisement in the Council is named explicitly, there is the potential of suspending an indefinite range of member state rights while continuing to subject them to EU law.[10] Wojciech Sadurski notes that, as a sanction, this is 'functionally almost equivalent to temporary expulsion' (2009: 390). But the question of ultimate membership of the EU by a member state in 'serious and persistent breach' of EU fundamental values (Article 7.2 TEU seems to remain formally within the purview of the state in breach; as such, other members and EU institutions must seemingly resign themselves fatalistically to supranational union with even a frankly autocratic state.

Depoliticizing conflicts over values: The failed cordon sanitaire against the FPÖ

The procedure in the Treaty of Nice (2001/2003) was not identical to that in the Treaty of Amsterdam (1997/1999), however, and to understand why we need to turn to the case of Austria. The first real test of the sanctions mechanism came sooner than expected and from a surprising corner—Austria, who had joined in 1995. In 2000, four years before the 'big bang' expansion of the EU to the east, the far-right Freedom Party of Austria (FPÖ) formed a coalition government with the centre-right Austrian People's Party (ÖVP). With the next big expansion on the horizon, one may imagine that such a challenge would cause other EU states to harden their resolve regarding EU fundamental values, and potentially expand the sanctions mechanism in the Treaty of Nice, which was under negotiation. In fact, the opposite happened. Instead of an EU-led response through the sanctions mechanism, the other fourteen member states imposed short-lived unilateral diplomatic sanctions against Austria. The specific circumstances and failure of these sanctions delegitimized the idea of significant repercussions for conflicts over fundamental values in the EU. A political response to such conflicts, which could be both more effective and more coherent, with a commitment to democracy as a fundamental value, was sidelined in favour of increasingly technocratic and legalistic responses. And far from being expanded in light of the failed response in 2000, the sanctions mechanism was rather weakened.[11]

The FPÖ had been founded in the 1950s by former members of the Nazi Party before undergoing a period of reform in the 1970s and 1980s, with a number of leaders adopting more liberal and centrist positions (Pelinka 2001). Jörg Haider had been appointed leader of the party in 1986 following a brief *Rot-blaue Koalition* in 1983 in which the FPÖ governed with the centre-left Social Democratic Party, the SPÖ. Under Haider's leadership, however, the party shifted back to the far right, and became known for its anti-immigrant and nationalist views as well as its Euroscepticism. Haider managed to unite disparate parts of the Austrian populist and far-right electorate, balancing nationalistic patriotism through 'Austria first' politics with the trivialization of Nazism[12] and the Holocaust typical of pan-German nationalists (Pelinka 2001; Mitten 2002). Many voters also saw the FPÖ as the only alternative to the 'grand coalition' of the social-democratic and centre-right parties[13] who had governed together for 34 out of the 54 years since 1945, and whose influence had predominated not only politics but also social and economic life.[14]

The resulting ideological shift was a big vote winner for the FPÖ. In the first elections contested under Haider's leadership, in 1986, the FPÖ almost doubled its vote share, from 5% to almost 10%. This trend continued throughout the 1990s, with the party winning 16.6% in the 1990 parliamentary election and breaking the million-vote barrier in 1994 with 22.5%. Campaigning on slogans such as 'We guarantee [to] stop over-foreignization',[15] the FPÖ finally managed to squeak past the centre-right ÖVP to second place, by barely 400 votes nationally, in the 1999 general election. While the social-democratic SPÖ still won a plurality of votes with 33.2%, this was a historically weak result for them. For months, negotiations ensued between the SPÖ to form a continuation of their 'grand coalition' government with the third-placed ÖVP. When these talks broke down, the SPÖ briefly explored the possibility of a minority government. It quickly became apparent that this would amount to nothing so, given that the SPÖ refused to negotiate with the FPÖ, the SPÖ Acting Chancellor Viktor Klima made way for the FPÖ and ÖVP to open negotiations.

The European response to the eventuality of a governmental coalition including the FPÖ was immediate, unprecedented, and ultimately deeply ineffective. The initial reaction was characterized by coordinated bilateralism (rather than multilateralism) and political pressure. On 31 January, while the ÖPV and the FPÖ were still negotiating an eventual coalition, then Portuguese Prime Minister António Guterres, on behalf of the Portuguese rotating presidency of the Council of the EU, informed the President and Chancellor of Austria that the remaining fourteen EU member states planned to impose a diplomatic boycott if the incoming Austrian government were to include the FPÖ. This would downgrade relations with Austria to a 'bureaucratic' level, meaning that each of the fourteen remaining EU states would refuse to hold official meetings with members of the Austrian coalition government, isolating Austria at the European level. The intention of this threat, quite explicitly, was to undermine the ongoing negotiations between the FPÖ and the ÖVP and try to impose a *cordon sanitaire* from the outside. However, this initial goal fell flat almost immediately, with the FPÖ and the ÖVP quickly coming to an agreement and forming a government as of 4 February.

The formation of this coalition was met with broad condemnation from other European countries, as well as groups within Austria. Domestically, opposition was widespread, with Jewish groups especially concerned about Haider's history of antisemitic comments and his trivialization of the Holocaust. Israel even recalled its ambassador from Vienna in protest. Critics argued that the FPÖ's far-right views were at odds with Austria's commitment to liberal democracy. Many European leaders also spoke out against the new government. While one can wonder as to the purity of motivations by European governments (Merlingen, Mudde and Sedelmeier 2001: 69–70; Gehler 2017: 188–94), the threatened diplomatic boycott of the EU-14[16] was implemented with immediate effect. While this took the form of essentially fourteen separate bilateral boycotts, there was also a moderated collective EU response. The Commission unanimously declared support for the concerns of the EU-14 and stated it would not hesitate to use the values mechanism in the Treaty of Amsterdam if Austria were to violate EU fundamental values. The European Parliament passed a resolution condemning FPÖ participation in Austria's government by a large majority, as did the Committee of the Regions. And of course, the diplomatic boycott, while formally bilateral, did take the guise of European multilateralism in that it was coordinated and communicated by the Portuguese presidency of the Council (Merlingen, Mudde and Sedelmeier 2001: 60).

It is worth being precise about the controversies and tensions of these developments. On the one hand, the member states were surely correct that the inclusion of the FPÖ in the Austrian governmental coalition was at least potentially a threat to the fundamental values of the EU, which include, beyond democracy and the rule of law, commitments to respect human rights (particularly those of minorities) in the spirit of tolerance and non-discrimination (Article 2 TEU). Nevertheless, the FPÖ had clearly received a strong democratic mandate from Austrian voters in elections that no one seriously contested for being both free and fair. In this context, a political response seems appropriate. After all, the European Court of Justice (ECJ) could hardly penalize Austria for *potentially* violating the rights of, say, migrants and religious minorities. But attempting to pressure Austrian political parties to freeze out the FPÖ could be reasonably considered anti-democratic interference in Austria's domestic affairs. The inclusion of the FPÖ in the coalition certainly did not in itself constitute an example of democratic backsliding. Regardless, the decision by the EU member states to impose sanctions against Austria was a significant event in the history of the organization. It marked the first and only time that EU member states have taken joint diplomatic action against another member state for violating collective norms.

For our purposes, the most important aspect of the response the EU-14 chose was that it was singularly ineffective. An early symbolic concession came when, response to the furore, and as a precondition set by then Austrian President Thomas Klestil on the acceptance of the coalition, the ÖVP and the FPÖ issued a joint statement reaffirming their commitment to 'the principles of pluralistic democracy and the rule of law common to all members of the European Union' and to the 'protection and promotion' as well as the 'unconditional implementation' of human rights (Ahtisaari, Frowein and Oreja 2001). Another concession was that ÖVP's Wolfgang Schüssel was appointed Chancellor of Austria, instead of Jörg Haider, who, as leader of the party with a stronger performance at the general election, would have been the more obvious candidate. Indeed, Haider bowed out of government participation entirely, ceding the vice-chancellorship and the chairpersonship of the FPÖ to Susanne Riess-Passer. But after this modest gain, the Austrian coalition continued with little regard for their temporary ostracization in the fourteen European capitals. Furthermore, the Commission and the European Parliament did not take any concrete further steps, and, while sidelined from informal meetings, Austrian representatives—including those of the FPÖ—continued to participate as equals in all formal European institutions.

Sanctions were eventually lifted after only a few months. On 5 May, the Austrian government, exploiting rising disagreements among the EU-14 on the continuation of the sanctions, threatened to put them to a national referendum in Austria if they were not lifted by the end of the Portuguese presidency of the Council on 30 June. Heedful of this threat, the European Parliament, on 13 June, resolved that relations with Austria should be reevaluated to search for an acceptable solution to the crisis. A so-called 'Council of Wise Men' was mandated by the President of the European Court of Human Rights to examine the commitment of the Austrian government to European fundamental values and find a way out on behalf of the EU-14. On 8 September, former Social-Democratic

MEMBERSHIP FATALISM AND DEPOLITICIZATION

President of Finland Martti Ahtisaari, German legal scholar Jochen Frowein, and Spanish former EU Commissioner Marcelino Oreja concluded that, while it was too early to say whether the FPÖ had really changed its stripes to become a 'responsible governmental party' (Ahtisaari, Frowein and Oreja 2001: 119 §106), the participation of its ministers in the Austrian government over the previous seven months could not be 'generally criticized' (ibid.: §104) and that a continuation of the diplomatic boycott would be counterproductive (ibid.: 120 §117). Four days later, the EU-14 announced an immediate cessation of the boycott.

This humiliating about-face had the effect of delegitimizing political responses to fundamental values conflicts between EU member states. As Richard Mitten (2002) wrote:

> If, indeed, there is a more general European lesson to be learned from the Austrian case, it is that any strategy for combating the populist right which depends primarily on the talismanic invocation of democratic values against what are described as these parties' atavistic ideological impulses, hoping that by doing so these groups can be kept in political quarantine and hence out of power, will probably fail.

Rather than rethink how and when political responses to such crises should take shape, member states returned to the legal mechanism for addressing the violation of EU fundamental values. On the direct advice of the 'Wise Men Report' looking into the Austrian controversy (ibid.: §117–8), the sanctions mechanism of the Treaty of Amsterdam was revised. The organizing logic of the revision was the idea that the mechanism had not been used against Austria because it was *too strong*. The revised procedure, accepted by all member state governments (including the Austrian government, with the involvement of the FPÖ) retained the unanimity requirement for the application of any sanction, but added an additional step of dialogue and monitoring before the sanctions mechanism could be used for any punitive end (Article 7 Treaty of Nice). The fatalistic rationale that member states committed to democracy, equality, human rights, and the rule of law were bound to continue their association with a member state in open violation of these norms was reinforced. Delegating the contestation over values conflicts to this highly formalized and legalistic arena had the dual effect of depoliticizing such conflicts and adding further steps to the pathways available for when EU member states actually started to dismantle democracy and the rule of law.

In the end, the inclusion of the FPÖ in the Austrian government did not lead to any significant political repercussions in Austria. Despite the criticism, an ÖVP-FPÖ coalition remained in power until 2005, when the BZÖ, a breakaway party from the FPÖ, took over the governmental functions from the FPÖ amid internal disagreements. This ÖVP-BZÖ coalition lasted until 2007. After another period with a grand coalition government constituting the ÖVP and the SPÖ (between 2007 and 2017), the FPÖ even briefly returned to government in a new coalition with the ÖVP, this time led by Sebastian Kurz. Electorally, results have been somewhat mixed but remain strong overall, the party achieving its best ever electoral result (in terms of total votes) in the 2017 general election.

What then can we learn from the failed *cordon sanitaire* that other EU states tried to impose on Austria after the FPÖ's first inclusion in government in 2000? One of the main practical problems with the sanctions was that they were taken bilaterally by the governments of the fourteen EU member states, not through the EU or other multilateral institutions (Gehler 2017). The sanctions were a classic example of a bark that was worse than its bite—loud, but lacking in real teeth—and they ultimately served only to expose the limits of the EU's ability to enforce its own values. A second problem with the sanctions was that they were largely symbolic. While the sanctions did lead to widespread concern and condemnation, they failed to achieve their intended effect.

This is not to say that the sanctions *ought* to have strong-armed the ÖVP into rejecting a coalition partnership with the FPÖ. As noted above, the FPÖ had a strong democratic mandate. Instead of trying to pressure the ÖVP to cut them out of a coalition, it would have been wiser for the EU-14 to be steadfast in rejecting the FPÖ's ideology and political project, while waiting to see whether the Austrian government would uphold their obligations to respect EU fundamental values. Keeping up discursive pressure on the ÖVP-FPÖ government without resorting to empty threats would have been a far more sustainable strategy for guarding against democratic backsliding. But by barking early and biting meekly, the EU-14 undermined the very idea of a collective political response to values conflicts. This paved the way for the overly legalistic, depoliticized approach to responding to democratic backsliding a decade later.

The failure of the sanctions to achieve their intended effect was a key factor in delegitimizing the idea of using robust repercussions as a means of responding to backsliding by member states. The choice to sideline EU institutions undermined the idea of robust sanctions at the EU level. Even the appointment of the 'Council of Wise Men'—by the President of the European Court of Human Rights, and mandated by the Portuguese presidency of the Council—undermined the role of the EU Commission, who could of course have been involved in this process. In the end, the findings of the 'Wise Men Report' directly led to the weakening of the Article 7 procedure. And all this came at a significant cost, with the diplomatic boycott galvanizing support for the far-right in Austria (Gehler 2017: 181, 208; Ahtisaari, Frowein and Oreja 2001: 120 §116) and for Eurosceptic right-wing populist parties across Europe. While it was coordinated among the EU-14 governments, opposition to the sanctions was widespread amongst opposition parties in Europe, especially on the right. The FPÖ and the ÖVP felt that they were being punished by other member states and that the FPÖ's inclusion in the government was questioned solely on the basis of their political beliefs. The sanctions also seemed to fail to contain Euroscepticism or the far right beyond the Austrian borders in the immediate aftermath. For instance, Denmark voted against adopting the euro on 28 September, mere weeks after the EU-14 boycotts had reached their ignominious end, and the populist radical right party Vlaams Blok (now Vlaams Belang) came first in Antwerp and Mechelen in the local council elections of 8 October.[17]

Linking depoliticization and membership fatalism to Hungarian and Polish backsliding

The Austrian sanctions, which proved to be singularly ineffective in addressing the inclusion of the far-right FPÖ in the government, were the harbinger of a developing fatalism about EU membership and the depoliticization of fundamental values violations within the EU. This section explores how EU institutions tolerated Hungarian and Polish backsliding on democracy and EU fundamental values without significant consequences. By analysing the experiences of these two countries, we can gain a deeper understanding of the implications of membership fatalism and depoliticization for the future of democratic governance in the EU.

The story of Hungary's democratic regression starts, perhaps surprisingly for those still unfamiliar with this story, with a liberal youth organization in the late 1980s. Viktor Orbán was one of the founding members of the Fiatal Demokraták Szövetsége (Alliance of Young Democrats), known by its acronym Fidesz. He played a prominent role in organizing anti-communist protests and demonstrations, calling for political liberalization and a transition towards democracy. Orbán was elected a Member of Parliament in 1990—the first democratic elections in Hungary since 1945—and led Fidesz' small group of eight parliamentarians. In 1993, Orbán became president of the party, which continued to perform modestly, barely reaching the 5% threshold in the 1994 general elections. However, in this period, Orbán shifted the party's ideological orientation towards a more conservative platform that emphasized national interests, economic liberalism, and traditional values, which would prove electorally profitable. In 1998, despite coming second in terms of total vote share (behind the centre-left Hungarian Socialist Party, the MSZP), Fidesz won the largest number of seats and Orbán formed a government with two small right-wing parties. In the 2002 parliamentary elections, Fidesz—now competing as a conservative party[18]—again squeaked past MSZP in terms of seats though winning fewer votes, but was kept from government by a coalition between the socialists and the Alliance of Free Democrats (SZDSZ), whose twenty parliamentarians allowed MSZP to form a government in 2002 and again in 2006. In the 2010 parliamentary elections, Fidesz won a decisive victory, securing a two-thirds majority in the National Assembly, a supermajority it has maintained in the 2014, 2018 and 2022 general elections.

Under Orbán's leadership, Hungary has seen a steady erosion of democratic norms, with the government increasingly taking steps to consolidate its power and limit the influence of opposition voices.

MEMBERSHIP FATALISM AND DEPOLITICIZATION

This included the passage of a new constitution in 2011 that limited the powers of the Hungarian Constitutional Court, weakened the independence of the judiciary, and curbed the rights of the media and civil society. In addition to these legal changes, Fidesz sought to stack the deck in its favour through gerrymandering and changes to the electoral system. These efforts have included the redrawing of electoral districts in ways that favour Fidesz, the introduction of new campaign finance rules that limit the ability of opposition parties to compete, and partisan changes to the composition of the National Election Commission. One of the key ways in which the government has sought to consolidate its power has been through the appointment of loyalists to key positions in the civil service and the judiciary. The independence of Hungary's central bank has come under scrutiny, with Orbán attempting to exert greater control over its operations by appointing allies to key positions and taking steps to limit the bank's autonomy. The government has also implemented changes to the criminal code that have increased its power to prosecute its opponents, using the justice system as a political weapon.

Equally troubling has been the government's crackdown on civil society and the media. This has included the passage of a new law in 2017 that requires non-governmental organizations (NGOs) receiving foreign funding to register with the government and label themselves as foreign-backed, as well as efforts to limit the freedom of the press through changes to media ownership rules and the intimidation of critical journalists (Bátorfy and Urbán 2020). The Central European University, long a haven for students and academics critical of Hungary's authoritarian turn, was forced to relocate to Vienna (Enyedi 2018; Bárd 2018). The Orbán government's efforts to suppress civil society have been particularly detrimental to the democratic landscape in Hungary. In addition to the changes to NGO registration requirements, there have been reports of harassment and intimidation of human rights activists and organizations, as well as efforts to limit the ability of civil society groups to access funding from international sources. Such developments are all the more pernicious—and difficult to grasp—given the Fidesz government's penchant for eroding civil freedoms not only through formal but also through informal routes (Zgut 2022).

PROTECTING DEMOCRACY IN EUROPE

After a decade of neglect, Hungary's democratic backsliding has slowly become a focal point of EU concern. Despite a range of responses from the EU, the triggering of Article 7 proceedings and, more recently, budget conditionality, the Hungarian government has so far mostly avoided serious consequences for its actions. The fatalistic attitude towards EU membership has allowed Hungary to backslide on democracy and EU fundamental values without facing significant repercussions. The idea that Hungary's membership of the EU is somehow inevitable and that there is little that can be done to change the course of the country's political trajectory has allowed the ruling Fidesz party to pursue anti-democratic policies with impunity. Wary about a repeat of the debacle of the Austrian sanctions, the EU's response has been characterized by a lack of political will to confront Hungary over its democratic deficiencies (Oleart and Theuns 2023), a failure to understand the nature and scope of the problem, and a willingness to accept cosmetic changes as genuine reform.

Depoliticization has also played a role in Hungary's democratic backsliding. Even by 2015, a full five years into Orbán's project of dismantling a free democratic playing field in Hungary, then Commission Vice-President Frans Timmermans grounded caution at robust action against Hungary on the Austrian experience saying, 'I believe that the case of Austria, with Jörg Haider's party joining the government, has weakened the EU's capacity to react [to Hungary]. It was a political response which completely backfired' (Timmermans 2015). The EU's response to Hungary's democratic backsliding has instead been largely characterized by examining Hungary's technical compliance with EU regulations in a piecemeal fashion rather than on the broader political and social implications of Hungary's actions. This has allowed Hungary to pursue broader anti-democratic policies while making minor concessions on particular controversial reforms.

The EU's response to Hungary's democratic backsliding has included investigations, dialogue with Hungarian authorities, and the triggering of Article 7 proceedings. But these actions have been largely ineffective in addressing the root causes. The investigations have been slow, the dialogue has been largely symbolic, and the triggering of Article 7 proceedings has been more about (virtue) signalling EU concern than about actually holding Hungary accountable for its actions. Take for instance the long delay of the Council to launch Article 7 proceedings against Poland and Hungary. EU officials were reluctant to pursue this option, convinced that proceedings against Poland and Hungary were doomed to fail because of the unanimity requirement of the Article 7 procedure. But this conviction was itself a product of depoliticization and membership fatalism, as can be seen in the 2018 Council Legal Services opinion that argued responses to the violation of the EU fundamental values taken outside the framework of Article 7 would be *ultra vires* (Oliver and Stefanelli 2016; Scheppele, Pech and Kelemen 2018). As was the case after the Austrian climbdown, there always seems to be an excuse that what is needed is one more mechanism, or one further reform, or a good discussion between (former) friends, rather than the level-headed use of existing possibilities to protest and sanction violations of core values. This is the essence of the culture of delay. As Scheppele and Pech note ironically, 'the precedent that Austria seems to have set is this: every time there is a challenge to EU values, the EU seeks refuge in a new framework that avoids using its existing powers' (2018).

More recently than in Hungary, but still over a period of almost a decade, the Polish Law and Justice (PiS)-led government steadily regressed on democracy and rule of law standards until it lost power in the 2023 general election. PiS was founded in 2001 as a right-wing, nationalist political party in Poland. In the 2005 parliamentary elections, the party won the most number of seats, but was unable to form a majority government. Between 2005 and 2007 it governed as a minority government with two smaller nationalist parties. In the 2007 parliamentary elections, and again in 2013, PiS improved its vote score, but emerged as the second-largest party in the Sejm (the lower house of the Polish Parliament) after centre-right party Civic Platform (PO), who formed a government with the agrarian Polish People's Party (PSL) from 2007 to 2015. In the 2015 parliamentary elections, however, PiS led the United Right (ZP) alliance, winning an outright majority, enabling it to form a majority government. Since then, the party has implemented a number of controversial policies, including reforms to the judicial system and media that undermine democracy. Despite this, the party has remained popular and won a strong second mandate in the 2019 parliamentary elections.

The PiS government's reforms since 2015 significantly undermined the rule of law in Poland. In particular, the party weakened the independence of key institutions such as the Constitutional Tribunal, the Supreme Court, and the National Council of the Judiciary. The Constitutional Tribunal was subject to controversial changes that seriously hampered its ability to act as an independent check on the government's power (Gajda-Roszczynialska and Markiewicz 2020; Kochenov and Bárd 2020). For instance, in 2015, the PiS government passed a law that lowered the quorum required for the tribunal to make decisions, making it easier for the government to pack the court with its own appointees. Moreover, the PiS government overruled the tribunal in 2015, appointing its own judges to the court, resulting in a constitutional crisis. Additionally, PiS passed a law in 2017 that allowed the Justice Minister to appoint the heads of regional courts, allowing the government to exert more control over the judiciary at a local level. Furthermore, the PiS government gave the Justice Minister greater control over the appointment of judges to the Supreme Court, allowing the government to replace sitting judges with its own appointees. In 2020, the infamous 'muzzle law' was passed, making it illegal in Poland for judges to question the legitimacy of the PiS judicial appointees. Those who persisted faced sanctions up to being fired.

As Fidesz did in Hungary, the PiS government also attempted to undermine media freedom in Poland. In 2016, the government passed a law that allowed it to appoint the heads of public broadcasters without the need for a public competition, effectively giving the government greater control over the editorial direction of these outlets. This led to concerns that the government was attempting to control the media and to stifle critical voices. The PiS government was also accused of using state advertising to reward friendly media outlets and to punish critical ones. Public broadcasting in Poland was increasingly used as a tool of PiS propaganda, including through the vilification of opposition politicians (Żuk 2020). This resulted in a significant decline in media pluralism and raised concerns about the ability of the media to serve as an independent watchdog over the government's actions. The Organization for Security and Co-operation in Europe election mission to Poland in 2020 noted that public broadcaster TVP 'acted as a campaign vehicle for the incumbent' (OSCE Statement of Preliminary Findings and Conclusions after the first round of the Polish election, 29 June 2020: 4). In a galling case of intimidation, a law professor was sued by public broadcaster TVP for referring to it as 'Goebbels media' after Paweł Adamowicz, the opposition mayor of Gdansk, was murdered in 2019. Adamowicz had been vilified on TVP, who mentioned him on air 1,773 times in 2018 alone. The criminal case against this professor was finally rejected by the Polish Supreme Court in 2022 (TVP appealed two earlier acquittals).

Membership fatalism, especially considering the high level of support for continued membership of the EU amongst the Polish public, allowed the PiS government in Poland to undermine EU values without much fear of significant consequences. The question of Poland possibly leaving the EU was derided by Kaczyński, leader of PiS and *de facto* of the Polish executive at the time, as 'a propaganda invention that has been used many times against us' (Euronews 2021). Furthermore, the depoliticization of conflict over fundamental values played a clear role in allowing backsliding to occur. Rather than being a source of political contestation, values such as the rule of law and democracy have been treated as technical issues to be resolved through legal and administrative means. While the EU took some action against Poland over these reforms, such as initiating Article 7 proceedings, these actions were largely symbolic and did not have a significant impact on the Polish government's actions.

Where the EU did respond to rule of law backsliding in Poland under the PiS-led government, the response was weak and fragmented, with member states divided on whether and how to sanction Poland. Moreover, the EU institutions themselves were slow and ineffective in responding to these challenges. For instance, while the European Commission took legal action before the ECJ via infringement proceedings for the most egregious violations of democratic and rule of law standards in Poland, it failed to do so systematically and generally held back from using all the tools at its disposal to hold member states accountable. Fines imposed via infringement procedures were left outstanding, and the court cases were spun by the PiS government keen to exploit the narrative of a heavy-handed Brussels elite subverting Polish sovereignty. The 2021 Rule of Law Conditionality Mechanism (discussed in more detail in Chapter 4), supposedly a powerful tool to withhold EU funding to EU states backsliding on fundamental values, was watered down so as to be a practically toothless multiplication of existing tools. The weakness of the Rule of Law Conditionality Regulation meant that it was mostly sidelined, the Commission instead attempting to impose some financial conditionality on Poland via the Recovery and Resilience Plan. Besides this, the Polish government was able to continue with its reforms without facing significant consequences. The European Council has generally been too focused on maintaining consensus among member states (de Búrca 2022), a weakness frequently exploited by the PiS-led government in Poland and Fidesz in Hungary when threatening to veto key decisions if it does not get concessions on the so-called 'rule of law dossier'.

This combination of membership fatalism and political passivity has been thoroughly exploited by actors pursuing an authoritarian agenda in domestic politics, especially where they gained executive power, as was the case in Hungary and Poland. For example, in recent years, the PiS-led Polish government used its veto power to block EU action on a number of important issues: in 2017, Poland threatened to veto the EU's budget unless it was given greater control over EU funds, and in 2018, it threatened to veto the EU's migration policy unless it was allowed to refuse to take in refugees. Similarly, the Hungarian government has also used its veto power as a weapon to block EU action on issues that are important to the rest of the Union: in 2019, Hungary threatened to veto the EU's budget unless it was given more funds to boost its own economy, and in 2020, it threatened to veto the EU's response to the COVID-19 pandemic unless it was given more support. Where vetoes have been unsuccessful or are ineffective, as when responding to rulings of the ECJ, the Polish and Hungarian governments often resorted to what Gráinne de Búrca has called a 'cat and mouse game', withdrawing contested legislation only to reintroduce similar measures in other legislation (2022: 27).[19] The combination of these threats and games has been brutally effective in undermining the EU's ability to respond effectively.

MEMBERSHIP FATALISM AND DEPOLITICIZATION

Conclusion: Moving past the Haider hangover

In conclusion, the cases of Austria, Hungary, and Poland serve as cautionary tales, highlighting the urgent need for the EU to reevaluate its strategies and take decisive action to safeguard democracy, human rights, and the rule of law. The failed *cordon sanitaire* in response to the inclusion of the far-right FPÖ in the Austrian government in 2000 set a precedent of ineffective political responses and paved the way for a more legalistic approach. This depoliticization of conflicts over values allowed Hungary and Poland to gradually erode democratic norms and institutions without facing significant consequences.

Membership fatalism—the belief that EU membership is fully a sovereign matter of each member state and that little can be done to change the political trajectory of a backsliding member state—played a key role in enabling democratic erosion. The fear of repeating the Austrian sanctions debacle and a lack of political will to confront democratic deficiencies resulted in a reluctance to take robust action when real authoritarianism rose within the EU's borders. Instead, the focus shifted towards endless dialogue and monitoring of technical compliance with EU laws and regulations, overlooking the broader political implications of Hungary and Poland's actions. The depoliticization of conflicts over fundamental values further undermined the EU's response. Rather than being treated as urgent sites of political contestation, values such as democracy and the rule of law were reduced to technical issues to be resolved through legal and administrative means. The EU's actions, such as investigations, dialogue, and the triggering of Article 7 proceedings, have been largely symbolic and ineffective in addressing the root causes of democratic backsliding.

The Haider affair in Austria was taken by EU officials and national politicians as a case study in the limitations of bilateral sanctions. However, the subsequent revision of the sanctions mechanism in the Treaty of Nice weakened the EU's ability to respond effectively. The unanimity requirement of Article 7 and the emphasis on dialogue and monitoring before imposing sanctions create further obstacles to addressing violations of fundamental values. The combination of membership fatalism, depoliticization and fragmented responses among member states has allowed actors pursuing authoritarian agendas to exploit the EU's weaknesses. Hungary and Poland, in particular, have used their veto power and threats to block effective action. The watering down of the Rule of Law Conditionality Regulation (see Chapter 4) and the focus on maintaining consensus among member states have further hampered democracy protection in Europe.

To effectively address democratic backsliding and protect fundamental values, the EU needs to confront membership fatalism, re-politicize conflicts over values, and take decisive and coordinated action. An example of this, discussed in more detail in Chapter 5, is the Commission finally imposing budget conditionality on Poland and Hungary in 2022 via the Recovery and Resilience fund, largely bypassing the Conditionality Regulation that machinations in the European Council had rendered impotent. Indeed, unlocking the tens of billions of euros on the line in this was a key political message for Poland's opposition, and has played a part in their electoral success in October 2023. The Polish example offers hope that democratic backsliding in Europe can be halted—possibly even reversed—where membership fatalism and depoliticization give way to a more robust democracy protection policy. Further developing such strategies is the subject of the second part of this book. It requires a shift towards a more proactive and assertive approach that holds member states accountable for their actions. Each member state and all EU institutions need to wake up to the fact that the collective political freedom of EU states is at stake when one or more member states become authoritarian. Strengthening the rule of law, protecting media freedom, safeguarding civil society and ensuring independent judicial systems are crucial for preserving democratic governance within the EU.

3

'DEMOCRACY WITHOUT POLITICS'

UNPACKING COMMISSION SPEECHES

> *Democracy is gray ... It chooses banality over excellence, shrewdness over nobility, empty promise over true competence ... It is eternal imperfection, a mixture of sinfulness, saintliness, and monkey business.*
>
> Adam Michnik[1]

The numerous shockwaves that followed the 2008 financial crisis have raised normative questions about democracy, and particularly about the democratic backsliding of some European Union (EU) member states (Bellamy and Kröger 2021; Müller 2015; Theuns 2020, 2022; Wolkenstein 2020). The wider political and academic debate about democracy being in a state of crisis is well established in recent years (cf. Levitsky and Ziblatt 2019; Mounk 2018; Runciman 2018). At the core of this debate there is an overwhelming focus on executive overreach and the rule of law. This tracks with a broadly liberal conception of democracy that emphasizes the separation of the branches of government, particularly the independence of the judiciary. This focus on the rule of law is especially true in the EU, since the internal constitutional diversity of EU member states challenges a more substantially developed conception of democracy. Indeed, it is in part this conceptual ambiguity combined with the constitutional pluralism of EU member states that has allowed Hungary's Prime Minister, Viktor Orbán, to present his vision for Hungary as an 'illiberal democracy'. In the previous chapter, I examined critical junctures in recent European integration to help us understand the depoliticized and fatalistic attitude of EU actors faced with democratic backsliding in member states. This chapter addresses the rhetoric of EU institutions: how are these flaws in the European response reflected in the way EU actors talk about democracy?

Given the ever-increasing salience of democratic backsliding in the EU context, it may be surprising that the academic literature has not paid much attention to the underlying conception of democracy that has informed EU institutions' policy choices. Instead, the literature is dominated by political scientists and legal scholars that describe (and criticize) the (in)appropriateness of EU policies vis-à-vis backsliding member states. These studies have enhanced our understanding of democratic backsliding in the EU context, but they have not problematized the Commission's conceptualization of democracy.

In this chapter, I unpack the prevailing understanding of democracy within the European Commission, which, I argue, is reflected in its largely legalistic and technocratic approach. Methodologically, I analyse a set of 155 speeches delivered by European Commissioners that mention democracy in the European context. EU Commissioner speeches are an appropriate corpus for this endeavour (see De Ville and Orbie 2014) given their central role in constructing meaning by the European Commission in the public sphere, as the speeches are given not only to the specific audience but also to the public at large, since they are later published online. The framing analysis performed on the Commission's speeches departs from the understanding of framing as 'adopting an interpretive framework for thinking about a political object' (Pan and Kosicki 2005: 177). In this case, the 'political object' is democracy, and I analyse the interpretive framework that European Commissioners mobilize when making sense of it. In accordance with this definition, the framing analysis was undertaken inductively through successive rounds of coding.

The rationale for doing so in this way is that the meaning-making process constructed discursively not only facilitates the understanding of political action, but also shapes it. The literature on the role of ideas in politics helps us to understand that the obstacles to political action are not only institutional, but also ideational (see Gofas and Hay 2010). Thus, understanding these obstacles might be helpful to overcome them, and different political proposals might flow from changing the understanding of democracy. This is not a causal argument, but rather a way to look at the interplay between discourse and institutional policymaking (see Schmidt 2010, on 'discursive institutionalism'), and how ideas underpin the EU's actions and policies. There is a rich literature on the role of ideas in shaping the EU's policies (Crespy 2010; Fairbrass 2011); this chapter contributes from this perspective to the specific policy domain of (countering) democratic backsliding, as the literature has, so far, prioritized a legal perspective.

The timeframe for the corpus of speeches I analyse departs from the European Parliament's vote on 12 September 2018 to trigger the Article 7 procedure against the Hungarian government's attacks on democratic institutions (which also coincides with the 2018 State of the Union address by Commission President Jean-Claude Juncker), up until when the European Commission referred Poland to the European Court of Justice for violations of EU law by its Constitutional Tribunal on 15 February 2023. The specific chronology was chosen to gather a manageable dataset of speeches for in-depth qualitative analysis while also taking into account a meaningful timeframe related to EU institutions' responses to democratic backsliding.

While in previous research I looked at speeches by all the Commissioners over a shorter period[2] (Oleart and Theuns 2023), here I chose to look at the speeches of Commissioners with dossiers key to democracy and the rule of law. In the Commission presided over by Jean-Claude Juncker, I examined, besides his own speeches, the speeches of Frans Timmermans (First Vice-President, Commissioner for Better Regulation, Inter-Institutional Relations, Rule of Law and Charter of Fundamental Rights), Věra Jourová (Commissioner for Justice and Consumers) and Johannes Hahn (Commissioner for European Neighbourhood Policy and Enlargement Negotiations). For the Commission presided by Ursula von der Leyen, I again analysed Věra Jourová (Commissioner for Values and Transparency—the closest approximation of Frans Timmermans' previous rule of law brief),

PROTECTING DEMOCRACY IN EUROPE

Olivér Várhelyi (Commissioner for European Neighbourhood Policy and Enlargement Negotiations), and Didier Reynders (Commissioner for Justice). As well as covering the key Commissioners in terms of the relevance of their portfolios substantively, this selection also provides decent variation in terms of geography and partisan allegiance. The total number of speeches (i.e. all speeches by these Commissioners mentioning the word 'democracy') amounted to 155 in the period studied. To increase the granularity of the analysis, I coded each instance of the use of the word 'democracy' rather than the speeches overall. The result was 480 references to democracy made by these Commissioners in their public speeches.

The period covered by the dataset is around fourteen months for the Juncker Commission and almost three and a half years for the first von der Leyen Commission. This discrepancy in duration results in there being considerably more speeches for the latter period (116) than the former (39). That the results of this study are nevertheless close to the findings from the previous research, which was skewed towards speeches from the Juncker Commission (ibid.), shows how the Commission's conceptualization of democracy is rather stable over this period of time.

The driving research question I ask in this chapter is: Which understandings of democracy have shaped the European Commission's response to democratic backsliding in recent years? I address this question through both a qualitative-empirical and a normative-theoretical analysis. Empirically, I analyse European Commissioners' speeches from the Juncker and von der Leyen Commissions and connect the Commission's discourse with its policy responses to democratic backsliding. The link between the European Commission's framing of democracy is relevant, as it matches the EU's policy responses to democratic backsliding in EU member states. I do not aim at establishing causal mechanisms at play that explain the Commission's policy choices. Rather, I am interested in how the Commission's discourse of 'democracy without politics' reflects the philosophy behind the policy choices. I show how democracy is conceived by the Commission in a largely depoliticized manner, prioritizing a 'technocratic legalistic' perspective over a democratic pluralist one. This depoliticized understanding of democracy and the legal toolbox deployed to counter democratic backsliding miss important aspects of democracy, such as ideological pluralism, democratic contestation, and the recognition of the role of a legitimate opposition. Incorporating these elements would, I argue, reflect a healthier and normatively more attractive conception of democracy.

The next sections present the speeches and analyse them, making the case that the Commission's conception of democracy in this period can be characterized as 'democracy without politics'. Next, I move from the empirical analysis of the speeches to a normative engagement of this conception of democracy. I argue an alternative democratic ideal—pluralist democracy—gives more room to elements such as robust public dialogue, the inclusion of diverse political perspectives, and the vibrancy of civil society (Theuns 2021). This conception of democracy better captures the essence of the democratic ideal as impartially navigating between divergent and potentially conflicting notions of the common good. In order to foster a more comprehensive and inclusive democratic framework, we must place genuine political engagement, open dialogue, and the active involvement of civil society central to our democratic politics. Finally, I argue that by embracing these elements, the European Commission can enhance its approach to democracy and ensure that its actions align with the principles and aspirations of a vibrant and participatory democratic system. This entails moving beyond a narrow technocratic focus and embracing a more holistic understanding of democracy that incorporates the richness and diversity of political life.

The rule of law as a prerequisite for democracy—or vice versa?

Close attention to how Commissioners speak about democracy in their public speeches reveals a rather stable conception of democracy between members of both the Juncker and the first von der Leyen Commissions—one that is both legalistic and technocratic. What is noteworthy is the near total absence of ideological pluralism or democratic contestation, even though the lack of pluralism is at the heart of the liberal conception of democracy under threat when member states regress on democratic values. I label this conception 'democracy without politics'. In this section, I demonstrate 'democracy without politics' in speeches of European Commissioners empirically. I first describe the democracy frames mobilized by the Commission between September 2018 and February 2023, and later relate the framing of democracy with the policy choices made in regard to democratic backsliding in EU member states.

After coding the 155 speeches in the corpus using the word 'democracy', I identified 480 uses of the term 'democracy', of which 432 were coded into 10 frames (the remaining 48 references were too vague or empty to give any insight into the speaker's conceptualization of democracy and were put aside). The following frames were identified in order of prevalence: the rule of law and fundamental or human rights (141 references), the quality of information (63), geopolitical threats (58), media freedom (40), international cooperation (36), data protection and cyber security (26), pluralism (24), elections (20), problem-solving (12), and respect for minorities (12). The frames were developed inductively, through iterative coding, on the basis of each reference to 'democracy' made by the Commissioners.

As we will see, the different frames do not necessarily contradict one another; rather, they tend to highlight different aspects of democracy, which is understandable given that the Commissioners under study deal with different policy portfolios. In this way, most of the frames can be seen as complementary, and give rise to a unified and fairly stable conceptualization of democracy. To this end, the goal of the framing analysis is to trace the elements that the different frames have in common. Each reference was categorized in terms of its main frame, even where it could be associated with more than one frame. The relative distribution of the frames throughout the corpus provides an overview, yet the core of the qualitative analysis consists of analysing which elements are shared throughout the main frames, as well as the absence of other dimensions. I argue the most common frames share a depoliticized conception of democracy at odds with democratic pluralism. In the remainder of this section, I analyse these frames in more detail, to prepare the ground for a general conceptualization of the Commission's understanding of democracy.

Out of the 155 speeches analysed, 'democracy' is most often connected by European Commissioners to the frame I labelled 'Rule of

Fig. 1: Democracy frames in speeches of European Commissioners, 2018–23.

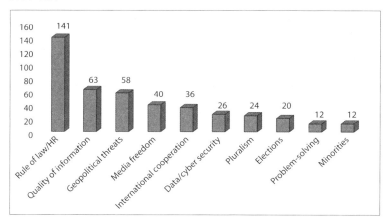

law and fundamental or human rights' (hereafter referred to as 'rule of law/HR', 141 references). This frame emphasizes the 'liberal' dimension of democracy, framing democracy as a set of liberal legal principles centred around the separation of the branches of government. The frame articulates democracy as being on an equal footing with the rule of law, or dependent on it. Frans Timmermans, the Commissioner in charge of Rule of Law and Fundamental Rights during the Juncker Commission, explicitly situated the rule of law as a precondition for democracy: 'The rule of law has a particular role: it is a prerequisite for the protection of all the other fundamental values, including for fundamental rights and democracy. Without the rule of law you cannot really protect them' (Timmermans 2019a). Commissioner Didier Reynders made a similar claim about the interdependence of the rule of law and democracy: 'What makes the rule of law so important is that it guarantees the respect of all other values, including democracy and fundamental rights' (Reynders 2020), while Commissioner Vera Jourová took this logic further still, seemingly placing the rule of law on a higher level and democracy in the supporting role: '*Defending the rule of law requires a resilient democracy*, an active civil society and free and independent media' (Jourová 2020, emphasis added). Most notable about the rule of law/HR frame is its sheer frequency—it is used in Commissioner speeches more often than the second and third most common frames combined (see Fig. 1).

PROTECTING DEMOCRACY IN EUROPE

The second most common interpretive framework the European Commissioners draw on in their discourse on democracy by European Commissions is 'quality of information' (63 references). This frame emphasizes the importance of a fact-based political debate, and the threat that disinformation poses to democracy. For instance, in a speech to the Fundamental Rights Forum, Commissioner Jourová warned: 'In democracy, irresponsible politicians can easily take advantage of the freedom of speech by using fear for their political gains' (Jourová 2018). Many of the speeches framing democracy in this way point explicitly to the threats posed by disinformation. This quote from a speech Commission President Ursula von der Leyen gave is a typical example: 'we must nurture our democracy every day, and defend our institutions against the corrosive power of hate speech, of disinformation, fake news and incitement to violence' (von der Leyen 2021a). Few of these references are directly about democratic backsliding. Instead, they are often more closely related to geopolitical concerns such as the intensification of Russian aggression against Ukraine. However, this frame is important to understand the Commission's general technocratic and depoliticized perspective on democracy. Too much attention to getting 'the facts' right undermines the pluralist reality that democratic politics consists not only in grappling with what the facts might be in a given situation, but also which facts are relevant, what ways they matter, what to do about them, and so on.

It is also important to note that the negative focus on the risks of disinformation in speeches framing democracy in terms of quality of information is overwhelming; indeed, there are no examples in the corpus of the quality of information frame being used to raise the importance of epistemic diversity (of viewpoints and perspectives), scientific or intellectual uncertainty, or any concession to contextual or relative notions of truth. Several references by Commissioner Jourová warning against a too stringent approach to combating disinformation come closest. For instance, in a speech where she presents several new or updated tools in the Commission's 'fight against disinformation', she also notes that 'freedom of speech is fundamental' and concedes that 'disinformation as such is not *always* illegal' (Jourová 2022, emphasis added). However, I did not find a single example of a Commissioner reflecting on how or why the expression of multiple and potentially contradictory perspectives on truth may be important for democratic government. Instead, the importance of the quality of information for democracy is generally understood by Commissioners simply as the perseverance of 'truth and facts' over 'lies and falsehoods' (von der Leyen 2022).

As I have noted, the quality of information frame is frequently adjacent to the 'geopolitical threat' frame, the third most common frame (58 references), that we find increasingly in Commissioner speeches after the full-scale military invasion of Ukraine by Russia in February 2022. This link can be seen clearly for example in a speech given by Commissioner Jourová in Tallinn, where she said: 'the Russian state has engaged in the war of ideas to pollute our information space with half-truth and lies to create a false image that democracy is no better than autocracy' (Jourová 2023). Other references to this frame, especially by Commission President von der Leyen, are even more explicit in framing the Russian invasion as a war against democracy in Europe overall. For example, 'Not only is Putin waging a war against Ukraine's integrity and freedom but also against Europe's energy, economy and democracy' (von der Leyen 2023). The geopolitical threat frame is also notably the most common frame used by von der Leyen; out of the 141 references coded in her speeches, this frame was used 42 times, well above the rule of law/fundamental rights frame (26 times), international cooperation (20 times), and the quality of information (13 times).[3]

Also closely connected to the 'quality of information' frame, we find the 'media freedom' frame, used a total of 40 times. While the two frames relate to one another, the latter emphasizes the protection of journalists, whereas the former tends to highlight the growing role of social media in (manipulating) public debates. In 2018, for instance, Commission President Jean-Claude Juncker made this link clearly in his State of the Union speech when he said 'Europe must always be a place where freedom of the press is sacrosanct. Too many of our journalists are intimidated, attacked, murdered. There is no democracy without a free press' (Juncker 2018). Interestingly, the media freedom frame is in some cases also connected to the rule of law/HR frame. For instance, when discussing the government attempts to silence free media in Poland, Hungary and Slovenia, Commissioner Jourová argued that, 'media are not just an economic sector, but an important pillar of democracy and the rule of law. Press freedom and media pluralism are vital to democracy' (Jourová 2021). This is an interesting argument to make that reflects the overall conceptualization of democracy by the European Commission. Rather than treating media freedom as a key guarantor and facilitator of political pluralism, the Commission has shifted the political arena towards legal institutions by connecting media freedom with the rule of law.

'International cooperation' is the next most used frame (36 references). This frame sometimes comes up in the context of EU relations with countries in its 'near abroad', for example, and in the context of enlargement. Not without irony, Commissioner Olivér Várhelyi, the Hungarian Fidesz-affiliated nominee for the first von der Leyen Commission appointed to the enlargement and neighbourhood dossier, said the following: 'I strongly believe that supporting enlargement and closer engagement means investing in long-lasting peace, stability, democracy, and prosperity in the region and beyond' (Várhelyi 2022).[4] The other context in which this frame is most often used is in the EU's relation with established democracies, particularly the United States. We can see a typical example to this effect in the following quote by von der Leyen, speaking about Joe Biden's Summit for Democracy: 'proving to people that international cooperation and democracy can deliver is our biggest test with like-minded partners' (von der Leyen 2021c).

After this, the frames become much more infrequently used. Indeed, the relevance of the following frames, 'data protection and cyber security' (26 references), 'pluralism' (24 references), 'elections' (20 references), 'problem-solving' (12 references) and 'minority protection' (12 references) for exposing the Commission's conception of democracy lies, in part, in how rare such elements are. While the 'data protection and cyber security' frame—focused on how the EU can strengthen protections in the face of digital threats—does not reveal much of interest here, the notable absence of many references to democratic pluralism and democratic elections is highly revealing. Even when these frames are implied, they are often done so indirectly or vaguely. For example, Johannes Hahn, Commissioner

'DEMOCRACY WITHOUT POLITICS'

for European Neighbourhood Policy and Enlargement Negotiations in the Juncker Commission, said the following: 'Younger voices are crucial in public debate and democracy in your countries. We need your creativity, ideas and commitment to build the societies everyone deserves' (Hahn 2018). I coded this in the pluralism frame because by mentioning the public debate that 'younger voices' can contribute their ideas to, Hahn implied that the interests or ideas of younger citizens may be different from those of older citizens. But it is hardly a strong endorsement of the importance of representing ideological pluralism or the divergence of interests. Similarly, I coded typical references to the European Parliament, sometimes described as the 'beating heart of European democracy' (Juncker 2019), in the pluralism frame given that the European Parliament is a diverse body with a direct democratic mandate. Yet the references to the European Parliament as a democracy frame—as well as being infrequent—are mostly abstract, conceiving it as a symbol of European democracy, rather than emphasizing the ideological confrontation and negotiation between competing political groups it facilitates.

The above quotes are typical examples of the few references Commissioners make to democracy that can be framed as pluralistic in that they avoid any direct reference to ideological or interest divergence—the idea that people might have contrasting, potentially incommensurable views that democracy serves to adjudicate neutrally. A rare exception, coded in the elections frame, can be seen in the following quote by Commission President von der Leyen: 'each of our democracies is slightly different and unique … But ultimately, democracy in all its forms comes down to the same thing. It gives people a voice. *It gives the ability to change things at the ballot box*' (von der Leyen 2021b, emphasis added). But what is most striking in the review of all 480 references to democracy in the speeches in the corpus analysed is that these frames are so rare in Commissioner speeches, given how pluralistic elections constitute the absolute core of how political scientists usually understand democracy.

The 'problem-solving' and 'minority protection' frames are the least frequent, at twelve references or 2.5% of total coded references each. Again, these frames are noteworthy less for their frequency than for how these uses help us grasp the overall understanding of democracy at the level of the European Commission. The minorities frame emphasizes minority rights as key to democratic government. Significantly, while the overall uses of this frame of democracy are very low, it is the second-most used frame by Commissioner Frans Timmermans.[5] Several times, Timmermans puts minority rights at the core of his conception of democracy, for instance arguing 'the respect for the position of minorities is more important than always putting through the will of the majority' (2019b). While the importance of this frame should not be overstated, we can note that it coheres with the liberal emphasis on limitations to public authority that we see more predominantly in the rule of law frame. Lastly, the problem-solving frame refers to those references that link democracy to a specific desired outcome. For instance, when discussing the importance of economic development in the European Neighbourhood Policy,[6] Commissioner Hahn posited that democracy was 'the best way to address social unrest' (2019). Despite the relative paucity of such references, they too share the general technocratic orientation of the Commission's conception of democracy, reflecting the idea that democracy can help in achieving certain ends that are defined as desirable independently of processes of democratic contestation.

'Democracy without politics' in responding to democratic backsliding in the EU

What brings together the vast majority of the different democracy frames of the European Commission is their depoliticized nature. I conceive of depoliticization as the process by which political choices are presented as if they are purely 'technical' or 'administrative' (Hay and Rosamond 2002), thereby removing 'the political character of decision-making' (Burnham 2001: 128). This characterizes to a great extent what the European Commission does when mobilizing the term 'democracy' in the corpus of speeches I have examined. In most of the Juncker and von der Leyen's Commission's discourse I analysed, democracy has little to do with actual *politics*. The frames related to the rule of law, fundamental and human rights, quality of information, or media freedom are normatively important, yet share, in the Commission's discourse, a common technocratic and legalistic nature. The rule of law dimensions of democracy are addressed through the (negative) focus on the question on whether there are violations of the separation of powers or legal accountability. The quality of information frame similarly focuses on a negative element (a threat), addressing disinformation campaigns that circulate on social media, which Commissioners frequently suggest ought to be addressed by the regulation of social media companies. Media freedom in turn is broached by emphasizing the importance of protecting the safety of journalists, mainly through the improvement of law enforcement mechanisms. All these democracy frames share an overall coherent technocratic and liberal understanding of democracy and, crucially, generally lack a pluralist or contestatory perspective. In this sense, the Commission seems to conceive itself as a sort of 'ombudsman' of the EU, rather than the EU's main political executive actor.

So far, the European Commission's response to democratic backsliding has been centred around this legal dimension. The most famous of these is the much criticized (but nevertheless underused) Article 7 of the Treaty on European Union (TEU) procedure, whereby the European Council can—in theory, if not in practice—determine 'serious and persistent' breaches of the EU fundamental values listed in Article 2 TEU. Article 7 proceedings were launched against Poland in December 2017 and, on the prompting of the European Parliament, against Hungary in September 2018 (I discuss the reticence of the Commission to launch Article 7 proceedings against Hungary in Chapter 5). For years, it was obvious that proceedings could never realistically lead to sanctions, however, given an alliance of support between the governments of Poland and Hungary on the one hand and, on the other, the unanimity requirement in Article 7 (see the discussion of the weakness of the legal tools to respond to democratic backsliding in Chapter 4). It remains to be seen at the time of writing if the 2023 victory of Polish opposition parties to unseat Law and Justice will have a decisive effect on changing this, or whether Giorgia Meloni's populist radical right government in Italy or Slovakia's populist government headed by Robert Fico will take over from Poland to protect Hungary from sanctions. In any case, besides the slim prospect of the so-called 'sanctioning arm' of the article ever being used, the core takeaway from over six years of ongoing Article 7 hearings has been one of dialogue and delay (or to use the words of one legal scholar, 'de-dramatization').[7]

If we briefly review the main responses of the European Commission to democratic backsliding in EU member states besides Article 7, we can see how this depoliticized conceptualization of democracy tracks through most of the Commission's actions. Since 2013, all EU member states are assessed by the European Commission for the 'efficiency of justice' (in relation to their judicial systems and the rule of law), resulting in the 'EU Justice Scoreboard'. A Commission-led monitoring and dialogue procedure—the 'Rule of Law Framework'—was added to this in 2014, adding steps prior to a Commission recommendation for Article 7 to be activated against a backsliding member state. The appetite for monitoring was not exhausted, though, and in response to resolutions adopted in the European Parliament in 2016 and 2018, the Commission published its first 'Rule of Law Report'—evaluating all member states' performance on rule of law criteria in September 2020 (these monitoring tools are discussed in more detail in Chapter 6). In December 2020, the European Parliament and the Council adopted the 'Rule of Law Conditionality Regulation' (regulation 2020/2092). This facilitates some economic conditionality as a response to rule of law backsliding in member states (the Regulation is analysed in detail in the following chapter). Concurrently, the European Public Prosecutor's Office was launched on 1 June 2021 to 'help promote a coordinated judicial response' to 'protect the EU's financial interests if there are generalized deficiencies linked to the rule of law' (a euphemism for wide-scale corruption concerning the use and disbursement of EU funds by backsliding member states) (Regulation 2017/1939). All of these responses were geared to addressing democratic regression only indirectly, via the rule of law, and they can mostly be characterized as the Commission trying to 'manage' rather than 'enforcing' democratic values (Priebus 2022). Thus, the Commissioners' framing of democracy matches the policy choices made in regard to democratic backsliding.

I conceive of the Commission's approach as 'technocratic legalism', insofar as democracy is framed in a depoliticized way (hence the strong technocratic component), facilitating a legal toolbox to address democratic backsliding. This is not a causal argument; I do not aim at establishing the causal mechanisms at play that explain the Commission's policy choices. Rather, from the above analysis I conclude that the Commission's depoliticized understanding of democracy reflects the philosophy behind the policy choices. A different conception of democracy would justify a different toolbox. These findings are not necessarily surprising, since presenting political issues as 'technical' tends to be the Commission's general modus operandi. But this actually underlines the pertinence of the analysis rather than undermining it. It is not by an external constraint of legal determinism that the Commission must interpret its role in a largely technocratic way, it is precisely its own conception of democracy that hinders its capacity to act politically. Indeed, the fact that the Commission depoliticizes issues—including its responses to democratic backsliding in EU member states—by presenting them as 'technical' problems to be solved does not mean that it is not a (transnational) political actor with a wider capacity to operate politically than it allows itself.

What we see in the European Commission's speeches is a vision of 'democracy without politics'. The traditional output-oriented approach to legitimacy of the EU (de Jongh and Theuns 2017), and particularly the European Commission, can be clearly identified in how the Commission frames democracy in Commissioner speeches, and aligns the Commission towards taking narrow and legalistic positions. To be fair, the rule of law is not conceived in an overly narrow way, and Commissioners do point to media freedom as an important element. However, 'media freedom' is not equivalent to 'media pluralism'. The mere fact that journalists do not fear for their lives—while clearly essential for democracy to function—does not mean that there is pluralism, nor that a healthy democratic public sphere is prioritized. Political pluralism requires more than the 'rule of law', 'quality of information' and 'media freedom'. Stripped of democratic contestation, these frames seem to indicate an administrative understanding of democracy. Pluralist democracy contrasts markedly with both the Commission's discourse and its approach to responding to democratic backsliding. The contestation of political ideas in the public sphere is at the very core of a political conception of democracy (or so I will argue in Chapter 7). These contrasting ideals inform alternative pathways for responding to democratic backsliding in EU member states.

Indeed, political contestation is largely left outside of the scope of the Commission's understanding of democracy, with few exceptions. Rather than democracy being about the confrontation of plural voices discussing how society should be organized, the Commission's discourse emphasizes mostly the safeguarding of quality of information, media freedom, elections in which there is no foreign interference, and a constant amalgamation of democracy, the rule of law and fundamental rights. Obviously, this is not to say that democracy is unrelated to these dimensions. Indeed, they are necessary conditions for a democratic polity to exist. However, they are not sufficient in themselves, and incorporating the missing aspects of democracy (ideological pluralism, contestation, the recognition of the role of a legitimate opposition, etc.) would reflect a fuller, healthier, and normatively more attractive conception of democracy. Moreover, these missing frames track similar lacunae in the Commission's policy response to democratic backsliding.

While much has been said in regard to the EU's response to democratic backsliding, the literature has so far barely addressed the normative conception of democracy underpinning the EU's policy choices. And through a systematic framing analysis of Commissioner speeches, we can see that the Commission's conception of 'democracy without politics' tracks their technocratic legalism in how they respond to democratic backsliding in EU member states. The Commission has developed myriad legal monitoring tools to assess member states' judicial systems and the rule of law. Yet, none of these mechanisms (and few of the infringement actions) assess the ailing health of the public spheres of backsliding member states, the suppression (through death by regulation, co-option, and intimidation) of critical voices in academia, civil society and the media, or the disadvantages increasingly stacked against opposition actors and parties to compete as equals. Sanction mechanisms are focused on cutting off EU funds to backsliding states who use them corruptly, and the eventual (though seemingly hopeless) exclusion of backsliding governments from EU political decision-making via Article 7 TEU. These may be important elements—not least to try to contain the influence of budding autocrats on EU legislation (see Chapter 6) and to reduce the complexity of the EU in member states' backsliding (see Chapter 5)—but they do little in themselves to protect pluralist democracy and foster a healthy public sphere.

Attention to democratic pluralism and contestation reveals some of the lacunae of the Commission's current approach. Such a vision of democracy must go beyond a technocratic concern with the quality and accuracy of public discourse and the formalism of a narrow focus on the rule of law. Instead, it highlights the importance of pluralism, the public sphere, and a vibrant civil society that holds the government to account. For democracy to be vibrant, processes of representation and contestation must include real alternative visions of society, and open deliberation on these alternatives in civic spaces that facilitate such exchanges—in other words, in healthy public spheres. Quality of information is of course important, but an over-emphasis on the quality of information (that is, the role of 'facts' in public discourse) depoliticizes democracy. It is in the contestation and negotiation of which facts are salient for a public policy, how to interpret, contextualize and use those facts, and what to do about them that a democratic polity's politics is forged. In other words, pluralism is a feature of democratic politics, not a flaw.

Conclusion

What emerges from the analysis in this chapter is that EU Commissioners do not think enough about how they can support domestic opposition to backsliding governments, and thereby stimulate more vibrant democratic contestation where democratic pluralism is at stake (a core point I develop further in Chapter 7). And while the urgency of this task is where the risks of democratic collapse are greatest, this wider understanding of democracy in the EU context should not only address extreme cases such as that of Orbán's Hungary. With a more pluralistic conception of democracy in mind, we can ask whether the Commission should be content with buttressing legal processes (notwithstanding the importance of a robust legal-democratic framework). As Guardian of the Treaties, and therefore of the EU's fundamental values, should the Commission not also encourage healthy democratic contestation in the public spheres of EU member states much more broadly, especially where these are moribund? After all, using a broader understanding of democracy that explicitly included democratic deliberation, Anna Gora and Pieter de Wilde found that declining democratic deliberation was on the whole more significant than rule of law setbacks in EU member states (2022). At the very least, the Commission should ensure that its activities in protecting democracy in Europe do not have the effect of further depoliticizing the sphere of member state politics at the domestic and European level, a concern that has been around for some time (cf. Mair 2007). Accordingly, revising the dominant understanding of democracy in the context of democratic backsliding is not only a conceptual question, but one that would have real political and normative implications for the EU's response to democratic backsliding.

In Chapter 6 and especially Chapter 7, I make the case that pluralist democracy could be more effective in containing and potentially even reversing democratic backsliding in EU member states. However, adding a pluralist approach would be normatively valuable irrespective of its efficacy in reversing democratic backsliding because it would communicate a commitment to (the value of) democracy in its full sense. It is valuable in its own right to reaffirm the importance of EU fundamental values and to commit to them. This is not to say that legal measures against governments leading democratic backsliding are necessarily inadequate on their own terms. Indeed, I will argue in Chapter 5 that the unrestrained use of existing legal measures is critical in correcting EU complicity with democratic backsliding. But the blinkered focus on legalism and the rule of law that we see throughout the corpus of Commissioner speeches I have analysed misses certain critical aspects, especially when combined with a depoliticized approach that tries to de-escalate democratic backsliding in EU member states through endless cycles of monitoring and dialogue with bad faith actors.

I recognize that this idea faces significant obstacles. The main one is that legalistic understandings of democracy are a better fit with traditional consensus-oriented EU political dynamics (see Hix and Bartolini 2006). There may also be a worry that a focus on more political pluralism may lead the European integration process towards a 'constraining dissensus' (Hooghe and Marks 2009). However, there are also significant risks to the European Commission maintaining its aversion towards pluralistic democratic politics by emphasizing its 'technical' and 'non-political' role (Haapala and Oleart 2022). Blocking 'agonistic' forms of politicization and democratic contestation opens the door towards the antagonistic forms of conflict such as those offered by the populist appeals of, for instance, Viktor Orbán or Marine Le Pen. If 'democracy without politics' is a threat to democratic pluralism, we should not lose sight of the fact that authoritarians' projects are a much more fundamental challenge to pluralism. The solution to political heterogeneity and disagreement is more democracy, not less.

The findings in this chapter have important political and academic implications. Much scholarship has (rightfully) paid attention to the 'rule of law' breaches by Poland and Hungary; however, as with the European Commission, some scholars have been tempted to overlook the political and deliberative dimensions of democratic backsliding in the EU. This is not to say that the rule of law is not an important pillar of democracy, but rather that it is not the only pillar. The goal of an objective and value-free political science is misguided in this context; we must be clear about what is valuable about democracy to be able to critically assess (and even identify) violations of democratic ideals, and to evaluate policy responses to the deterioration of democratic government in some member states. Consequently, academics should engage the debate on democratic backsliding using a full and healthy conception of democracy that situates democratic pluralism at its centre. If my conception of 'pluralist democracy' is convincing, it gives us both a normative framework to assess democratic backsliding in EU member states, and an ideal to aim for when developing a policy response that goes beyond legal mechanisms. So far, most political, policy and academic analyses of democratic backsliding have overemphasized the rule of law, the separation of powers and executive overreach, much like the European Commission. This is to the detriment of adequate attention to the degradation of political pluralism and the public sphere. Given this, a fuller and healthier conception of democracy is needed to protect what is valuable in European democratic life.

4

AN IMMANENT CRITIQUE OF EU TOOLS AGAINST DEMOCRATIC BACKSLIDING

Good to be bold; but mettle is dangerous in a blind horse. Spit in the wind's face, and you know the consequence.

Hewson Clarke, *Herwald De Wake or, The Two Apostates*

We have seen that the recent history of the European Union's (EU) responses to anti-democratic politics and the Commission's approach to conceptualizing democracy suffers from several serious flaws. But does the so-called 'toolbox' that EU actors have to respond to anti-democratic threats fare any better on its own terms? In this chapter, I use political theory methods that are designed to test the coherence of these tools with the fundamental values that they are supposed to protect. I argue that some of the key sanctions mechanisms the EU has at its disposal are seriously flawed on these terms. Specifically, I argue that the flagship procedure to sanction state violations of fundamental values described in Article 7 of the Treaty on European Union (TEU) is normatively incoherent. The sanction it describes itself undermines the values of democracy and equality it is supposed to protect. The same is true, I argue, of a lesser-known procedure that can be used to deregister anti-democratic political parties in the European Parliament. If this critique is valid, this not only poses a serious problem for armchair philosophers and others who care about moral hypocrisy, but also has a vital practical dimension: normatively incoherent mechanisms cannot succeed on their own terms as they undermine their own conditions for success, or so I will argue.

This chapter assesses the existing toolbox the EU has to respond to democratic backsliding in EU member states. The bulk of my analysis critically engages the best-known procedure for responding to member state violations of EU fundamental values: Article 7 TEU. The methodology I use here is quite different from the approach of the previous two chapters. In Chapter 2, I tried to understand how depoliticization and membership fatalism—key problems in how the EU has responded to democratic backsliding over the past decade—have emerged. In Chapter 3, I used a different empirical approach—discourse and framing analysis—to explore how the European Commission thinks about democracy, analysing 155 speeches by European Commissioners in the Juncker and first von der Leyen Commissions. Here, in contrast, my goal is primarily philosophical rather than empirical. I want to assess the extent to which key EU democracy protection tools live up to or undermine EU fundamental values.

Normative political theory does not seek principally to ascertain 'the facts' in order to better understand or explain empirical phenomena. Instead, normative theory analyses political phenomena through systematic reflection on their legitimacy, justification, authority, and their coherence with relevant political values. The goal of normative theory when thinking about politics can be—i.e. evaluatively—to look at existing or past politics, evaluating the (il)legitimacy, (in)justice or (in)coherence of these states of affairs. Alternatively, it can be to look forwards—i.e. prescriptively—at recommending specific institutional, constitutional or societal changes to better live up to certain values or ideals. Here (and in this first part this book more generally), the goal is evaluative and the orientation backward-looking. In the second half of the book, I present a more prescriptive and forward-looking agenda of how the EU can better protect democracy.

Studying the normative question of what, if anything, the EU ought to do about the fact of democratic backsliding in EU member states raises challenging methodological issues concerning how to bridge 'fact' and 'value'. While empirical facts may be necessary for this reflection, facts alone cannot suffice. This is sometimes referred to as the gap between 'is' and 'ought' (Rippon et al. 2020: 17). In either the evaluative or prescriptive mode, normative theory must make a choice regarding the appropriate degree of idealization. 'Ideal' theories seek to evaluate states of affairs or prescribe actions based on a utopian vision of a perfectly just or perfectly legitimate polity. We can use such theories, in a second stage, to criticize existing politics for failing to live up to these ideals and defend reforms that should take us closer to the ideal. 'Non-ideal' theories, in contrast, take more seriously the limitations of what may be plausible or realistic to push society from how things are in the here and now to a more just and legitimate near future (Zala et al. 2020).

As discussed in Chapter 1, the normative-theoretical approach taken in this book is 'non-ideal'. My project is not to debate different utopian visions of European politics, but to identify paths for improving the legitimacy, authority and justification of the existing EU in light of democratic backsliding among member states; in other words, to protect democracy in Europe. That is not to say that ideal theory in general is necessarily misplaced or mistaken; I take no position on that question here. Rather, non-ideal theory seems well suited to the task at hand because the nature of democratic backsliding requires identifying a regression on democratic standards relative to a prior baseline. We say a country is backsliding at a certain point in time relative to how democratic it was at a specific previous point in time. Such an 'ordinal' comparison of current versus past performance on democratic indicators does not require—and I think would be hampered—by continually needing to refer back to the sorts of transcendental evaluative standards that ideal theorists pursue (Sen 2006). Rather than arguing from (or taking as given) externally derived 'cardinal' values, the methods I use in this chapter are practice-dependent, using values derived from political and legal practice of EU integration (Sangiovanni 2007, 2015; cf. Erman and Möller 2015). As such, instead of first developing or adopting a philosophical account of the absolute or universal value of democratic government, I look internally to identify the values and norms that are implicitly or explicitly embedded in EU law and policy.

PROTECTING DEMOCRACY IN EUROPE

This chapter applies two specific normative methodologies to evaluate the existing legal and policy toolbox the EU has to respond to democratic backsliding: the study of normative (in)coherence and the study of expressive consistency. Both the study of normative coherence and the specific method to test for expressive consistency belong to the family of approaches to normative political theory sometimes called 'immanent critique'. Immanent critique departs from the position that a minimal normative standard of a political practice is that it does not violate its own normative premises (Nicolaïdis 2013; Theuns 2017). There are many ways immanent critique has been interpreted, but the analyses here consist of the critical normative evaluation of legal and political practices grounded not on an external set of normative values but on justificatory standards drawn internally from legal and political praxis. As such, it operates on an 'internal' rather than an 'external' mode of practice-dependent critique (Sangiovanni 2007, 2015; cf. Erman and Möller 2015).

There are two elements to such an immanent critique. First, we need to isolate the evaluative standards from the 'evolving aspirations, tensions and contradictions within this world observed' (Nicolaïdis 2013: 357). Second, we must evaluate the extent to which the practice lives up to its normative commitments. Immanent critique has as an advantage that any observer drawn or committed to the internal values and norms of a particular legal and political environment can feel implicated by the normative analysis. Like other non-ideal approaches to normative theorizing, this means it is ecumenical in that it does not demand an overarching philosophical commitment to fully worked-out values.[1]

The first normative theory analysis that I use in this chapter is the study of the normative coherence of the EU's response to democratic backsliding in EU member states. For a law or policy to be normatively coherent, it must be the case that the contents of the policy do not undermine the values justifying the policy. Following a distinction by Joseph Raz (1992), coherence here is used in the weak sense whereby a set of laws and policies are taken to be normatively coherent if they do not stand in opposition to one another, rather than in the strong sense whereby they are all derived from the same normative commitments, values or presuppositions. Normatively incoherent policy and law is not only a problem for political philosophers, but has very concrete political consequences: if two policies pursued simultaneously by the same actors or institutions run at cross purposes then they cannot both succeed on their own terms. To test for normative incoherence, then, it is first necessary to determine which evaluative standards emerge from a specific legal or political practice before assessing whether a set of laws or policies live up to those self-same standards. Specifically, I will elucidate the core values through a reading of European treaty texts (centrally Article 2 TEU) and test various legal responses to democratic backsliding in EU member states.

The second immanent critique method I adopt in this chapter is testing EU policy and legal responses to democratic backsliding for expressive consistency. There are many ways a communicative act can be expressively inconsistent. For instance, a communicative act can be ambiguous, in that several different interpretations of the message are valid; or it can be vague, in that it lacks precision over key ideas or concepts. One radical way that a communicative act can be expressively inconsistent is that it can be a 'performative contradiction'. A performative contradiction, in its simplest form, is 'when the content of a particular statement is in conflict with its utterance' (Poama and Theuns 2019: 800), such as when saying 'I do not exist' (Hintikka 1962: 32) or 'I never tell the truth'. In the context of the expressive purpose of a rule or law, the relevant performative contradiction is when a rule or law intended to express commitment to certain values itself undermines those values.

Like the study of normative coherence, tests of expressive consistency are geared towards ascertaining whether a policy or law can undermine its own preconditions, but which are focused on communicative or expressive aspects. Essentially, tests of expressive consistency are more specific ways to test for normative coherence that focus on the performative aspect of political praxis. This is especially important where we are interested in the communicative value of a particular policy or law. If, for instance, the procedure or sanctions of a democracy protection policy undermine the values it purports to express, then supporting the policy cannot unambiguously mark an actor as pro-democratic, nor can it draw member states committed to democracy closer together as a value community. Perhaps even more importantly, an expressively inconsistent response to democratic backsliding in an EU member state cannot adequately notify that state of the content and importance of the democratic values they threaten nor, consequently, give clarity on what would be necessary for reform. Such expressive failings are all the more malignant given the general confusion over the scope and specification of the EU's fundamental values, something that is exploited by those seeking to undermine those values (Mos 2020).

The bulk of the remainder of this chapter first draws out the relevant values that serve as standards in the consequent immanent critique before applying those to the procedure in Article 7 TEU, testing that legal mechanism for normative coherence and expressive consistency. In the final part of the chapter, I assess the normative coherence of three further tools that include the possibility of sanctions more schematically.[2] I first analyse the possibility of the European Commission or member states bringing 'systemic' infringement procedures against member states backsliding on EU fundamental values, including democracy, under Articles 258–60 of the Treaty on the Functioning of the EU (TFEU). Second, I examine the Rule of Law Conditionality Regulation,[3] adopted in late 2020, which allows the Commission to propose suspensions or reductions in EU funding to a member state with a 'generalised deficiency as regards the rule of law'. Third, I evaluate a little-known procedure for deregistering European political parties or foundations for breaches of the requirement that they uphold EU fundamental values in their programmes and activities.[4]

Analysing these four tools of the current EU toolbox for responding to violations of EU fundamental values and democratic standards shows that the current toolbox is deeply flawed. As well as being expressively inconsistent, I argue the Article 7 sanction and EU Regulation 1141/2014 on deregistering EU political parties and foundations are normatively incoherent in that the sanctions they propose violate the values they purport to defend. In contrast, I argue that the Rule of Law Conditionality Regulation and (systemic) infringement actions under Articles 258–60 TFEU do not raise the same concerns regarding their normative coherence. This critique suggests that one of the ways to design a coherent and effective system for protecting democracy in the EU would be to widen the application and scope of budget conditionality and infringement actions. I take up these possibilities and other ways to correct EU complicity in democratic backsliding and contain autocratic actors in EU member states in Chapters 5 and 6.

What values does the EU claim to uphold?

In keeping with the immanent critique approach, the analysis of the normative coherence of EU responses to democratic backsliding must start with careful attention to the values the EU claims to uphold. This is because tests of normative coherence use internal rather than external values, drawing their normativity from the political and legal practices themselves rather than from predetermined philosophical or ideological commitments. Legally, much of the bedrock of EU responses to democratic backsliding in EU member states is framed through the lens of such backsliding violating fundamental EU values, as listed in the European treaties. The main source for such values is Article 2 of the TEU, the core legal document of European integration, which clearly states that:

> The Union is founded on the values of respect for human dignity, freedom, democracy, equality, the rule of law and respect for human rights, including the rights of persons belonging to minorities. These values are common to the Member States in a society in which pluralism, non-discrimination, tolerance, justice, solidarity and equality between women and men prevail. (Article 2 TEU 2012)

The formulation of Article 2—which holds that the values listed 'are' shared and that normative commitments 'prevail'—is at odds with current trends towards democratic and rule of law backsliding in some member states. In effect, this already points to a form of incoherence, as clearly the values listed in Article 2 are *not* shared by each member state government. The fact that we are forced to interpret the article as listing ideals to be attained rather than as a declaration of shared normative commitments illustrates the urgency of the task at hand. It directly challenges us to reflect on what the EU should do to guarantee the democratic character of member states and EU institutions when member states are backsliding on fundamental values.

Besides Article 2, there is another important legal source of the commitment to specifically democratic government in the TEU: Article 10. This both stipulates that 'the functioning of the Union shall be founded on representative democracy' (Article 10.1 TEU 2012) and clarifies that, alongside the direct representation of European citizens in the European Parliament, 'Member States are represented in the European Council by their Heads of State or Government and in the Council by their governments, *themselves democratically accountable* either to their national Parliaments, or to their citizens' (Article 10.2, emphasis added). Finally, Article 10.3 also appears relevant, demanding that 'every citizen shall have the right to participate in the life of the Union'.[5]

The core treaty mechanism for sanctioning violations of fundamental values: Article 7

Since the Lisbon Treaty came into force in 2009, the EU has a core treaty mechanism to respond to violations of fundamental values in EU member states: Article 7 TEU. My contention is that a study of the normative and expressive value of Article 7 shows it to fall short of minimal standards of normative coherence and expressive consistency. To argue this point, we first need to start with a careful review of the procedure and precise mechanism detailed in Article 7. Almost each paragraph of Article 7 is relevant to my demonstration, so it is worth quoting the relevant sections in full.

Article 7 states that:

1. On a reasoned proposal by one third of the Member States, by the European Parliament or by the European Commission, the Council, acting by a majority of four fifths of its members after obtaining the consent of the European Parliament, may determine that there is a *clear risk of a serious breach* by a Member State of the *values referred to in Article 2* [...]
2. The European Council, *acting by unanimity* on a proposal by one third of the Member States or by the Commission and after obtain-

ing the consent of the European Parliament, may determine the *existence of a serious and persistent breach* by a Member State of the values referred to in Article 2, after inviting the Member State in question to submit its observations.
3. Where a determination under paragraph 2 has been made, the Council, acting by a qualified majority, may decide to *suspend certain of the rights* deriving from the application of the Treaties to the Member State in question, *including the voting rights* of the representative of the government of that Member State in the Council. In doing so, the Council shall take into account the possible consequences of such a suspension on the rights and obligations of natural and legal persons. *The obligations of the Member State in question under this Treaty shall in any case continue to be binding on that State.*
4. The Council, acting by a qualified majority, may decide subsequently to vary or revoke measures taken under paragraph 3 in response to changes in the situation which led to their being imposed [...]. (Article 7 TEU, emphases added)

Though the procedure has not gone very far, at the time of writing, Article 7 proceedings are officially ongoing against Hungary. After seven years of relative inactivity, Article 7 proceedings against Poland were officially withdrawn by the Commission on 29 May 2024.[6] Key stated concerns in both cases have been the dismantling of judicial independence, executive overreach, the suppression of independent critical voices in the media and academia, and violations of minority rights—specifically the rights of LGBTQ+ people and migrants. Yet, the Hungarian government, as well as the PiS-led Polish government between 2015 and 2023, have argued that, far from backsliding on democracy, they are implementing the sovereign will of their people and have a democratic mandate to do so.

Commentators have focused much of their ire on the unanimity requirement of Article 7.2, but have also criticized the very slow speed of the proceedings, as well as their politicized nature (e.g. Kochenov and Pech 2016; cf. Sedelmeier 2017). For instance, while concerns with Hungarian democratic backsliding have been around at least since Fidesz won the 2010 general election in Hungary, and have intensified progressively after their re-election in 2014 (Oliver and

Stefanelli 2016), 2018, and 2022, the first concrete steps towards rule of law proceedings against Hungary under Article 7 were made in the autumn of 2018. Procedures against Poland were quicker to start following the constitutional crisis of 2015, but anti-democratic actions by the Law and Justice-led government have intensified since 'dialogue' with the European Commission started (Kovács and Scheppele 2018), and continued until their electoral loss in 2023. Regarding the politicization of the proceedings, it has been argued that Fidesz, though now a defector from the European People's Party (EPP) group, was protected for a long time at the EU level by their EPP membership given their dominance in the Council and Parliament (Kelemen 2017: 220).

Further, because Article 7.2 requires the unanimity of the European Council at ascertaining a serious and persistent breach of Article 2 values, a simple alliance of Poland and Hungary (or any two member states) was sufficient to block any sanctions from being imposed. The unanimity requirement is thus a barrier to the practical efficacy of the Article 7 procedure. Another element which is said to block the working of Article 7 is the fact that the type of sanction it proposes is a slow, blunt instrument, often (although not without critique) described as the 'nuclear option'. Since stripping a member state's votes in the Council is symbolically weighty, observers think it is unlikely ever to be used to sanction a member state (e.g. Oliver and Stefanelli 2016; Sedelmeier 2017). Some also note that the sanction amounts to a sort of 'moral quarantine' rather than directly addressing the fact of backsliding in a member state (Müller 2015: 144).

Proposals for alternative sanctions mechanisms abound, and tend to focus on swifter, milder political sanctions, on depoliticizing the procedure by giving a stronger weight to the courts, or complementing political with economic sanctions (e.g. Kochenov and Pech 2016; Blauberger and Kelemen 2017; Pech and Scheppele 2017; Theuns 2020; Bellamy and Kröger 2021).[7] The justification for this move is usually framed as an issue of necessity: given the (assumed) salience of the Article 2 values, and continued democratic and rule of law backsliding by EU member states despite the Article 7 procedure, new procedures and tools are needed. Proposals for these new procedures are evaluated on their perceived ability to reverse democratic and rule of law backsliding, or at least to effectively contain it.

The normative incoherence of the Article 7 sanction

Critically engaging, as others have done, the procedural requirements, slow speed, severity and type of sanction currently formalized in Article 7 is important, but it misses another line of critical reflection that looks at the normative coherence of the rule of law procedure. Such a reflection asks whether the sanctions mechanism that Article 7 lays out for member states in breach of EU fundamental values is itself in line with those values. From the perspective of normative coherence, I argue that Article 7 is in conflict with the principle of democratic equality in that it violates a minimum democratic standard whereby all who are legally subject to a law ought to have a formally equal stake in its authorization. This is important, because this critique would remain valid even if the concerns regarding the procedural requirements and slow speed of the Article 7 TEU would be resolved.

The precise view I want to defend here is that the Article 7 mechanism is normatively incoherent because stripping a member state of their vote in the Council would be a violation of the fundamental values of democracy and equality, and especially of the procedural expression of the intersection of these values—democratic equality. The main reason that Article 7 is in conflict with democratic legitimacy is that it breaks with a minimal standard of democratic processes whereby all those legally subject to a rule or policy ought to have a formally equal stake in authorizing it. Article 7 allows for the eventuality of a member state losing its right to vote in the Council—a key legislative body of the EU—while continuing to be bound to the rules and policies (co-)determined by Council votes.

The importance of this argument for Article 7 being at 'mixed purposes' normatively is grounded on the value of normative coherence. I use the term 'normative coherence' to refer to any set of rules, policies and principles that do not undermine one another (that are mutually compatible if you will), rather than a stronger notion of coherence that would require that they all follow from a unitary foundational principle (Raz 1992). To say that Article 7 is normatively incoherent in light of the values of democracy and equality, then, is to say that it undermines those values. This normative incoherence is not mere moral 'hypocrisy' but has an important practical dimension. If the sanctions mechanism detailed in Article 7 cannot be used without undermining the grounds for its existence—the values of democracy and equality—then the procedure laid out in Article 7 can never be successful. Even if the procedure succeeds in reversing democracy and rule of law backsliding in a given member state, it does so at the cost of democratic equality.[8]

The purpose of Article 7 is to try to prevent and, if necessary, sanction breaches of the fundamental values of the EU listed in Article 2. Those values include, as we have seen, a commitment to democracy and equality. Nonetheless, I claim that the sanction laid out in Article 7.3 is in conflict with these fundamental values. What would it mean to respect the values of democracy and equality?

At the level of individual citizens of a democratic state, a minimal democratic standard holds that all those legally and permanently subject to a legally binding rule or policy (in short, a law) ought to have an equal stake in co-authorizing that law. In democratic theory, this standard is known as the 'all those subjected' standard or 'All-Subjected Principle'. What such a standard does is give a principled reason for the inclusion or exclusion of any given person into the body of democratic citizens with equal civil and political rights—the *demos*. Being 'permanently subjected to the binding laws' of a polity interferes with a subject's autonomy and must therefore be justified to them (Scherz 2013: 4). The democratic process offers a way of justifying such interference or 'subjection' in a neutral manner by granting all permanent residents of a given territory the right to participate in a formally equal fashion in democratic processes (Song 2012), typically an equal vote to elect the legislative body.

It is important to note that the standard whereby 'all subjected' must have an equal stake in democratic decision-making processes is not the only standard in the literature in democratic theory over the legitimate boundaries of the *demos*. Some argue that democratic equality requires that all those 'affected' by a decision ought to have an equal stake in it (Goodin 2007) or that all those 'coerced' by a law ought to co-authorize that law (López-Guerra 2005). This is not the place to weigh in on this complex debate. It is enough to note that the All-Subjected Principle, when limited territorially, constitutes the least expansive criterion for inclusion in the *demos* amongst these views; the other dominant criteria that have been proposed would all include many more people in the *demos*, especially those criteria that seek to extend the *demos* beyond a territorial polity (Goodin 2007; Abizadeh 2008; cf. Song 2012). Thus, for the sake of this chapter, I assume the validity of the All-Subjected Principle. If a more expansive principle of inclusion is correct, my critique of the normative incoherence of Article 7 is all the stronger.

The case for the normative incoherence of Article 7 in light of the Article 2 fundamental values of democracy and equality is straightforward with the All-Subjected Principle in mind. Were the sanction in Article 7.3 to be activated against a member state such that the state in question loses its right to vote in the Council, that state could not legitimately be subjected to the (otherwise legally authoritative) decisions of the Council. However, Article 7 states explicitly that, for such a disenfranchised state, 'The obligations [...] under this Treaty shall in any case continue to be binding' (Article 7.3 TEU 2012). Binding a state to obligations that result from procedures that exclude them seems to run in the face of the All-Subjected Principle.

One complicating factor, however, is that the All-Subjected Principle (and the alternative normative principles for inclusion in the *demos*) was designed for citizens, and the context of Article 7 concerns the votes of the representatives of governments. While democratic legitimacy principles posit strong normative reasons to treat all citizens as free and equal, the same cannot be assumed to be true for governments (Gaedeke 2016). Ordinarily, there is little trouble in applying such a principle of democratic equality to argue that states subject to the laws of the EU ought to have voting rights in EU institutional decision-making bodies such as the Council (and, proportionally to their population, in the European Parliament).[9] However, the particularities of democratic and rule of law backsliding throw up an additional hurdle: it is only when we assume that a given government is the democratically legitimate representative of its citizens that their authority to (co-)decide in institutions like the Council is justified.

But if a state has seriously regressed on democracy and the rule of law, is it still a legitimate representative of its citizens in this multi-level democratic structure?

The answer must be no—there will be a point of democratic and rule of law backsliding when an EU member state's government can no longer be considered the legitimate representative of its citizens.[10] But this does not help the legitimacy and normative coherence of Article 7. States that are sufficiently democratic ought, under the All-Subjected Principle, to have an equal stake in democratic rule-making and rule-authorization (in this context, an equal vote in the Council). But states that are insufficiently democratic cannot legitimately be bound to the Council's decisions—at least not if those obligations are premised on decisions of the Council being authoritative in light of the Council's democratic legitimacy. Nor can such a non-democratic state participate in Council decision-making if one wishes to protect the democratic legitimacy of such procedures (this is a key point I develop in Chapter 8). In other words, if a backsliding member state is still 'democratic enough', its right to an equal vote in the Council must be guaranteed, whereas if it is not, it must lose its vote, but cannot be bound to Council decision-making.

Expressive consistency: Article 7 as a performative contradiction

The critique developed in the previous subsection holds that Article 7 is normatively incoherent in that the sanction undermines the values it purports to defend. Another perspective focuses not on the normative coherence of the mechanism, but on its expressive consistency. In an important sense, normative coherence and expressive consistency are related. Where a law or policy is normatively incoherent, it is difficult to suppose that it can be an effective vehicle for communicating the importance of the values it purports to uphold. Yet, the focus of these critiques and their scope is distinct. While normative coherence examines the philosophical consistency of a law or policy with the values immanent to a legal and political community, expressive consistency raises the question of precisely what the purpose of a law or policy is in terms of how it can contribute to discursively constructing that value community. One of the key purposes of Article 7, I claim, is to express commitment to the fundamental values listed in Article 2. Yet, in this section, I argue that it fails in this purpose in the way it undermines the values of equality and democracy. In other words, it falls into a performative contradiction.

An interesting aspect of Article 7 is that at every stage of the process the modality 'may' is invoked (e.g. 'the Council ... may determine/decide'). This guarantees a margin of manoeuvre even once the European Council has determined a serious and persistent breach; this text does not create a legal 'duty' for the Council to sanction a backsliding state, and provides for no role for the European Court of Justice (ECJ; Sadurski 2009: 394). In other words, it is politics 'all the way down'. This gives us an important clue that one of the purposes of Article 7 is centrally political—to communicate something—rather than being geared solely at the rectification of a legal wrong. Article 7, in this sense, is not only the 'enforcer' of Article 2 values, but also their 'loudspeaker', functioning to underline the EU's supposedly unequivocal and deep commitment to the fundamental values listed in Article 2.

It is also not immediately clear from the wording of Article 7 what its purpose is. Yet it is crucial to interrogate its purpose if we are to take a position on whether it is expressively consistent. As a sanctions mechanism, it is useful to look to the extant theories justifying penal sanctions for illumination. With this in mind, several possible purposes or functions of Article 7 can be imagined.

- A *dissuasive* purpose. On this line of thought, the existence of weighty sanctions themselves could motivate member states to respect Article 2 values. This purpose would be similar to the justification of criminal law sanctions that grounds these in their deterrent function.
- A *punitive* purpose, to avenge the supposed wrong that transgressing Article 2 values may constitute. This purpose would be structurally similar to justifications of criminal sanctions that emphasize their retributive function.
- An *expressive* purpose, to express the EU's continuing commitment to, and the importance of, Article 2 values. This function tracks the denunciative rationale of penal sanctions.

- A *reformative* purpose, where the aim is centrally to change the behaviour of the member state putatively in violation of Article 2 values. This purpose would track justifications of penal sanctions focused on rehabilitation.
- An *inoculative* purpose. If the main intention is to prevent governments backsliding on democratic values to influence Council decisions (by stripping them of a vote), we might say the purpose is inoculative. This purpose is similar to justifications of penal sanctions focused on incapacitating the offender.

It is likely that elements of each type of justification for a sanctions-based response can be identified in Article 7 in some shape or form. The expressive inconsistency I wish to highlight, however, focuses on the intersection of the expressive and the reformative purposes.

These functions of Article 7 can be understood along two lines. First, Article 7 has the function of underlining the normative importance of the values listed in Article 2 for the European Union. It is this sort of purpose Sadurski has in mind when he writes that sanctions 'should be seen as a general ideological declaration setting the limits of what is politically acceptable within the Union' (2009: 405). Regardless of whether certain states in fact are (at risk of) breaching Article 2 values, the specification of a weighty political sanction for such a breach serves to bring the member states (closer) together around a shared perspective of which values are of fundamental political importance. This could be called the 'declarative' expressive function of Article 7. Second, Article 7 can have the function of expressing to member states the costs and the weightiness of breaching fundamental values. This second perspective focuses on the 'instructive' reformative aspect and is geared towards pushing backsliding member states to reform practices that lead them to be in breach of those values (Poama and Theuns 2019: 797). These perspectives are related to one another in that, in order to instruct member states regarding their breach of fundamental values, these values must be clearly expressed; that is, the reformative purpose of Article 7 rests in part on the clarity and coherence of the expressive purpose.

For both the expressive and the reformative functions of Article 7 to be successful, it must at a minimum be the case that the procedure described in Article 7 does not itself undermine the values it purports to express. Even so, Article 7 fails to live up to the values of democracy and equality, and thus falls into a performative contradiction, or so I will argue. My specific claim is that stripping a member state in serious and persistent breach of EU fundamental values of their right to vote in the Council itself undermines the EU fundamental values of democracy and equality. As such, Article 7 is in a performative contradiction with the fundamental values listed in Article 2: it cannot adequately express them and, consequently, is hampered in both its declarative and instructive functions.

As with the test of normative coherence, testing the expressive consistency of Article 7 in line with these purposes requires first asking oneself what, minimally, a commitment to the fundamental value of democracy and equality requires in the context of EU decision-making. The values of democracy and equality are notably hard to pin down (Mos 2020). However, not 'everything goes' when expressing a commitment to these values. Supporting democracy and equality requires agreement to the normative principles whereby each agent in a political process has a formally equal stake in that process, that no agents' interests are arbitrarily weighted more than any other, and that agents themselves are able to determine how their vote will be cast (Christiano 2008: 75ff.). Of course, expressing support for democracy and equality in this way does not require pretending that agents' interests or views are equally valuable in some objective sense,[11] but rather requires acknowledging that their views, filtered through a political procedure that accords them formally neutral weighting, are *treated* equally.[12]

What does this mean for a supranational and multilevel polity such as the European Union? At the level of Council decision-making, it means accepting that each state subjected to an authoritative rule co-determined by Council voting ought to have a proportionally equal stake in determining that rule. This approach to democratic legitimacy overlaps with what I have described above as the All-Subjected Principle, whereby all those permanently subject to a rule ought to have an equal stake in authorizing it (Theuns 2020; cf. Beckman 2014). The idea here is that it is necessary and sufficient to be a permanent subject of a particular rule in order to be authorized to have a democratic stake in its formulation. It is enough, under such a principle, to be formally bound by a rule or decision, even if one is not otherwise heavily affected by that rule or decision.[13]

While I am partisan to a version of the All-Subjected Principle in democratic theory (Theuns 2021), the task here is not to defend it. Rather, as is more appropriate to the 'immanent' method of testing expressive consistency, it is sufficient to note two things. First, it is the standard that best corresponds to the juridical framework of the EU legal order, where only those states that are full members of the European Union are ordinarily and automatically bound by EU law.[14] Second, it allows us to clearly identify which persons or agents are and which are not legally subject to EU law. Once jurisdictional boundaries have been drawn, as they have in the EU, it is not technically complex or politically controversial to determine the corresponding *demos*. This is especially true of Council decisions, as all member states are subject to the rules and decisions co-legislated in the Council, within the boundaries of the scope of its authority and prerogative that are stipulated in the EU treaties. We must therefore interpret the demands of equality in democratic decision-making (via the Article 2 fundamental value of democracy) to apply, immanently, between EU member states in those supranational processes that collectively bind them.[15] To sum up, the fundamental values of democracy and equality, as interpreted through the lens of the EU legal and political order, require that states subject to EU law—EU member states—expressively commit to their status as co-equals in EU law-making and governance.[16]

Does the sanctions procedure in Article 7 live up to this demand of democratic equality? I have already argued that it does not. Recall that the final political sanction outlined in Article 7.3 includes the suspension of 'the voting rights of the representative of the government of that Member State in the Council'. Importantly, as we have noted, a member state sanctioned in this way would lose their right to vote in the Council while still being subject to the decisions made in the Council (given Article 7.4). This violates the demand that all member states subject to EU legislation are recognized as equals in EU law-making. Indeed, as Wojciech Sadurski has noted, disenfranchisement under Article 7 is 'functionally almost equivalent to temporary expulsion, with the crucial difference that the *obligations* of the

Member State in question remain in place' (2009: 390, emphasis in original). Pursuing the disenfranchisement of a member state in the Council, the sanction detailed in Article 7.2, thus violates a commitment to viewing that member state as an equal partner. This undermines the values of democracy and equality stipulated in Article 2, and means the sanctions procedure of Article 7 is expressively inconsistent in that it falls into a performative contradiction. A consequence of this incoherence is the impossibility of Article 7 adequately declaring a commitment to EU fundamental values and instructing backsliding states in returning to the democratic fold.

How can disenfranchising an autocratic government be anti-democratic?

One may think that disenfranchising an autocratic state could not violate a commitment to expressing democratic principles as, *ex hypothesi*, the autocratic state's government would no longer be a legitimate democratic representative of its people.[17] How could it be problematic from the perspective of democratic principles to call for the disenfranchisement of an autocratic member? After all, autocratic governments have no democratic claim to represent their peoples in supranational democratic procedures.

This objection goes astray as it focuses on the wrong aspect of the problem. Indeed, autocrats, by definition, cannot be legitimate democratic representatives. Empowering autocrats does not further democratic ends. However, ruling over such disenfranchised governments (and their citizens) by holding them subjected to the decisions of a body in whom they have no democratic representation is no solution. It is this 'subjection without equal representation' that is the crux of the objection I have made to the procedure outlined in Article 7. Granted, one may consider that this objection is tempered somewhat by the continued representation that the citizens of a disenfranchised state would enjoy in the European Parliament (Bellamy and Kröger 2021). However, given the fundamental legislative importance of the Council, the citizens of a disenfranchised state would still be subject to EU laws without having an equal/proportional stake in their authorship. We must therefore conclude that Article 7 is currently both normatively incoherent, expressively inconsistent, and democratically illegitimate.

PROTECTING DEMOCRACY IN EUROPE

Examining other tools on the grounds of normative coherence

In the previous sections, we have seen how the critiques of normative coherence and expressive consistency come apart methodologically yet cohere in grounding an immanent critique of the flagship EU response mechanism to democratic backsliding in EU member states—Article 7 TEU. We now look to the normative coherence of some other responses—systemic infringement actions—which could be brought under Articles 258–60 TFEU, the Rule of Law Conditionality Regulation 2020/2092, and the possibility to deregister European political parties and foundations for violating EU fundamental values.[18] I focus on these tools because they include sanctions and therefore can, in principle, raise the problems of normative incoherence that I discuss above. With the methodology laid out and worked through in previous sections, it will not be necessary to analyse each measure in as much detail as I have done with Article 7 TEU. The goal here is, more modestly, to see if other sanctions mechanisms also raise similar concerns.

Using infringement actions to sanction democratic backsliding

The first measure, then, is the possibility of the European Commission or member state governments bringing (systemic) 'infringement actions' against member states backsliding on democracy and EU fundamental values. While the infringement action procedure has never been used to respond to democratic backsliding in an EU member state in a systemic way (and its effectiveness has therefore been limited so far), I will argue that it does not pose the same problems with regards to normative coherence compared to Article 7 TEU.

The procedure for infringement actions brought against member states, detailed in Articles 258–60 TFEU, was not designed directly for use as a response to democratic backsliding. It is the general procedure whereby the Commission (Article 258 TFEU) or aggrieved member states (Article 259 TFEU) can take a member state they consider to be in violation of EU law to court. Yet, as argued by Kim Lane Scheppele, Dimitry Kochenov and others, this procedure could be used to respond to member state autocratization, the gravest threat to democracy in the EU, especially where regression on democratic norms is systemic (Scheppele 2016; Kochenov 2015; Scheppele, Pech and Platon 2020). The infringement procedure is also not toothless, as the ECJ can impose both lump sum and daily fines if states fail to comply with their judgements. Indeed, a recent decision of the Court did exactly that. In mid-June 2024, a lump sum fine of €200m and additional daily fines of €1m were imposed on Hungary for failing to comply with a 2020 decision (following an infringement action brought by the Commission in 2019)[19] to bring its immigration policy in line with EU law.[20] However, the way infringement actions have been used thus far has always been directed to the infringement of EU law in specific, targeted areas.[21] In the above case, Hungary was penalized for illegally pushing back migrants at the border, for example, and for requiring asylum seekers to pre-register at a Hungarian embassy abroad prior to their arrival on Hungarian territory. A more robust use of Articles 258–60 TFEU would be to combine a broader series of violations of democratic and rule of law standards across different domains, in what has been called 'systemic infringement actions' (Scheppele 2016; Kochenov 2015; Scheppele, Pech and Platon 2020).

Unlike the Article 7 mechanism, however, systemic infringement actions are not targeted to the political participation of actors threatening democracy, but are responses that target proscribed actions generally. Infringement actions can result in a financial sanction that, at least in theory, would apply to all member states found in violation of their obligations under EU law by the ECJ. This point is easily misunderstood: clearly, as a matter of legal fact, any infringement action must be brought against the government of a specific member state. Furthermore, when used to address systematic processes of autocratization, actions would specifically target anti-democratic actors. So why do systemic infringement actions not raise the same concerns that we can see with the normative incoherence and expressive inconsistency of Article 7?

As in the national context, it is possible at the EU level to defend democracy with general rules or norms that bind everyone equally. These need not raise any normative incoherence as long as the proscribed behaviour is applicable to everybody and the sanction does not undermine equal political participation. Systemic infringement actions against backsliding member states under Articles 258–60 TFEU function in this way. The EU fundamental values of Article 2 TEU are binding on all. When these values are violated systemically, Articles 258–60 TFEU permit the ECJ to demand rectificatory measures and, failing rectification, to sanction any backsliding member states. Crucially, the sanction the ECJ can implement for failing to rectify a deficiency is a financial penalty imposed on the sanctioned member state. Such a sanction does not undermine that states' equal political participation, and thus does not raise the same normative incoherence with the values of democracy and equality listed in Article 2 as the one we see with the Article 7 procedure.

Using EU budget conditionality to protect the rule of law

Another measure that can be used to impose sanctions on member states backsliding on democracy and the rule of law is the Rule of Law Conditionality Regulation 2020/2092, adopted in late 2020. The term 'rule of law conditionality' gives away some of the original *ratio legis* of this regulation, which in theory allows the Commission to propose that EU funding to a member state is suspended or reduced if there are 'breaches of the principles of the rule of law' (Article 4.1). Given the sorts of amounts transferred in the EU budget, such a conditionality mechanism would seem to be a powerful response to democratic backsliding. However, much of the ambition of the initial regulation was watered down over the course of negotiating the mechanism.[22] Specifically, the adopted measure only allows the Commission to propose budget conditionality when the integrity of the EU budget itself is at stake, and when the link between the breach of the principle of the rule of law undermines the 'sound financial management of the Union budget or the protection of the financial interests of the Union in a sufficiently direct way' (Article 4.1). In other words, it is not enough for an EU member state to systematically undermine democracy and the rule of law—they must be doing so in a matter that directly implicates the EU's finances. As such, the 'rule of law conditionality' amounts to a sanction on fiscal corruption and grift (Hillion 2021: 270–4).

Regardless of this regrettable narrowing down of the Rule of Law Conditionality Regulation, it may still be considered a response to anti-democratic activities in some cases, such as where a member state government undermines democracy by corrupting the rule of law in such a way as to put the EU budget at risk. And indeed, the Regulation has played some part in EU budget conditionality imposed on Poland and Hungary recently. However, as with the possibility of systemic infringement actions and unlike the Article 7 procedure, the sanction in the Regulation does not undermine the equal political participation of the anti-democratic actor (i.e. backsliding member state governments). Instead, the Regulation proscribes and sanctions a specific illicit action (i.e. the corrupt use of EU funds) by withholding EU funds. Making EU funds conditional on member states maintaining the rule of law in a manner sufficient as to protect the EU budget's integrity is a general demand made by the Regulation of all member states.

Like with systemic infringement actions and in contrast with Article 7 TEU, it therefore seems that the Rule of Law Conditionality Regulation does not raise issues of normative coherence vis-a-vis the EU's fundamental values. In both cases, the proscribed behaviour is general (it binds all member states) and the sanctions do not target core civil or political processes in a way that may clash with the democratic norms of equal civil and political rights. Responding to anti-democratic action via the Regulation, as in the case of systemic infringement actions, does not threaten the EU's commitment to democratic values and equality. If the Regulation can be used or redesigned in such a way as to be more effective, then it should clearly be preferred over the current Article 7 procedure by those committed to democracy.[23]

Deregistration of European political parties and foundations

The last measure I will examine for normative coherence is the possibility under EU Regulation 1141/2014 for European political parties and foundations to be deregistered using a regulatory authority (Morijn 2019; Wolkenstein 2021; Norman 2021). This regulation generally governs the funding and status of European political parties, but also sets out the legal framework for the Authority for European Political Parties and European Political Foundations[24] 'for the purpose of registering, controlling and imposing sanctions on European political parties and European political foundations' (Article 6.1). In this context, both the registration and the deregistration roles are interesting.

To register a political party or association political foundation, the Authority must assess whether that party or foundation observes the fundamental values of the EU formulated in Article 2 TEU 'in its programme and in its activities' (Articles 3.1c, 3.2c, 6.2, 9.1 and 10). However, Article 9.3 states that the Authority shall consider as 'sufficient' a mere declaration by the political party or foundation. The procedure regarding deregistration in Article 10, though, is more thorough, as the Authority is tasked with verifying that political parties and foundations continue to respect EU fundamental values, and allows for the possibility of deregistering the party or foundation if it is deemed to violate those values. Considering that democracy and the rule of law are amongst the fundamental values in Article 2 TEU, it seems that the sanction of deregistering European political parties and foundations under Regulation 1141/2014 is an apt measure to respond to anti-democratic political actors in the EU. It should be noted, however, that the Regulation has yet to be used in this way to respond to violations of democratic norms, or indeed any violations of EU fundamental values, a fact that has led some observers to decry the Authority as obstructionist.[25]

Sanctions under Regulation 1141/2014 can be directly imposed on political parties and foundations for undermining Article 2 values in their programmes or activities, and target actors' equal political participation. The only further substantive demand is that these activities and/or programmatic alignments breach Article 2 values in a manner that is 'manifest and serious' (Article 10.3). Deregistration of European political parties and foundations is, in this way, clearly a targeted measure to tackle, *inter alia*, European political actors that threaten democratic governance in Europe. The Regulation is not purely designed to respond to violations of EU fundamental values in how it functions; for instance, European parties and foundations can also be deregistered on the basis of the party failing to (continue to) meet other more formal conditions of registration, particularly the demand that it has representation at the European, national or regional level in at least one quarter of the EU member states or received at least 3% of the national vote in the most recent elections for the European Parliament in one quarter of the member states (Article 3.1b). Still, since the Regulation includes a measure specifically for responding to Article 2 values, which include the value of democracy, the Authority is legally authorized to deregister parties and foundations on the basis of anti-democratic activities.

Given that Regulation 1141/2014 is suitable for responding to anti-democratic threats and is targeted to anti-democratic actors, sanctioning them through their political participation, it remains to be seen whether the specific sanction proposed in the Regulation undermines democratic equality and is normatively incoherent in the same way that I have argued is the case with Article 7 TEU. Here, I think we must answer that it does. The sanction of deregistration has profound effects undermining political parties' and foundations' equal political rights, as deregistration would mean that the European political party or foundation is not entitled to a proportionally equal share of European funding. The scale of this restriction should not be underestimated, as registration under the Regulation allows European political parties to claim up to 90% of their expenses from the EU budget and foundations to claim up to 95% (Article 19.3). Excluding a European political party or foundation from these sorts of budget contributions would clearly undermine the equal democratic playing field vis-a-vis other parties and foundations that are financed from the EU budget.

While sympathetic to the legitimacy of the Regulation, arguing that 'the deregistering of European political parties by no means entails an absolute "exclusion from the democratic game"', Fabio Wolkenstein concedes that deregistration 'would mean a big blow to any European party ... reducing its capacity to make its voice heard in the European Parliament' (2021: 20; see also Müller 2015: 144). However, in contrast to my analysis that the Regulation is incoherent with the EU fundamental values of democracy and equality, Wolkenstein argues that the measure is democratically legitimate since EU member states have agreed to be bound by it. I find this unconvincing, though, as it assumes (in my view wrongly) that member states can agree to un- or anti-democratic terms in EU treaties with no consequence to democratic legitimacy.[26] Ludvig Norman, in an article tracing the development of the Regulation, agrees with this assessment, arguing that the Regulation 'demonstrates a clear shift from a democratizing logic to a more protective one' (2021: 733), a logic he defines by commitment to the idea that 'democracy must be protected, even at the cost of sometimes infringing on democratic principles' (ibid.: 725).

Conclusion

Some of the existing policy and legal 'tools' for EU institutions to respond to anti-democratic politics fail to live up to even minimal standards of normative coherence. The Article 7 TEU procedure, supposedly the core mechanism for violations of fundamental values, is not only normatively incoherent (in that the sanction undermines the very values it is supposed to protect), but it is also deeply inadequate in expressive terms. This means that even were the mechanism to be used to impose the sanction of disenfranchising a member state in the Council, it would do so at the cost of democratic legitimacy. Another measure for attempting to secure compliance with fundamental values, Regulation 1141/2014, is similarly disappointing. Like Article 7, this measure has never been used to sanction a Europarty for violating core values such as democracy, equality and the rule of law. More importantly, though, even if the Regulation could overcome the sclerosis of the authority charged with its implementation, the sanction of deregistration undermines the EU's commitment to democratic equality. While rejecting the Regulation may mean funding political parties and foundations committed to repulsive views, I have argued that it would be anti-democratic to target their fair participation in political life. Restrictions on extremist political speech and behaviour had better proceed via general prohibitions enforced by standard sanctions (such as fines) than by targeting the democratic rights of extremists, thereby sullying democratic norms.[27]

While other tools which involve sanctions have proven woefully inadequate to contain anti-democratic forces, they nevertheless seem less problematic from the perspective of normative coherence. The sanctions that can be imposed via the rule of law conditionality mechanism or infringement procedures do not themselves undermine democratic fundamentals. Perhaps partially for this reason, we have seen some modest applications of these mechanisms, while Article 7 and Regulation 1141/2014 have, as yet, amounted to nothing. That is not to say that budget conditionality and infringement procedures are currently used effectively. The largely self-imposed limitations to their scope and application have meant that these mechanisms have proven toothless to curb democratic backsliding in EU member states. Indeed, the bulk of funding withheld from Hungary and Poland—which featured strongly in the Polish opposition's successful bid to remove Law and Justice from power in 2023—came not from the Conditionality Regulation supposedly designed for that purpose but from the preexisting and more broadly applicable Common Provisions Regulation.

Our conclusion from this investigation into the normative coherence and expressive consistency of the EU's legal tools to respond to fundamental values violations is stark. The sanction of disenfranchisement in the Council in the core provision, Article 7 TEU, should be abandoned as it is itself anti-democratic. The same is true of the possibility to deregister European political parties that violate fundamental values. On the other hand, infringement actions and budget conditionality warrant their scope and application being radically enlarged. These tools are coherent with the fundamental values the EU seeks to protect. While this may not successfully reverse democratic backsliding in all cases, at least it would reduce the complicity of EU institutions and pro-democratic member states in the EU's autocracy crisis.

PART TWO

INTRODUCTION TO PART TWO

LOOKING FORWARD
PROTECTING PLURALIST DEMOCRACY

The first part of this book has examined what has gone wrong in the past fifteen years or so of responses from the European Union (EU) to democratic backsliding in some member states. I have argued that we can best understand these failings through the lenses of depoliticization and membership fatalism, attitudes that developed throughout the 1990s and early 2000s (Chapter 2). Such attitudes fostered a minimalist, conciliatory, technocratic and legalistic approach to responding to democratic backsliding, corresponding to a prevailing conception of 'democracy without politics', which we can see permeating the discourse on democracy that EU Commissioners use in their public speeches (Chapter 3). This conception of democracy is a far cry from the ideal of pluralist democracy, motivated by the political and normative equality of each citizen and animated by contestation over what each of us might believe to be true and good. What is more, some of the tools available for sanctioning the violation of fundamental values by EU member states—especially the key Article 7 of the Treaty on European Union (TEU) procedure—are not only hampered by procedural veto points but are also incoherent with the very values they are intended to protect (Chapter 4).

The second part of the book looks at how democracy can be protected coherently by the EU. It largely focuses on the responses available to EU actors, be they European institutions like the Council, the European Council, the Commission or the European Parliament, or those represented in these institutions such as the governments of EU member states, European political parties and foundations, and, ultimately, EU citizens. The broad lines of the approach I set out aim to re-politicize the violation of fundamental values such as democracy and the rule of law, with the ideal of pluralist democracy in mind. This ideal, further spelled out in Chapter 7, puts at the centre the political and normative equality of each EU citizen, and recognizes that political disagreement and contestation over values is an ordinary part of democratic politics that should not be shunned. The fundamental values listed in Article 2 of the TEU—especially democracy, equality and the rule of law—protect exactly this ideal. Citizens do not need to share a commitment to one monolithic vision of politics, of the good life, or even of truth. Democratic procedures, when they proceed in vibrant public spheres and with the protection of core civic and political rights, facilitate the adjudication between different political ideas and ideals with respect for the normative equality of each person. The rule of law demands that each be subject to the laws passed by the people's representatives, including, crucially, members of the government and their agents and officials. At the ballot box, each counts as one and nobody as more than one.

Prospective authoritarians are keen to frame their acts of democratic sabotage as part of an ordinary partisan preference for a different political ideal. Opponents to their authoritarian projects are framed as enemies of the nation, of Christianity, or even of democracy itself. But undermining the procedural conditions for fair democratic contestation is not part of ordinary democratic life. It imposes one vision of politics above others, undermining political equality. We should not lose sight of the fact that the first victims of democratic and rule of law backsliding in EU member states are the citizens of those states themselves. But given how EU member states have chosen to pool sovereignty in some areas, co-legislating at the European level, democratic backsliding in one member state affects all EU citizens. Because of the involvement of national governments in European legislation (centrally via the Council, but also less directly through the European Council and European Commission), democratic backsliding submits each to laws co-legislated by increasingly authoritarian actors.

The following chapters articulate an alternative pathway for protecting democracy in Europe to the depoliticized, technocratic and legalistic approach that has often been taken in the near past, which has proved to be so toothless in the face of would-be authoritarians. The analysis here cannot be exhaustive, nor is it intended to be a policy blueprint. This would run against the ideals I am setting out to defend. Beyond the minimal procedural core necessary to guarantee fair and equal participation, democratic politics is open-ended. As such, the precise approach and content of EU democracy protection ought itself to be the result of democratic contestation and compromise. Instead, I want to advocate for a different way of responding to democracy and rule of law backsliding in EU member states. In this line, rather than a policy blueprint, I develop a series of principles for coherently protecting democracy in Europe. The democratic ethos of equal citizenship, political pluralism and legitimate opposition must be central to both how we understand democratic decay and the responses we advocate.

The first priority is reordering European integration such that it no longer contributes to the problem. Democratic backsliding must be re-politicized to increase the political cost for authoritarian actors to dismantle democratic institutions and safeguards. EU governments that fail to safeguard democracy domestically must be held accountable transnationally and their influence over European law- and policymaking must be reduced as far as is possible without violating democratic values. Finally, it is imperative that the governments and citizens of European member states wake up to the fact that European integration is a mediated, negotiated, but ultimately voluntary association of European peoples. While EU institutions and member states may not dispose of tools that guarantee all member states respect fundamental EU values, they need not indefinitely tolerate the violation of these norms. If push comes to shove, limited European disintegration, however heartbreaking, may prove paradoxically to be the only way to ensure a democratic European Union.

To these ends, in this part of the book, I analyse who is complicit in EU democratic backsliding (Chapter 5), arguing that complicity amongst European political actors is much broader in scope than has been recognized in the academic literature (Wolkenstein 2020, 2021; Theuns 2020). If this is right, then we must think of duties for redress (correcting complicity) and reparations (remedial duties owed to those wronged) beyond those member state governments who are the primary instigators of democratic backsliding. The European Commission, the European Parliament, the Council and the other member states all hold a share in this complicity, as well as certain European political parties.

In the next chapter (Chapter 6), I focus on what should be done to limit the influence of authoritarian governments in EU member states. I argue for a three-pronged strategy of containment. Authoritarian actors must be deprived of economic resources (via conditionality) and political legitimacy and prestige (via isolation). They must also be sidelined as far as possible from EU political procedures. However, a balance must also be struck, I argue, between the need to maximally isolate these actors from European politics and legislation and the need to uphold the values of democracy, equality and the rule of law in EU responses, both procedurally and substantively.

Correcting complicity and containing autocracy coherently may slow the downward trajectory of democratic and rule of law backsliding, but may not in themselves reverse these trends. Indeed, the first line of resistance to authoritarian politics in EU member states must be the citizens of those states themselves. The last of this trio of chapters therefore explores some of the ways that different EU actors can cultivate pluralist democratic actors in EU member states where democratic pluralism is most under threat (Chapter 7). The thrust of the argument, like the chapter on complicity, is that it is legitimate and appropriate for a much broader range of actors to become involved in supporting civil society, critical media, independent judges and even opposition politicians in EU countries at risk of becoming autocratic.

That I present these three approaches separately does not mean that they are divisible into neat and self-contained conceptual boxes. There is overlap. For instance, one of the reasons that may ground a duty of EU actors to cultivate pluralist democracy in EU member states undergoing democratic backsliding is their complicity in these harms.

INTRODUCTION TO PART TWO

Indeed, in Chapter 7, I develop one version of that argument which looks at how cultivating pluralist democracy may be one way to meet the duties of reparation arising from complicity in democratic backsliding. In a similar vein, empowering pluralist political and civil society actors may reduce the relative influence of autocratic politics in the EU; where this is the case, cultivating pluralist democracy also functions as a strategy of containment. Nevertheless, it is useful to keep the three separate, as they broadly identify different priorities and different motivations. Chapter 5 centrally analyses how EU actors ought to correct for the moral and political failure to hold backsliding governments accountable using existing measures of EU law ('redressing complicitous omissions' to use the terminology of Chapter 5). The approach focused on containing autocracy developed in Chapter 6 is, in contrast, generally more instrumental. Given the value of democratic government in general and supranational cooperation shaped around a democratic ethos in particular, EU institutions as well as member state governments and their delegates (for instance in the Council and the European Council) have a direct stake in trying to ensure that anti-democratic actors in European politics are limited and constrained. Chapter 7 focuses instead on the domestic impact of EU responses to democratic backsliding, and more broadly on whether EU actors have duties to provide direct support for pro-democratic actors in member states where democracy is under threat.

While I make the case that a wide range of EU actors should do a great deal more than they have done so far to protect democracy in Europe, the scope of legitimate EU responses to democratic and rule of law backsliding is not unlimited. Not all types of responses are coherent with democratic values, and, in my view, EU actors should not use sanctions that challenge those values, sometimes called 'militant democratic' responses (Wagrandl 2018; Theuns 2023). What then is the appropriate and legitimate response to authoritarian EU member states where correcting complicity, containing authoritarian actors and cultivating pluralist democracy fails? In the last chapter of this second part of the book, I argue that the final sanction, the *ultima ratio*, must be to expel such frankly autocratic states from the European Union altogether (Chapter 8).

5

CORRECTING EU COMPLICITY IN DEMOCRATIC BACKSLIDING

Why do you see the speck in your neighbour's eye, but do not notice the log in your own eye? Or how can you say to your neighbour, 'Let me take the speck out of your eye,' while the log is in your own eye?

Matthew 7:3–5, the Bible, NRSV

Much of the first part of this book has focused on how responses to democratic and rule of law backsliding in European Union (EU) member states—namely Hungary and Poland—have been ineffective, depoliticized, technocratic, legalistic and incoherent. As my approach so far has consisted of a critical examination of what little has been done, I have not extensively mapped out all missed opportunities that may have led to a different outcome. Instead, the focus has been on how EU actors have tried and failed to contain authoritarian politics in Europe. This reflects a general orientation in the literature on analysing and criticizing ineffective responses and proposing legal alternatives (Blauberger and Kelemen 2017; Kochenov 2015; Oliver and Stefanelli 2016; Pech and Scheppele 2017; Priebus 2022; Theuns 2020; von Bogdandy and Spieker 2019). My contribution to this debate in the first part of this book and in previously published work (Oleart and Theuns 2023; Theuns 2020, 2022, 2023) has been to use tools of political theory to assess responses from a different angle: genealogically, discursively, and with attention to expressive and normative coherence. In this chapter, I draw attention to a different aspect of the problem: some policies and choices of EU actors have actually, or at least potentially, *contributed* to democratic and rule of law backsliding in EU member states. Where this is the case, or reasonably might have been, these actors are complicit in democratic backsliding and owe special duties of redress and reparation.

Some authors have already explicitly raised the idea that EU actors may be complicit in democratic backsliding in member states (Bárd and Kochenov 2021; Theuns 2020; Wolkenstein 2020, 2021). Generally speaking though, attention has been drawn to the 'worst offenders': actors who knowingly and perhaps even maliciously tolerated would-be authoritarians in exchange for some benefit (cf. Bárd and Kochenov 2021: 43–6). A key case in point is how the European People's Party continued to accept and protect Viktor Orbán's Fidesz as a member party despite clear violations of fundamental values (Kelemen 2020a; Meijers and van der Veer 2019; Wolkenstein 2021). I wish to cast a wider net. Some EU actors may potentially contribute to democratic backsliding unintentionally.[1] Similarly, some EU actors may share in the blame of permitting democratic backsliding, or in turning a blind eye to it, without making a direct contribution. Here we might want to speak of a 'culpable omission'. While these cases are less severe than the knowing or malicious contribution to democratic and rule of law backsliding, they may still be wrong in ways that we may think generate special duties of redress and reparation.

To get at these types of complicity in EU democratic backsliding, and make the case that a far wider range of EU actors owe duties of redress and reparation, this chapter first clarifies the notion of 'complicity in EU democratic backsliding'. Drawing on the theoretical and conceptual framework developed by Chiara Lepora and Robert Goodin (2013) to analyse the ethical complexities of providing medical aid in conflict areas, I argue that complicity in EU backsliding is much more widespread than reflected in the current literature. Not only are virtually all actors in the EU institutional context complicit in democratic and rule of law backsliding, but so are all member states to some degree. If it is correct that normative responsibility for democratic backsliding in EU member states is widely shared, then we should look not only at how authoritarian actors in the EU can most effectively be sanctioned and contained, we must also think much more about how the full range of EU political actors can ensure that they do not contribute to the processes of democratic decay in Europe, how they can use their legal authority and political clout to resist authoritarian politics, and how they can fulfil their remedial duties to those harmed by democratic backsliding.

The rest of the chapter proceeds as follows. First, I engage the notion of complicity at the conceptual and philosophical level. I specify how complicity as I understand it is a specific but secondary form of wrongdoing, and that one can be complicit through both blameworthy omissions as well as actions. Next, I examine a set of EU actors and institutions that I want to argue hold some normative responsibility for democratic and rule of law backsliding in Europe, albeit to different degrees. I therefore assess in turn whether the European Commission and the European Council have potentially contributed to democratic and rule of law backsliding through their actions or failures to act.[2] I do not aim to be exhaustive in this assessment, but rather aim to provide illustrative examples that show how each of the above agents share some responsibility for democratic backsliding and therefore can be held accountable politically for duties of redress and reparation. Finally, in the last section, I reflect on the main ways complicit actors in EU democratic backsliding can act to correct their complicity. Sometimes this will simply involve stopping doing something that makes that actor complicit, but in other cases it will require more ambitious action.[3]

A final caveat: while I make my case for each EU actor listed above, the core argument of this chapter does not turn on these individual examples. If we accept my definition of complicity as including blameworthy omission then we must think much more broadly about who is responsible for democratic backsliding in Europe. This is, ultimately, the point of this chapter. And it tracks with a simple yet vital political message: rather than passing the buck, pointing fingers at others or hoping that the problem, if ignored, will eventually go away of its own accord, European political actors should first and foremost face up to their own responsibilities in protecting democracy in Europe.

PROTECTING DEMOCRACY IN EUROPE

Complicity, redress and reparations

Complicity, as I intend it here, should be understood as a normative wrong.[4] It pertains to a specific kind of ethical failing that occurs when an agent, through their wrongful actions or omissions, enables, induces, encourages, or permits another wrongful action. In that sense, complicity is a *secondary* wrong. This means that, conceptually, the wrong of complicity is necessarily associated with a different, primary act of wrongdoing. In the case of complicity to democratic backsliding, the primary wrong consists of actions to deliberately undermine democratic government and its institutional and societal foundations. So, if we agree with Wolkenstein that the European People's Party is complicit in democratic backsliding by Fidesz, then the primary wrong is democratic backsliding by Fidesz, and the secondary wrong is some wrongful action or omission by the European People's Party (Wolkenstein 2020). This sort of complicity belongs to the general category of complicit actions or blameworthy omissions by an EU actor that make a potentially crucial contribution to democratic backsliding in an EU member state. Following Wolkenstein (2020), I call this 'EU transnational complicity'.

The general notion of complicity this is based on has several features that it is important to draw attention to. First—and this considerably extends its application—the concept is not limited to positive actions. It extends to those who, though having the capacity to avert a wrong, wrongfully fail to do so. This is a crucial point, as it opens the scope of analysis from all those who acted to enable, induce, encourage or permit a primary wrong considerably. Indeed, the starting point for ascertaining complicity by omission most fruitfully does not start from an act of wrongdoing to try to identify who provided a potentially causal contribution to that wrong, but rather starts from the question of who had the means (materially, epistemically, and so on) and authority to prevent the wrong. Where those actors who had both the means and the authority to act to prevent the wrong failed to do so, those actors may be complicit by omission.

Second—and this, conversely, considerably narrows the scope of this notion of complicity—it is not enough for the complicit actor to have enabled, induced, encouraged or granted permission for a primary wrong. These actions or omissions must themselves also be wrongful. Where, for example, a putatively complicit actor in fact was coerced into an action that enables a primary wrong, such that they could not be reasonably expected to act otherwise in those circumstances, then they are not complicit in that wrong. This idea turns on a widespread view in moral philosophy that to be blameworthy in a certain situation it must have been possible to act otherwise—an implication of the view that 'ought implies can'.

Complicity as a normative wrong is a matter of degree. Consider the following three relevant axes for assessing the relative wrongfulness of complicity.[5] First, other things being equal, being complicit in a more severe type of primary wrongdoing is worse than being complicit in a more minor type of wrongdoing. Second, making a more significant potentially causal contribution to a primary wrong is worse than making a more incidental potentially causal contribution. Third, in an extension of the idea that 'ought implies can', complicit actions and omissions are worse if acting otherwise imposed relatively low costs on the complicit agent; the higher the burden of preventing a primary wrong (in the case of complicit omissions) or not enabling, inducing, encouraging or permitting the wrong (in the case of complicit acts), the less blameworthy the complicit omission or action. These three criteria for assessing the severity of wrongfulness by complicity interact. The morally worst incidents of complicity occur when an agent makes a significant causal contribution to a terrible primary wrong where doing otherwise would have imposed only a trivial burden. The morally least serious occurrences are when an agent makes an incidental contribution to a minor primary wrong where acting otherwise would have been very burdensome. The graver the wrong in complicity, the weightier the subsequent duties of redress and reparation.

While moral complicity is related to causality, a complicit action or omission does not need to make a causal contribution to a wrongful act; it is enough that it makes a potentially causal contribution. If, at the time of a potentially complicit action or omission, the agent could reasonably expect their action or omission to make a causal contribution to a primary wrong, then they are complicit in the subsequent primary wrong. For example, if I were to lend a faculty colleague the keys to my *pied-à-terre*, knowing that they wanted to use it for an affair with an undergraduate student,[6] then I am morally complicit in that affair, even if my colleague ended up taking a room in a hotel.[7] I would even argue that the ultimate causal contribution to a primary wrong is largely irrelevant to whether an agent is complicit and the relative wrongfulness of their complicity. If this is correct, I am equally blameworthy in the case my apartment is used for the affair as in the case that my colleague eventually went to a hotel.

The wrongfulness of complicity in a primary act of wrongdoing ordinarily generates special duties of redress and reparation in the complicitous agent. I use redress, which comes from the French verb *redresser* (set upright, straighten), to refer to the correction of a previous complicitous course of action, be that by omission or positive action. By reparation, I mean the special duties that a complicit agent has to those harmed by the primary wrong. These duties of redress and reparation are generally less than the corresponding duties of the primary agent of wrongdoing, given that complicity in a wrongful act is always less than the primary wrong.[8] But they are usually greater than general duties that might be owed to those who suffer a wrong by agents who are in no way responsible for that wrong, like for instance humanitarian duties to provide assistance to the victims of a natural disaster. It is a difficult and contentious exercise to calculate the respective duties of redress and reparation in an adequately precise manner in each individual case of complicity. Suffice to say for our purposes that complicity does raise such special duties, and that these duties will usually track the overall degree of wrongfulness of the complicit action or omission. As a result, when trying to judge the relative burdens of redress and reparation that a complicit agent may owe, we need to look at the three criteria of the wrongfulness of complicity: we need to ask how bad the primary wrong was; we need to ask how extensive the potential contribution of the complicit agent was to the primary wrong; and we need to ask how burdensome it would have been for the complicit agent to act otherwise.

It may not be the case that complicit agents always owe a duty of redress; that is, it may not always be morally required of them to stop acting or omitting in the ways that make them complicit in a primary wrongdoing. One strength of Lepora and Goodin's careful analysis of complicity, for example, is that they explicitly confront this problem (2013: 151–69). Sometimes it may be justified to act in a way that makes one complicit in a primary wrong in service of some other greater good, or on the balance of reasons. Lepora and Goodin give the example of doctors who are asked to attend to the medical needs of a prisoner who has been subject to torture. Accepting may make them complicit in the primary moral wrong of torture. And yet, in some circumstances, it may be better to accept than to refuse to treat the victim-cum-patient, even from the perspective of the wronged individual.

Or take an argument closer to our subject at hand. In the context of the Russian war against Ukraine, Poland has proven a formidable ally to Ukraine and a staunch opponent of Russian aggression. Hungary, on the other hand, has proved much more ambivalent, maintaining close ties with Russian state actors and hampering both sanctions against Russia and EU support for Ukraine. In an op-ed I wrote with Jakub Jaraczewski in April 2022, shortly after Russia massively scaled up its aggression against Ukraine, I argued that the European Commission should try to exploit this difference between Poland and Hungary, withholding EU funding to Hungary via the Rule of Law Conditionality Regulation[9] while being more lenient with Poland, despite serious violations of the rule of law the Polish government was engaged in at the time (Jaraczewski and Theuns 2022; cf. Bárd and Kochenov 2021). This, we argued, could help to split apart Europe's 'authoritarian alliance' between Law and Justice-led Warsaw and the Fidesz government in Budapest. If we were right in our reasoning, then this sort of strategic manipulation could be justified in the name of the greater good of weakening ties between the two states most centrally concerned with democratic and rule of law backsliding. But going 'soft' (or softer) on Poland in the aftermath of the Russian invasion, because of their more constructive attitude towards Ukraine and despite serious violations of EU fundamental values by the Law and Justice government, might also have made the Commission complicit in these violations. The complicity in contributing to Poland's rule of law backsliding would not have evaporated, but might have been outweighed by other interests.[10]

Finally, it is helpful to draw a distinction between complicity as I use it here and other normative concepts that also entail an extension of moral responsibility for a wrong, like collective responsibility or being a co-author (or 'co-principal') in a wrongful act.[11] Collective responsibility, unlike complicity, primarily rests on the notion of collective agency, where an act of wrongdoing is a product of a group's concerted action or decision. For example, where a group of people agree, explicitly or tacitly, to pursue some shared wrongful aim, then we may ascribe collective responsibility for the harms of that wrongful act irrespective of their final individual material contribution to bringing about the harm. Indeed, it might not always be possible to separate each individual's causal contribution to the harm or identify an ultimate wrongdoer without whom the harm would not have occurred. Take a classic example from criminal legal theory. A group of hunters gets a little tipsy and goes boar hunting in the forest. A mist descends. The hunters, with some bloodlust, decide to continue despite the risks of reduced visibility. They hear the sound of a couple of boars grunting some distance away, obscured by the mist, and shoot in that direction, accidentally killing a hiker. It may not be possible to say which hunter was causally responsible for killing the hiker, but we might say that the group as a whole is morally responsible for the death due to their recklessness.[12] This group-based approach assumes a general agreement or implicit consensus among the individuals involved, who then act as a single, collective agent.

Sometimes, however, it is clear that several specific agents jointly bring about a wrong. Here their moral responsibility should be assessed in terms of their co-agency in the *primary* wrongdoing, rather in their (secondary) contribution to a primary wrongful act or collective agency.[13] Compared to collective responsibility for wrongdoing, complicity is less bound by the strictures of collective action. One does not need to be an active agent or directly involved in a wrongful act to be complicit. It is enough for one to have acted wrongfully, or wrongfully failed to act, in a way that one could reasonably expect may contribute to the primary wrongdoing. However, as noted above, this also means that (merely) complicit actors are less culpable than primary agents of wrongdoing—their specific duties of redressing and repairing the harms are less weighty than the obligations of the primary agents of the wrong.

The complicity of EU actors

The main argument of this chapter is that complicity for democratic backsliding in EU member states is much broader than is typically accepted. Many EU actors and institutions have failed to act, or failed to respond adequately, in the face of democratic backsliding. In some cases, EU actors have even positively contributed to democratic decay in some member states. Being complicit in EU democratic backsliding means being subject to special normative duties: duties of redress (to try to right the wrong of the complicitous action or omission) and duties of reparations (to try to compensate those harmed by the primary wrong). If this conception of complicity is correct, and if it is true that a wide range of EU actors and institutions are complicit in EU democratic backsliding, then it is crucial for complicit agents to stop finger-pointing and buck-passing and ask what they can each do to protect democracy in Europe.

It is not my ambition to offer a systematic analysis of each EU actor and institution's complicity in EU democratic backsliding. The specific contributions of various actors, through their actions and omissions, would be difficult to assign with precision. The extent to which various actors ought to have acted to prevent democratic regression—both in terms of their legal and their political responsibilities—will also be knotty and contested. And indeed, so is the specific question of which pathways most effectively correct such complicity and repair the harms of backsliding deserve exclusive and sustained analysis. I have more modest ambitions here. Specifically, I want to make the case that the European Commission and the European Council are complicit in EU democratic backsliding to varying degrees, as, by extension, are the Council of the EU and indeed all EU member states. This means that each of these actors variously ought to have done more to prevent democratic regression or respond to it, or that they ought not to have acted in ways that enabled, induced, encouraged or permitted these developments. If this analysis is correct, none can justifiably push responsibility to another actor without simultaneously addressing their own duties of redress and reparation.

PROTECTING DEMOCRACY IN EUROPE

The conciliatory Commission

A good place to start is the European Commission. In keeping with the definition of complicity developed above, there are three important elements to the analysis of the Commission's transnational complicity in EU democratic backsliding. The Commission is complicit if there are things it should have done to prevent, discourage, protest or proscribe democratic and rule of law backsliding in EU member states that it did not do. This is complicity by omission. The Commission is also complicit if it wrongly acted in ways that enabled, induced, encouraged or permitted backsliding.[14] If we judge the Commission complicit in either or both of these ways, we must then, in a third step, evaluate the relative wrongfulness of the Commission's complicity across the three criteria described above. In other words, we need to answer several questions: how bad was the primary wrong? How extensive was the potential contribution of the Commission to the primary wrong? And how burdensome would it have been for the Commission to act otherwise? The first and second steps require us to ask whether the European Commission had a duty to respond to democratic and rule of law backsliding, and whether it adequately fulfilled this duty. So, why might we legitimately expect the European Commission to act to try to combat democratic and rule of law backsliding in member states?

Of all the EU institutions and actors, the Commission's role in protecting EU values is maybe clearest, as it is tasked with ensuring member states live up to their commitments under EU law, including their commitment to uphold the EU's fundamental values, including democracy and the rule of law. This duty is described in Article 17 of the Treaty on European Union (TEU), which holds that the Commission 'shall ensure the application of the Treaties' and 'shall oversee the application of Union law under the control of the Court of Justice of the European Union' (Article 17.1 TEU).[15] This general task is given teeth in the Treaty on the Functioning of the European Union (TFEU), which lays out the Commission's role when it considers member states to have infringed their duties under EU law: 'If the Commission considers that a Member State has failed to fulfil an obligation under the Treaties, it *shall* deliver a reasoned opinion on the matter after giving the State concerned the opportunity to submit its observations' (Article 258 TFEU, emphasis added).[16] Consequently, '[i]f the State concerned does not comply with the opinion within the period laid down by the Commission, the latter may bring the matter before the Court of Justice of the European Union' (ibid.).[17] While member states may also bring so-called infringement actions against other member states before the European Court of Justice (ECJ), the Commission also plays a role in these procedures, both by delivering a 'reasoned opinion' on the supposed infringement (Article 259 TFEU), by evaluating whether a member state has sufficiently enacted a judgement of the ECJ to rectify an infringement in such cases, and by proposing the level of lump sum fine or penalty payment they consider 'appropriate' where that is not the case (Article 260.2 TFEU).

While these remain the most important legal tools that empower the Commission to respond to democratic backsliding, the Commission also has an important role in the ballooning range of new instruments developed by the Commission over the last decade or so. In the 'Justice Scorecard' introduced in 2013, the Commission evaluates each member state on the 'quality, independence and efficiency' of their legal systems. In the 'Rule of Law Framework', introduced in 2014, the Commission gives member states which show deficiencies in the rule of law that, while serious, do not meet the threshold of the Article 7 procedure an 'early warning' to try to prevent further degradation. In the 'Rule of Law Mechanism', introduced in 2019, the Commission evaluates all member states on their justice systems, anti-corruption frameworks, media freedom and pluralism, and checks and balances over a full year (in what is called the 'Annual Rule of Law Cycle'), leading to a yearly 'Rule of Law Report'.[18] And finally, in the newest 'tool', the 'Rule of Law Conditionality Instrument', adopted in late 2020, the Commission can propose to reduce EU funds to member states with 'breaches of the principles of the rule of law ... [which] affect or seriously risk affecting the sound financial management of the Union budget' (Article 6, Regulation 2020/2092).

These roles explain why the Commission is often referred to as the 'Guardian of the [European] Treaties'. The use of this term to describe the executive branch of European institutions dates right back to the earliest days of European integration, when Jean Monnet described the High Authority of the European Coal and Steel Community as the 'guardian of the rules laid down by the six countries which have signed and ratified the Treaty' (High Authority 1953: 31), terminology which was taken over by Walter Hallstein, the President of the first Commission (of the European Economic Community) as early as 1959. In a speech to the European Parliamentary Assembly on the creation of the common market, Hallstein said, 'True, the first to act must be the member states. But it was incumbent on the Commission also to give a strong helping hand, for the Commission is the *guardian of the Treaty*' (European Parliamentary Assembly 1959: 42, emphasis added). The widespread use of the term 'Guardian of the Treaties' as a shorthand to describe the Commission's role, both in contemporary academic and political discourse and, as we have seen, in more historical debates on European integration, points to the expectation that the Commission should act within its legal mandate to ensure member states uphold their obligations under EU law, including most fundamentally the values like democracy and the rule of law that are supposed to be at the core of European integration. And the fact that three of the four new tools supposed to combat rule of law decay in the EU described above were designed and promulgated by the European Commission on its own authority suggests that the self-understanding of the Commission largely reflects this historical guardianship role, including on fundamental values (the remaining Rule of Law Conditionality Instrument, as an EU Regulation, was passed in conjunction with the Council and the European Parliament).

We can see over multiple legal tools and a long history of political discourse that the European Commission is a key actor when thinking through legitimate European responses to violations of EU law and fundamental values by member states. Citizens and governments of European member states rely on the Commission to use this role to defend their rights and ensure that all member states live up to their duties under EU law. Are there then examples of the Commission failing to respond adequately to democratic backsliding or acting in ways that could reasonably be expected to exacerbate democratic decay? Complicity by omission in this context would mean identifying moments when the European Commission either did not act in the face of flagrant violations of democratic norms or hesitated in acting, making concessions to the primary wrongdoers. I want to argue that we can find examples of these, and therefore of complicity by omission by the European Commission.

A good example can be seen regarding the Article 7 procedure against Hungary. While the Commission did instigate Article 7 proceedings against Poland on 20 December 2017, it took a vote in the European Parliament on 12 September 2018 to start proceedings against Hungary. This was despite the fact that democratic violations in Hungary were both more fundamental and had started considerably earlier than the problems in Poland. We can see evidence of democratic backsliding right from the start of Orbán's second term as Prime Minister. Freedom House, for example, already listed Hungary as a notable case of democratic backsliding in 2011 (Puddington 2011), reporting on the first nine months of Fidesz government after Orbán won a landslide election, routing the Socialist Party (MSZP) in April 2010. Converting less than 53% of the vote with a turnout of just 46.7% into 68.1% of seats, the Fidesz-Christian Democratic People's Party alliance cleared a crucial two-thirds threshold of seats, allowing it to single-handedly change the Hungarian Constitution. Hillary Clinton, US Secretary of State at the time, expressed concern over a 'crackdown' on Hungarian democracy as early as December 2011 (Jenne and Mudde 2012: 149).

By 2012, Hungary experts were already speaking of an 'illiberal turn' in the country, Fidesz having amended over 50 articles of the Constitution in its first 12 months in office in 'a perfect storm battering Hungarian constitutionalism' (Bánkuti, Halmai and Scheppele 2012: 139) before pushing through a whole new 'unconstitutional constitution' (Scheppele 2012). A primary focus was bringing the Constitutional Court to heel, which they achieved through a combination of stripping it of authority in key areas like the judicial review of tax and budget matters, lowering the mandatory retirement age for judges and prosecutors from 70 to 62, increasing the size of the court, and getting rid of the Constitutional requirement for multi-party agreement on judicial appointments (Bánkuti, Halmai and Scheppele 2012). In another major reform in March 2013, all jurisprudence of the Constitutional Court before it was captured by Fidesz was nullified, undermining over two decades of case-law on democracy, human rights, and the rule of law (Venice Commission 2013: §88–99). Another early focus was mass media, with two major media laws restructuring the Hungarian Media Authority and creating a new Media Council which was duly packed with Orbán loyalists. This set the stage for a steady erosion of media freedom and pluralism in Hungary, with increasingly kleptocratic private media captured by Fidesz allies and Orbán associates, and public media used as a tool of Fidesz propaganda both by praising the party line and by vilifying or ignoring opposition (Wójcik 2022).[19]

While there was some measure of outrage among European officials, on the whole the Commission's material response was one of hesitation and concession. Rhetorically, there were some strong words. For example, then Justice Commissioner and Vice-President of the Barroso Commission Viviane Reding said that only 'actual changes' to the constitutional reforms or their 'immediate suspension' would suffice to address the Commission's concerns. On the occasion of this speech, the Commission announced three expedited infringement proceedings against Hungary for undermining the independence of its central bank, judiciary and data protection authorities, using the Article 258 procedure described above. The problem, however, is that these infringement actions focused only on very specific reforms, failing to take account of the bigger picture of the Hungarian slide to authoritarianism. Worse, the Fidesz government quickly developed a ruthless strategy for such targeted legal interventions by the Commission. Like the heads of the Hydra of Lerna, the Hungarian government became apt at sacrificing one problematic reform while replacing it with two new measures that ultimately worsened the state of Hungarian democracy further.[20] Or introducing a legal 'resolution' that acknowledges harm was done without remedying the damage. Or making *de jure* changes that addressed the Commission's concerns while doing little to change things on the ground, a strategy Agnes Batory calls 'creative compliance' (Batory 2016: 691–3).

Take the lowering of the mandatory retirement age of judges and prosecutors in Hungary from 70 to 62, the subject of one of the Commission's 2012 infringement actions. The ECJ indeed ruled on 6 November 2012 that the reform violated EU law, and demanded that the 274 judges who had been dismissed under this reform be reinstated if they wished.[21] However, while the Hungarian government did backtrack on the reform, lowering the retirement age to 65 instead of 62, and with a much longer transition period, only 56 of the forcibly retired judges were eventually reinstated, and few of them into leading positions (Halmai 2017). This back-and-forth technique of entrenching reforms that strike at democratic fundamentals—in this case, the independence of the judiciary—while making minor concessions to bring legislation within the narrow confines of the Commission's concerns are part of what Orbán himself has called his 'peacock dance' with EU institutions (de Búrca 2022). The European Commission's reactions to these developments are representative of the problems characterizing its responses to democratic backsliding in EU member states in general. Rather than acknowledging the lasting damage of this exchange, and opening Article 7 procedures, the Commission closed the infringement procedure on 20 November 2013, stating it was 'satisfied that Hungary has brought its legislation in line with EU law' (European Commission 2013).

These constitutional developments in Hungary contain just a few examples of how the Orbán regime has systematically undermined democracy and the rule of law in Hungary. The full list deserves book-length treatment in its own right—and indeed several books have been written on the subject (e.g. Körösényi, Illés and Gyulai 2020; Scheiring 2020; Pap 2017). Suffice to note that when the European Parliament pressed the European Commission to launch the Rule of Law Framework procedure[22] in June 2015, after incendiary rhetoric by Orbán linking migration to insecurity and calling for the death penalty to be reinstated, there were more than enough grounds to do so. The response by the European Commission declaring that they saw 'no systemic threat to democracy, the rule of law and fundamental rights in Hungary' (European Commission 2015) is a fitting summary of the Commission's dereliction of its duty to act as guardian of the treaties.

Capitulation on conditionality in the European Council

The second actor I want to consider from the perspective of transnational complicity in EU democratic backsliding is the European

Council. While the European Council does not have as direct a role in protecting the integrity of the European treaties as the Commission (as 'Guardian of the Treaties'), it is clear that it has weighty responsibilities in this area too, in accordance with the role it is accorded in the treaties. The European Council is a key actor in Article 7, the main sanctions mechanism for violations of EU fundamental values (see Chapter 4). Article 7.2 TEU tasks the European Council, by unanimity voting, to determine 'the existence of a serious and persistent breach' of the values listed in Article 2 TEU (incidentally, this is the first mention of the European Council in the TEU). Second, in the title 'Provisions on Democratic Principles' (Title III TEU), the legitimacy of the European Council, as representative of the member states, is directly tied to the democratic accountability of its composite heads of state or government (Article 10.2). This means that the European Council has a treaty responsibility vis-a-vis its own institutional legitimacy to maintain a (derivative) democratic character. If a non-democratic member state wields a vote (especially a veto) in the European Council, this institution can no longer be considered democratic, even in a derivative way, in violation of Article 10 TEU.[23] Third, protecting the democratic character of EU member states is crucial to retaining international credibility for actions to 'consolidate and support democracy, the rule of law, human rights and the principles of international law'. These are among the foremost of the self declared goals of the EU's external action (as per Article 21(2b) TEU). While responsibility for the EU's international engagements are shared between (mostly) the Council and the European Commission, the European Council has a key role in defining the guidelines, strategic interests and objectives of EU external action (see Article 26 TEU).

These are three important reasons why we can demand the European Council to act within its authority to protect democracy and the rule of law in EU member states. So, we can say that the European Council has a normative obligation to respond to democratic backsliding, within the remit of its competences, and a negative duty not to act in ways that may reasonably be expected to exacerbate democratic decay. And these are only some of the treaty-based justifications for this; one could make a wholly separate argument about the duty of each of the individual heads of state or government sitting in the European Council to protect the democratic character of their own states. Arguably, the democratic freedom of each EU citizen is tied to the freedom of all EU citizens in that each is tied to EU legislation co-authored by the governmental representatives (in the Council) of each other. But given my general methodological orientation in this book to immanent critique (see Chapters 1 and 4), I will not labour this point further.

Now that we have identified sources for the European Council's normative obligation to respond to democratic backsliding in EU member states, it remains to ask whether it had always adequately fulfilled these responsibilities. If not, it too shares in transnational complicity in EU democratic backsliding. And indeed there are numerous examples of the European Council's complicity, either by appeasement or by turning a blind eye to anti-democratic developments for political expediency. An illustrative example of this complicity in democratic backsliding concerns how it has dealt with the Rule of Law Conditionality Regulation. Essentially, the European Council allowed Hungary and Poland to hijack efforts to restrict EU funds to states violating rule of law norms, greatly limiting the possibility of weighty financial sanctions. The story of how we got there is a little convoluted, so bear with me.

The Conditionality Regulation was initially pitched by the European Commission as a stronger tool to tackle rule of law backsliding in member states by making the disbursement of EU funds conditional on sufficient performance on rule of law indicators. After some debate on a conditionality mechanism to protect democracy and the rule of law, the Commission made a proposal in May 2018[24] that would allow the Commission to withhold EU funds to member states where it found 'generalised deficiencies' with the rule of law, such as violations of the independence of the judiciary, or the failure to correct or legally sanction abuses of power by public authorities, where those deficiencies undermine the EU's budget or its financial interests.[25] Crucially, the Commission proposed that sanctions arising from the Conditionality Regulation would be adopted unless a qualified majority of the Council opposed the measures (what has been called a 'reverse qualified majority'). This meant that the Commission would have quite extensive powers to withhold EU funds where it identified rule of law backsliding.

It is not fanciful to imagine that budgetary conditionality could have a strong restraining effect on democratic backsliding. Take the two member states that have regressed furthest on democratic norms: Hungary and Poland. Of course, as members of the EU, Hungary and Poland have benefitted from being part of the single market, which allows for the free movement of goods, services, and people within its borders. This has led to increased trade and economic growth in both countries. But in addition to the benefits of being part of the single market, Hungary and Poland have also been net beneficiaries of various EU funding instruments. These include the European Regional Development Fund (ERDF), the European Social Fund (ESF), and the Cohesion Fund, which provide financial support for a wide range of initiatives, such as infrastructure development, research and innovation, and support for small and medium-sized enterprises. According to data from the European Commission, between 2014 and 2020, Hungary received a total of €12.3 billion from the ERDF, €8.7 billion from the ESF, and €1.9 billion from the Cohesion Fund. In terms of gross domestic product (GDP), this represents an average of around 1.7% per year. For Poland, the figures are slightly higher relative to the size of their economy, with a total of €35.3 billion from the ERDF, €18.5 billion from the ESF, and €8.3 billion from the Cohesion Fund between 2014 and 2020. This represents an average of around 2.7% of GDP per year. Making these funds conditional on democratic indicators would be a powerful incentive to roll back anti-democratic reform.

So, for once it seemed the Commission was showing its teeth when it came to democratic backsliding—at least where this was taken, narrowly, to refer to the degradation of the rule of law. The member states, though, failed to pick up the proposal for the Conditionality Regulation in the Council; few member states were initially keen to grant the Commission such extensive powers of control. It resurfaced however in the debate on EU recovery funds following the COVID-19 pandemic in 2020. In exchange for their agreement to authorize the European Central Bank to take on debt to finance member states' economic recovery, the so-called 'frugal states' (centrally the Netherlands) demanded that the recovery funds be made conditional to minimal standards on the rule of law. Initially, this renewed attention for the Conditionality Regulation seemed to work—despite opposition from Poland and Hungary, the 2018 Regulation looked like it was going to be passed by the Council. However, while the Conditionality Regulation could be passed by a qualified majority (that is, in the face of opposition by Hungary and Poland), certain financial aspects of the recovery funding itself did require unanimous agreement.

Predictably, Hungary and Poland latched onto this veto point, arguing they would block all the EU-level COVID-19 recovery funding—and indeed the entire EU budget (with a combined value of €1.9 trillion)—if the Conditionality Regulation was passed as it had been proposed by the Commission. This was one of those make-or-break moments in the recent history of EU responses to democratic and rule of law backsliding. Would Hungary and Poland succeed in neutering the Conditionality Regulation? Or would they be appeased by the other players in European politics? Unfortunately, under the leadership of Angela Merkel (Germany held the rotating presidency of the Council at the time), the Conditionality Regulation was first hollowed out beyond recognition and then kicked down the road.

The first victim was inversing the negative qualified majority; instead of needing a qualified (super-) majority in the Council to block Commission-proposed conditionality, a qualified majority in the Council would be needed to authorize the sanction. This radically changed the balance of power of the proposal in favour of member states. The second victim was the threshold needed to trigger the Regulation. The original proposal came into play when rule of law backsliding '*affects or risks affecting* the sound financial management or the protection of the financial interests of the Union' (draft Article 3.1, emphasis added). The hollowed-out version required rule of law backsliding to 'affect or *seriously* risk affecting the sound financial management and the protection of the financial interests of the Union budget or the protection of the financial interests of the Union *in a sufficiently direct way*' (Article 4.1, emphasis added). The third change hollowing out the original proposal was the introduction, in the preamble of the Regulation, of a sort of special appeals procedure

(Preamble, clause 26). This allows a member state who feels that the principles of objectivity, non-discrimination and equal treatment have been violated when the Regulation is used against them to request the President of the European Council to raise the matter there, and delays the adoption of any measures until the discussion in the European Council has taken place. This may seem innocuous, but as Sébastian Platon has pointed out, runs the risk of converting a qualified majority decision into a unanimous decision, since voting in the European Council is by consensus (Platon 2021).

Still, this was not enough. Hungary and Poland persisted in threatening to use their veto against the Multiannual Financial Framework, without which there could be no EU-wide coronavirus recovery fund (and indeed, no EU budget). Under pressure to find a solution to finally release the massive pandemic recovery funds that had been negotiated, the European Council proposed keeping the text of the hollowed-out Regulation as it had been passed in November 2020 with two far-reaching caveats. First, the Commission was instructed to come up with 'guidelines' on how it was to implement the Regulation. Second, these guidelines would have to be published after the ECJ had ruled on the pre-empted actions for annulment that Hungary and Poland were preparing. This meant, in practice, that the Conditionality Regulation was kicked down the road from the legal entry into force in January 2021 until some vague future time in 2022 or later (read: after the 2022 Hungarian general election).

These further compromises were presented in the 'conclusions' of the European Council meeting (European Council 2020). The problem is that the European Council had no legal authority to delay the implementation of the Conditionality Regulation. As Alberto Alemanno and Merijn Chamon argue, there were two key problems with this. First, the European Council is explicitly proscribed from having a legislative function in Article 15 of the TEU,[26] this role being shared by the European Parliament and the Council. But in mandating the Commission to draw up 'guidelines' and in delaying the implementation of the Conditionality Regulation until these guidelines were finalized, the European Council effectively forced an amendment on the Regulation, which it had no authority to change. Indeed, instructing the Commission in this way directly undermines the principle of balance between EU institutions, since the Commission is treaty-bound to be 'completely independent' and its members (the Commissioners) 'shall neither seek nor take instructions from any Government' (Article 17.3 TEU). Second, by in effect suspending the entry into force of the Regulation pending a case before the Court, the European Council overturned the legal norm that actions for annulment do *not* have such an effect (Article 278 TFEU), whereby only the Court can decide otherwise in its own judgements (Alemanno and Chamon 2020). Beyond being hollowed out substantively by the earlier concessions granted to Hungary and Poland on the content of the Conditionality Regulation, the regulation was also significantly delayed in an *ultra vires* intervention by the European Council.

Notwithstanding that the hollowed-out and delayed Conditionality Regulation has nevertheless eventually been used by the Commission with some success (Scheppele and Morijn 2023), these interventions by the member states acting in the European Council (and, when it came to the initial hollowing out of the proposed Regulation, in the Council) significantly hampered the development of democracy and rule of law conditionality. Underscoring this conclusion, Polish civil society movement Akcja Demokracja (Democracy Action) and the Hungarian civil society organization aHang (The Voice) said:

> Today's agreement is a political decision to push through the budget and sadly, the rule of law mechanism was sacrificed. The promised link between the EU budget and the rule of law conditionality has been weakened. It's almost toothless now. For the citizens of Hungary and Poland, rule of law delayed is rule of law denied. This capitulation could create an indefinite delay in the rule of law mechanism coming into force and … allows Orban to fund his next election with European taxpayers money. (Akcja Demokracja and aHang Hungary 2020)

Academic observers were equally scathing, with one group decrying the European Council conclusions as 'a great victory to Orbán and Kaczyński' who achieved 'years of non-enforcement and only weak, too-little-too-late enforcement after that' (Scheppele, Pech and Platon 2020).

Under the initial terms proposed by the Commission, the Conditionality Regulation might have proven a far stronger tool to respond to democratic and rule of law backsliding. And this not only to sanction would-be authoritarian governments, but also to ensure that EU funds do not finance their anti-democratic political takeover (Theuns 2020). As such, the member states capitulating to the hostage diplomacy of Hungary and Poland, hollowing out the proposal in the Council and then undermining EU law in kicking the Regulation further down the road in the European Council is a key example of transnational complicity in enabling democratic backsliding in EU member states.

Conclusion: Correcting complicity through redress

In this chapter, I have argued that the European Commission and member state governments acting in the European Council (and the Council) are all complicit in democratic backsliding in EU member states. While sometimes their complicity has taken the form of condoning democratic backsliding, more often it has been complicity by omission—blameworthy forbearance and unwillingness to use existing tools of enforcement to secure compliance with EU fundamental values. Correcting this sort of complicity is more demanding than correcting more active forms of complicity. In the second case, taken very generally, the first duty will be to desist from acting in the way or ways that can plausibly be expected to make a causal contribution to the primary wrong. When it comes to complicity by omission, more positive action is needed.

Complicit member states and EU actors must use all their legal and political authority to check autocratic politics in the EU. For example, it is crucial that the decade-long trend of the Commission stepping back from infringement actions it is empowered to bring against member states for violations of EU law under Article 258 TFEU is reversed (Kelemen and Pavone 2023). But it is also crucial—and is pointed out far less often—that while member state governments are authorized to bring infringement actions against member states violating EU law by Article 259 TFEU, in practice they almost never do (Kochenov 2015). This reticence is hard to understand given the urgency of the democracy crisis, and more attention to it will hopefully galvanize pro-democratic member states to act.[27] Both of these strategies to meet the duties of redress consequent to their complicity in democratic backsliding could be made more potent still by 'bundling' the violations of Article 2 related to democratic and rule of law backsliding and other fundamental values violations in what Scheppele has named 'systemic infringement actions' (Scheppele 2013b).

Another way that the member state governments (in the Council and the European Council) and the European Commission could meet their duties of redress in light of their complicity with democratic backsliding in EU member states is by ensuring that all tools of EU budget conditionality are used to their full potential. Such a strategy may be more effective in enforcing Article 2 values, including democracy and the rule of law, but I have argued that there are normative reasons to do this independent of such success—correcting complicity.

Bolder and more systematic use of EU budget conditionality would build on recent steps in this direction taken over the past few years. The first foray in imposing budget conditionality came from the Council and concerned the Rule of Law Conditionality Regulation that we are by now familiar with. After its bruising adoption, which all but hollowed out the Regulation of its intended scope and force, the Council nevertheless voted by qualified majority to withhold over €6 billion in EU funds to Hungary on 22 December 2022. Perhaps emboldened by these first steps (Kelemen 2024), the next step of budget conditionality came from the Commission in a more creative manner. The Regulation on the Recovery and Resilience Fund, which established the 'NextGenEU' facility earmarking huge sums to stimulate recovery after the COVID-19 pandemic, contained recommendations for each country. Every member state had to present a National Recovery and Resilience Plan for approval by both the Commission and Council. The Commission had the authority to reject the plan or withhold funds if the plan did not adequately address the recommendations for that country. For Hungary and Poland, the country-specific recommendations included rule of law criteria, something that had largely escaped notice or scandal (Scheppele and Morijn 2023). While approving the national plans in principle, the Commission used these rule of law criteria to withhold almost €6 billion from Hungary and over €35 billion from Poland until the two countries met a series of rule of law 'milestones'.

Scaling up one step further, the Commission then turned to the Common Provisions Regulation. The new rules of the Common Provisions Regulation, enacted in 2021, require that member states follow the Charter of Fundamental Rights when using funds from this regulation. But Article 47 of the Charter demands that all EU citizens are 'entitled to a fair and public hearing within a reasonable time by an independent and impartial tribunal previously established by law' (European Parliament 2000). And the repeated violations of the independence of the judiciary by Hungary and Poland, some of which I have detailed above, fall far short of this standard. Consequently, over €16 billion in EU structural and cohesion funds were withheld from Hungary in 2022 and around €75 billion from Poland.[28]

But before taking too congratulatory a tone, we should also note some of the failures in pursuing budget conditionality. A major problem is that the relevant EU actors have again proven willing to accept symbolic or merely *de jure* reforms rather than real systemic change. The milestones the Commission laid out for Poland to access NextGenEU funds, for example, did not even require that Poland uphold all the judgements of the ECJ on its violations of judicial independence. This even led to four major European judges organizations suing the Council and the Commission, seeking to overturn the approval of Poland's plans.[29] We can see a similar logic around the European Council summit in December 2023. Viktor Orbán threatened to veto EU accession talks and EU funding for Ukraine. When Orbán threatens with a veto in one area, you can always be sure he wants something elsewhere. And indeed, over €10 billion in withheld EU funding was released in exchange for his walking out of the room so as not to have to vote on Ukrainian accession talks (Kelemen 2024: 14), thus leading to the European Parliament taking the European Commission to court for 'horse-trading' fundamental values for political concessions (Liboreiro 2024).[30] We can see that despite some progress over the last couple of years, we have some way to go before we can say that EU actors are meeting their duties of redress in this domain (European Commission 2024b).

So far, I have focused on ways that EU actors complicit in democratic backsliding in EU member states could flesh out their normative duties of redress in order to correct their complicitous course of action, be that by omission or by positive action. But complicity generates a different class of duties too—namely those of reparation. If the European Council and the Commission are complicit in democratic backsliding, as I have argued, then they hold special duties to those harmed by the primary wrong. I return to this question in Chapter 7, when I argue that EU actors ought to be much more proactive in cultivating pluralist democracy in member states undergoing democratic decline.

6

CONTAINING AUTOCRACY IN THE EU

Point n'est besoin d'espérer pour entreprendre, ni de réussir pour persévérer.

Attributed to Charles Martin de Bourgogne[1]

This chapter takes up the challenge of how to coherently contain autocratic influences in European Union (EU) policy and law-making. The previous chapter examined special duties of redress and reparation for the harms of democratic backsliding in EU member states that I argued different European actors owed due to their complicity in processes of democratic backsliding. I specifically made the case that moral complicity grounds a duty of the European Commission to use infringement actions against violations of EU fundamental values in a more tenacious way, which would reverse the current trend of 'forbearance' by the Commission (Kelemen and Pavone 2023). Together with pro-democratic member states in the Council and the European Council, the Commission should also pursue a more thorough conditionality of EU funds. But above and beyond the matter of correcting complicity, pro-democratic actors in Europe have strong normative reasons to act where they can to contain autocratic influences in European politics.

The precise moral and political grounds for such containment will vary depending on the specific threat to democracy that is being contained and the specific actor or actors attempting to contain them.

PROTECTING DEMOCRACY IN EUROPE

Generally though, it will be ultimately based on the value of and commitment to democratic norms. And this is not some sort of imperial project of some European countries trying to impose their vision of political legitimacy on others (Morgan 2020). As I argued in Chapter 1, one of the core normative reasons for European political actors to combat democratic backsliding is essentially self-interested; given how the EU treaties have integrated European political decision-making and legislative authority, democratic decay in one member state undermines the democratic character of all member states and the civic freedom of all EU citizens. EU member states are therefore acting in democratic self-defence when they act to contain autocracy in other member states.

Before assessing the ways in which EU actors can legitimately and coherently act to contain threats to democracy in Europe, we have to specify what exactly is meant with the term 'containment'. The most common context for what is sometimes called the 'doctrine of containment' in political science and international relations is US foreign policy during the Cold War (Gaddis 2005). This strategy to counter the spread of communism is usually attributed to George F. Kennan, Deputy Chief of Mission at the US Embassy in Moscow in the mid-1940s. It consisted, roughly, in scaling up opposition to the USSR through economic, political and diplomatic means without engaging the USSR or established communist regimes to try to roll back communism directly. My use of the term containment in this chapter has some similarities to this doctrine, but also several important differences. As with Cold War containment, the approach I develop here opposes both inaction ('isolationism' in the language of international relations) and accommodation ('appeasement') with autocratic actors in EU politics. Like the doctrine of containment, it also emphasizes the need for a long-term and multilateral response to autocratic threats. And finally, in the same vein as some early formulations of the US strategy, it rejects the use of force in favour of economic and political tactics.[2] Indeed, the normative arguments I have made about how the integration of EU members' political, legal and economic systems justifies a collective response when governments of individual member states undermine democracy and the rule of law domestically can never be taken to justify violence and generally cannot even justify, in my view, 'militant democratic' responses by the EU (see Theuns 2023; I develop this argument further in Chapter 8).

These similarities notwithstanding, there are also important differences between containment as a strategy of EU democracy protection and Cold War containment. Cold War containment is sometimes used to refer to a strategy of domestic non-interference with communist states, which were supposed to eventually collapse under the inherent contradictions of their social, political and economic organization (an idea that shows striking similarities with Marxist historical materialism, for those who enjoy these sorts of ironies). As I argued in Chapter 1, and as I will develop further in Chapter 7, I do not think EU actors should shy away from acting in a partisan manner at the national level when democracy is threatened. Given this, the containment of autocratic actors in European politics presented here is not an alternative to trying to reverse autocratization at the domestic member state level, but a complement to correcting complicity in democratic backsliding (Chapter 5) and cultivating pluralist democracy in EU member states (Chapter 7). In short, while the legitimacy and desirability of 'rolling back' autocratic politics in EU member states should indeed be tempered and delimited both by a democratic ethos and a rejection of coercive measures, restoring all member states to liberal democratic norms is the core goal of EU democracy protection overall.

Working to contain autocratic actors in EU politics can therefore be specified as the strategy of systematically limiting, constraining and reducing the influence of autocratic politics within the EU. Containment understood this way has legal, political and economic dimensions.[3] Legal containment includes the implementation of existing legal frameworks and policies that can restrict the influence and power of autocratic actors within EU institutions and procedures. This requires proactive engagement with the established legal framework to try to make EU governance structures robust to attempts by autocratic actors to exert influence and control. The goal is not just to react to such attempts, but to create an environment where the influence of autocratic governments is systematically weakened. Where feasible, it could include developing new legal tools, though I think this is generally a waste of time (Kelemen 2023). The effectiveness of legal containment, I argue, depends on using current laws and regulations in a creative manner, while remaining within both the letter and the ultimate spirit of the overall legal framework the EU treaties provide.

With political containment, I mean the use of political strategies of isolation that seek proactively to undermine autocratic actors symbolically and, more passively, to deny them voluntary signs of prestige and legitimacy. This can take the form of various forms of political non-cooperation and starving autocratic actors of goodwill gestures like shared photo opportunities, exchanges of gifts, joint press conferences and public messages of congratulations.

Finally, economic measures of containment designate the use of economic tools such as financial conditionality to economically disincentivize and weaken autocratic regimes within the EU. While the logic of pro-democratic actors using economic tools for containment is an independent normative basis for their use from correcting complicity, the tools themselves (i.e. the Rule of Law Conditionality Regulation, the Common Provisions Regulation and the Financial Regulation) are by now familiar, so I do not further develop the notion of economic containment in this chapter.

Below, I work out in more detail the legal and political conceptions of containment. While the focus is on articulating the relevant normative principles that ought to guide the use of legal and political containment, I will work out illustrative examples that comprise both weak strategies of containment (what not to do) and more robust strategies (what to do). However, these examples should not be taken as a policy checklist or blueprint. They are instead suggestions for how the normative principles regarding a coherent approach to containing autocracy in Europe along these dimensions could be worked out more concretely. Identifying, working out and pursuing legal and political containment across myriad institutional and policy domains will necessarily be agent- and context-specific, and will require the creativity and courage of many different actors from civil servants in European institutions and member states to representatives of European and national political parties.

Furthermore, I cover only those strategies that can, I think, be coherently pursued in the context of the current treaties. More radical alternatives that would require reform of the treaties may be better at containing autocracy on paper but would require the unanimous assent of all member states—something which is unimaginable on this issue in the current political context. In keeping with the non-ideal orientation of this book, such 'ideal' (read 'unrealistic') proposals fall outside the scope of my study. Containing autocracy in the EU must also be normatively coherent with the fundamental values it seeks to protect. As I argued in Chapter 4, the core challenge for a normatively coherent approach is how to pursue containment without resorting to the sorts of anti-democratic action that are incompatible with democratic values. This is not only a core problem with the Article 7 sanction and Regulation 1141/2014 (Theuns 2023), but also with some new proposals such as disenfranchisement in the Council via Article 10 (Cotter 2022). Normative incoherence lies at the heart of my critique of existing legal tools for responding to democratic backsliding in EU member states, so it is logical this is a minimal standard of my own proposals too.

A final caveat concerns proportionality. Clearly, respect for fundamental values and standards is scalar. Containment should not be all or nothing, but should be tailored to the specific situation in a backsliding member state. There can even be concerns with developments in EU member states that are full liberal democracies, like when the Latvian Parliament decided in November 2021 to exclude members who were not vaccinated against COVID-19 from all parliamentary business, including online meetings (Theuns and Daemen 2021), or when over half of Dutch party programmes were found to include items conflicting with the principles of the rule of law in the run up to the 2023 election (Commissie Rechtsstatelijkheid in Verkiezingsprogramma's 2023).[4] However, while it is important to be vigilant regarding such matters, the situation in these countries is vastly different from the worst examples of democratic and rule of law backsliding in Europe. Indeed, it is not even helpful to compare them in some cases; while this may seem to play into the hand of neutrality, it in fact soaks up valuable resources of time and money.[5] The strongest measures of containment I lay out below are pitched at relations with a member state who is no longer a democracy. For instance, I argue that a non-democratic state should be maximally excluded from EU law and policymaking, to the extent that such exclusion is itself coherent with EU fundamental values. (In Chapter 8 I will go a step further, to consider the principles that should govern relations with a frankly autocratic member state).[6]

Legal containment

The strategy of legal containment is about harnessing the existing tools within the EU legal framework to mitigate the impact of autocratic actors on EU law- and policymaking. The standard approach to legal containment over the past decade or so has been *soft* legal containment: the use of social pressure, dialogue monitoring and negotiation to try to moderate autocratic actors. While such tools have their place when a member state intends to uphold fundamental values, they have proved to be naïve and ineffective in light of more confrontational and deliberate politics of democratic decay. Instead, as far as this is possible without undermining their commitment to fundamental values, EU actors should use *hard* legal containment to maximally exclude autocratic actors from legal and political procedures at the European level.

In an influential article published in the *European Law Journal* in 2015, Jan-Werner Müller wrote that Article 7 of the Treaty on European Union (TEU), the main provision in the EU treaties for responding to member state violations of EU fundamental values, amounted to a kind of 'moral quarantine' (Müller 2015: 144). The only sanction described explicitly in Article 7.3 is the suspension of the voting rights of a member state in the Council, which Müller argues is 'not an actual intervention' in the member state but rather 'a mechanism to *insulate* the rest of the Union from the government ... deemed to be in breach of fundamental values' (emphasis in original). As Ulrich Wagrandl put it pithily, '[Article 7] is simply a move to contain an illiberal Member State before it can affect common policy ... [It] essentially says: stay as you are, but do not mess with us' (2018: 161–2). For these reasons, Article 7 seems to fit well into a strategy that emphasizes containment. Despite this, as I argued in Chapter 4, Article 7 suffered from two insurmountable flaws. First, as has been widely noted, the requirement that the Council determines 'the existence of a serious and persistent breach' of fundamental values unanimously and with the (supermajority)[7] consent of the European Parliament (Article 7.2) makes it exceedingly unlikely that even flagrant violations are sanctioned. Second, I argued that stripping a sanctioned state of their right to vote in the Council while continuing to hold them subject to the legislation co-determined in that Council (as per Article 7.3) violates the commitment to democratic equality enshrined in Article 2 TEU by undermining the All-Subjected Principle in democratic theory. Legal containment therefore should not take the route of Article 7 disenfranchisement.

If European actors cannot use Article 7 to contain autocratic leaders in an effective and democratically legitimate way by excluding their representatives from the Council, how then should legal containment proceed? As I mention above, I think it is helpful to distinguish two general routes to tackling this question. The first is to try to mitigate the impact of authoritarian politics in EU law- and policy-making through soft measures: discursive pressure, socialization, negotiation, monitoring, etc. The second is to use hard measures to sideline autocratic governments from EU-level decision-making.

Soft legal containment: Social pressure, dialogue and monitoring

Prioritizing social pressure, dialogue, negotiation and monitoring—which we can call 'soft legal containment'—has been the dominant approach of the European Commission for much of the 2010s. Ulrich Sedelmeier advocates for this kind of approach, arguing that, with appropriate design and favourable conditions, naming and shaming member states in violation of EU fundamental values could foster a culture of compliance with democratic norms (Sedelmeier 2017). Such an approach is careful to avoid backlash against EU intervention, of the kind that arguably followed the bilateral diplomatic sanctions against Austria in 2000 (see Chapter 2; Schlipphak and Treib 2017). But it remains very much to be seen whether it has proven its worth, or whether it has been largely a waste of time (or even, as I will argue, that it may have had counterproductive effects).

Partly because of the procedural weakness of Article 7, the Commission has tended to prefer the soft approach to legal containment over the past decade or so, developing new tools of soft legal containment focused on dialogue and the monitoring of member state compliance with rule of law norms. The Rule of Law Framework and the Rule of Law Review Cycle were intended to try to hold governments backsliding on EU values (particularly the rule of law) accountable.[8] Proposed as a preventive tool in 2014, the EU Rule of Law Framework was supposed to pre-empt systemic threats to the rule of law in EU countries before they escalate to a level warranting the invocation of Article 7. The process is structured into three stages. First, the European Commission evaluates the rule of law situation in a member state. Where deficiencies are observed, the Commission can issue recommendations. Subsequently, the Commission is supposed to monitor the member state's compliance with these recommendations (European Commission 2014: 3; Priebus 2022: 1691). Despite acknowledging that the Commission 'has the responsibility of ensuring the respect of the values on which the EU is founded' (European Commission 2014: 2) and boldly claiming that the framework is designed to 'resolve future threats to the rule of law in Member States' (ibid.: 3), in practice the framework was quickly sidelined.[9]

This gap between ambition and effect is perhaps not so surprising when we pause to consider what a 'pre-Article 7' procedure entails. Already, the first clause of Article 7 TEU, for ascertaining a clear risk of a breach of EU fundamental values, requires a dialogue between the Council and the member state in question and opens the space for recommendations. The second clause—where the European Council determines the existence of a breach—also builds in dialogue, with the requirement the member state is invited to submit observations prior to the vote. By extension, a pre-Article 7 procedure is thus a monitoring and dialogue procedure that takes place *before* these steps: 'a dialogue before the dialogue before the dialogue before any sanctions might actually be imposed' (Kelemen 2023: 228).[10]

Introduced in 2020, the EU Rule of Law Review Cycle, also known as the Rule of Law Mechanism, is intended to promote and maintain the rule of law within the EU through a proactive and preventive approach. The Mechanism involves annual dialogue with rule of law actors geared to monitoring the extent of their compliance with rule of law norms, an annual Rule of Law Report for each member state, and a subsequent discussion with stakeholders focused on the implementation of rule of law recommendations (Regulation 2020/2092). At face value, this approach seems to have merits. For a start, by systematically reviewing all member states on rule of law compliance, the Rule of Law Reports seem to be more robust against member state bias, political partisanship and stereotyping. Such a general and broad-based approach is precisely what Sedelmeier argued might increase the efficacy of soft legal containment measures as they enhance 'formal process, impartiality and publicity … [through] continuous monitoring of compliance' (2017: 349, cf. Uitz 2019). Furthermore, by assessing rule of law deficiencies before they become widespread, and pushing towards cooperative solutions, the hope was that these might be 'nipped in the bud' while the costs of changing course are low (Pech 2021: 335, Priebus 2022: 1693).

Unfortunately, the specific form the EU Rule of Law Review Cycle has taken did little to build on this potential, and has arguably made the situation regarding member-state respect for EU fundamental values worse. In a lengthy study commissioned by the European Parliament, Laurent Pech and Petra Bárd evaluated the Commission's Rule of Law Reports. On the positive side of the balance, addressing concerns that the rule of law was conceptually too indeterminate for clear definition or implementation (see e.g. Mos 2020), the Commission managed a persuasive explanation of what the rule of law entails, along with its fundamental elements in line with the case law of the Court of Justice of the European Union and the European Court of Human Rights (Pech and Bárd 2022). The Commission also succeeded in underlining the fundamental importance of the rule of law as a prerequisite of the enjoyment of all the rights deriving from the EU treaties as well as more generally the mutual trust needed between EU member states, which contributed to increasing the political saliency of the rule of law crisis. Finally, the authors commended the scope of the reports, framed around the pillars of the independence, quality and efficiency of member state judicial systems, anti-corruption, media pluralism and checks and balances (ibid.: 60–6).

Notwithstanding these bright spots, the overall assessment of the study was deeply critical. The Rule of Law Reports create unsustainably high expectations as a tool of prevention, use 'extremely soft, diplomatic language' (ibid.: 70), ignore the broader context of rule of law backsliding, and fail to differentiate major and minor concerns. The result, the authors contend, is that the extensive reports and their recommendations (283 of them by a recent count; cf. Pech 2023) misallocated the Commission's finite resources of focus, energy and political capital, undermining the Commission's effectiveness in enforcing EU legal standards related to the rule of law. Along these lines, an op-ed responding to the publication of the very first Rule of Law Report made the following analogy:

> On September 30, with one democracy under its guard already burned to the ground and another in the midst of a three-alarm fire, the European Commission published an obscurantist treatise on the importance of fire safety and on warning signs of fire risk. (Kelemen 2020b)

To see how these critiques play out in practice in the Reports, contrast the recommendations of the most recent Rule of Law Report on Denmark and Hungary. These two countries are respectively the highest- and the lowest-ranked EU member states on the rule of law in the World Justice Project Rule of Law Index, the leading academic index measuring respect for the rule of law.[11] Similarly, Denmark scores highly in the V-Dem Liberal Democracy Index—it is in fact the top-scoring country worldwide based on 2023 data—while Hungary trails in 97th place, one spot above Kuwait.[12] Nevertheless, while coverage of Hungary is somewhat more extensive than Denmark, the 'extremely soft, diplomatic language' used in the two cases is often indistinguishable. Take for instance the paragraph on 'access to justice'. The Commission concludes that, in Hungary, 'access to justice for vulnerable groups could be improved', while in Denmark, 'the review of the legal aid system that commenced in 2020 has been put on hold' (European Commission 2024a: 10). Or compare the formulations in the paragraph on 'ensuring transparent lobbying'. In Denmark, 'no steps have been taken to introduce rules on revolving doors for ministers', while in Hungary 'post-employment restrictions and cooling-off periods are fragmented and apply only to a small group of public officials' (ibid.: 15). In the words of George and Ira Gershwin, 'potato, potahto, tomato, tomahto, let's call the whole thing off'.

The specific weaknesses of the EU's Rule of Law Framework and Rule of Law Review Cycle highlight a more generally applicable worry when it comes to soft legal containment. The creation of new soft instruments is often proposed as a way to address gaps in the existing legal framework or to respond to evolving threats. While this might seem like a proactive approach, it can lead to what Laurent Pech has termed 'toolbox navel gazing' (2023), whereby developing new legal tools functions as a distraction, leading to a cycle of perpetually drafting new tools while failing to address the immediate and urgent needs of countering autocratic politics, which is followed by yet more new tools *ad absurdum*. This problem is only exacerbated when, as has been the case, the tools in question are framed around additional dialogue and monitoring, tools that soak up extensive resources in an attempt to 'manage' values violations rather than 'enforce' fundamental values (Priebus 2022). Even so, it is not surprising that toolbox navel gazing has generally led to the multiplication of soft tools because many proposals for harder measures, for instance reforming the Article 7 procedure, would require treaty change and hence unanimity amongst member state governments, including the very authoritarian governments that would be threatened by such reforms.

Hard legal containment: Maximal coherent exclusion

The alternative to soft legal containment is to take a harder approach, maximally sidelining autocratic actors in EU legal and political procedures to the extent that such exclusions are coherent with the values that autocratic politics threaten (to remain normatively coherent). If we accept the argument I presented in Chapter 4, this cannot mean stripping a backsliding member state of its right to vote in the Council, but could, for example, mean denying them the rotating Council presidency (an example I work out below) and making much more extensive use of the tools of differentiated integration (an option I discuss in Chapter 8). Hard legal containment looks creatively for opportunities to curtail autocratic actors from within the existing legal framework.[13] The principle I defend here is a proportionality demand such that, within the appropriate limits set by normative coherence and the legitimate scope of EU authority, the less democratic an EU member state becomes, the less influence it should generally have on EU law and policymaking. When we reach a situation in which a member state cannot be called a democracy at all because of deterioration of some of the core criteria of democratic government, their influence should, other things being equal, be limited to the maximum possible extent.[14] And to be slightly more precise still, EU actors should maximally exclude authoritarian governments from European legal and political procedures, insofar as this is compatible with EU law and coherent with fundamental values—let us call this 'maximal coherent exclusion'.[15] If it seems self-evident that non-democratic governments should be maximally sidelined from EU law and policymaking, we shall see that it is almost the opposite to the current situation, whereby especially the competitive authoritarian Hungarian government searches out and exploits each and every veto point it may have to extract concessions from EU institutions and from other member states.

'Maximal coherent exclusion' as a principle for limiting the political and legal influence of non-democratic member states grounds a much harder approach to legal containment. The normative justification such a principle can take is twofold. First, and in light of the demonstrated inefficacy of soft legal containment measures, a harder approach to legal containment might be expected to be more effective as leverage on member states experiencing democratic backsliding. While empirical research is needed to test this hypothesis and flesh out maximal coherent exclusion strategies along these desiderata, the broad thrust of conditionality research supports the idea that more robust measures lead to a larger behavioural effect (Bapat et al. 2013; Peksen 2019). Second, there is a principled reason for maximal coherent exclusion based on the tainted democratic legitimacy of autocratic member state governments and the 'spillover' that this illegitimacy has on the legitimacy of EU law and policymaking (see Chapter 1).

To see how hard legal containment in accordance with the principle of maximal coherent exclusion could proceed, it is helpful to illustrate the approach with a concrete measure. Let us look more closely at one potential application of hard legal containment that briefly caught the headlines in spring 2023, when the European Parliament pushed discussion on the Hungarian presidency of the Council in the summer of 2023 (Rafaela and Theuns 2023). On 1 June 2023, a huge majority of the European Parliament (442 in favour, 144 against, 33 abstentions) voted for a resolution on 'Breaches of the Rule of law and fundamental rights in Hungary and frozen EU funds' (European Parliament 2023). Article 11 of the resolution was particularly explosive, and is worth quoting in full:

> [The European Parliament] underlines the important role of the presidency of the Council in driving forward the Council's work on EU legislation, ensuring the continuity of the EU agenda and representing the Council in relations with the other EU institutions; *questions how Hungary will be able to credibly fulfil this task in 2024, in view of its non-compliance with EU law and the values enshrined in Article 2 TEU*, as well as the principle of sincere cooperation; asks the Council to find a proper solution as soon as possible; recalls that Parliament could take appropriate measures if such a solution is not found. (European Parliament 2023, emphasis added)

This resolution added considerable urgency to the recent legal and political debate on the presidency of the Council. But before we tackle this legal puzzle, let us look briefly at the broader picture.

The rotating presidency of the Council is a system for sharing the leadership of this institution among the EU member states. Every six months, a different member state takes on this role, supposedly ensuring equality among member states, regardless of their size or power. In theory, this is one way that all EU countries can have a direct impact on the EU's policy and decision-making agenda. The presidency has several responsibilities. It sets the Council's agenda and highlights specific issues and priorities, although the real power to set the broader long-term agenda remains with the European Commission and the European Council. The presidency also chairs meetings of the Council, ideally facilitating dialogue, fostering consensus, and advancing the legislative process. The treaty basis of the rotation system is the TEU, where Article 16.9 holds that 'the Presidency of Council configurations, other than that of Foreign Affairs, shall be held by Member State representatives in the Council on the basis of equal rotation'. Article 236.b of the Treaty on the Functioning of the European Union (TFEU) in turn holds that decisions on the presidency of the Council—that is, decisions that give practical effect to Article 16.9 TEU—shall be taken by the European Council, and, importantly, only require a qualified majority.

In a report on the presidency of the Council, the Meijers Committee addressed the thorny question of a Hungarian presidency of the Council (Meijers Committee 2023). As highlighted in the European Parliament Resolution quoted above, there is something deeply unsettling about Hungary taking on this role given that Hungary has been found repeatedly in violation of EU fundamental values and is, by the reckoning of the European Parliament and broad agreement amongst academic experts, no longer a democracy. A particularly Kafkaesque possibility is Hungary chairing meetings in the Council on its own democratic decay (as part of the ongoing Article 7 hearings).[16] As such, the urgency of this question in May and June 2023 was acute: though Hungary has taken up the presidency only since 1 July 2024, the 'trio' system (whereby three member state presidencies closely cooperate over an 18-month period) meant Hungary would already be in pole position from July 2023.[17] Alongside a few more moderate suggestions, the Meijers Committee drew attention to the possibility that Article 235.b TFEU gave the European Council the authority to change the planned order of Council presidencies in order to postpone the presidency of a member state that has either Article 7 TEU procedures pending before the Council or has been subject to fundamental values-related budgetary conditionality decided by the Council (ibid.: 9–10).

The crux of the issue, as I highlighted in an op-ed in the EUobserver I wrote together with Samira Rafaela (2023), was the requirement under Article 16.9 TEU that the presidency of the Council should proceed under a system of equal rotation. What does it mean for the presidency of the Council to proceed in this way? One conservative reading would be that each member state must act as Council President for six months every 13.5 years (given 27 member states), with a 13-year gap between the end of their previous presidency and the start of their next one. But does it necessarily need to be interpreted in such a narrow way? As Rafaela and I noted, and as has been subsequently discussed (e.g. in van den Brink 2023: 12–13), Article 16.9 does not call for 'strictly' equal rotation, like for instance the very next Article of the TEU, Article 17.5, on the appointment of Commissioners. This seems to open up room for manoeuvre, even if the permanent exclusion of a member state from the rotating Council presidency would seem to violate Article 16.9 TEU.

Given this, what possibilities could this discrepancy between 'strictly equal' and 'equal' rotation give rise to? Martijn van den Brink, though generally sceptical of the proposals by the Meijers Committee, has suggested that it could plausibly be interpreted to mean 'that all states get their turn before others get their second turn' (ibid.: 14). This would mean that a Hungarian Council presidency could be delayed until the end of the currently ongoing 13.5-year period—until the end of 2030.[18] Another suggestion, discussed in the Meijers Committee report and elsewhere, was that Hungary take on the formal role of President of the Council but that the Hungarian presidency is tempered and limited, especially with regard to its handling of Article 7 proceedings; Alberto Alemanno has called this a 'depotentiated presidency of the Council' (Vinocur 2023). I think a qualified majority of the Council could go further. Essentially, my view is that there is no rigorous legal or philosophical reason to interpret 'equal rotation' as requiring that each member state presides over the Council for the same six-month period every 13.5 years. Legally, the basis for this is a 2009 decision of the European Council, taken in line with their authority under Article 235.b TFEU. But that decision could be overturned by a qualified majority decision in that same body.

A key consideration would be whether suspending an authoritarian state's presidency of the Council would be coherent with EU fundamental values. (If it is not, then the critique I developed in Chapter 4 on the illegitimacy of stripping a member state of their right to vote in the Council while holding them subject to laws co-legislated in the Council would have bite here too.) There is some reason for caution on this point. Van den Brink argues that delaying a member state's presidency of the Council 'for some time' would be in accordance with the equal rotation demand in Article 16.9 TEU. However, he argues denying a member state this role 'for as long as it continues to violate the rule of law and other EU values' would need to be done via the familiar Article 7 TEU procedure, and bypassing Article 7 TEU in this context 'would be a violation of the EU's very own rule of law' (van den Brink 2023: 7–8). Given that the rule of law is one of the EU's fundamental values explicitly listed in Article 2 TEU, this charge would be fatal for the normative coherence of my argument here to pursue maximal coherent exclusion. But van den Brink's interpretation of the principle of equal rotation is not necessarily the only one possible, nor does it follow from some of the standard philosophical considerations on equality in political and legal theory.

Philosophically, there is solid ground for differentiating between democratic member states and non-democratic member states in the interpretation of 'equal rotation'. Take perhaps the most classical philosophical source on the interrelation between equality and justice, Book V of Aristotle's *Nicomachean Ethics*. In Aristotle's account, we find a principle of equality not grounded in uniformity but in proportionality to circumstance. This is sometimes paraphrased as the idea that equality requires treating 'like things alike'. For Aristotle, this principle of equality means that equals should be treated equally—and unequals unequally—in accordance with their relevant differences, such as virtue or merit. This Aristotelian perspective underscores the idea that equality is context-dependent, requiring carefully weighing the specific criteria that would justify differential treatment. Such a contextual approach to equality also has a solid foundation in jurisprudence. Consider for instance the widespread idea that criminal law penalties ought to be personalized or adjusted to an offender's circumstance. Such personalization can be considered not only to be compatible with the principle of equality before the law (a key component of the rule of law) but a *consequence* of a commitment to equality.[19] Treating offenders who have relevantly different circumstances, such as their health, wealth or age, in the same way despite those circumstances would in fact mean treating them unequally—even if they have committed the exact same offence when taken from the perspective of the victim.

These considerations on a contextual approach to equality offer a different lens through which to view the 'equal rotation' of the Council presidency. It suggests that equality in rotation does not necessarily mean each member state presides for the same amount of time. Instead, the principle of 'equal rotation' could be argued to lead in precisely the opposite direction in the extreme circumstances we are considering, namely when a non-democratic state is set to take up the Council presidency. Equal rotation, interpreted in this light, could be taken to require that those member states that respect the value of political equality, as expressed in their commitment to democracy and the rule of law, should have equal opportunities to lead. But (all) members who show flagrant disregard for these principles should be excluded from the Council presidency. Differentiating between democratic and non-democratic member states in this way not only does not violate but in fact affirms and protects the principles of equality and the rule of law laid out in Article 2 TEU. The value of equality, on this interpretation, is preserved in that all member states have an equal claim to the Council presidency, tempered only by the demand that they are democratic (which is explicit in the EU treaties, e.g. Article 10 TEU). Of course, it also follows from this that if and when the member state in question were to recover its democratic character, it would again have the right to preside over the Council.

Political containment

Political containment, as I use the term here, is the use of political strategies of isolation that seek to undermine autocratic actors in EU politics symbolically. This could take the form of various forms of political non-cooperation and starving autocratic actors of goodwill gestures like shared photo opportunities, exchanges of gifts, joint press conferences and public messages of congratulations. And indeed, the general principle I will defend is that authoritarian actors in EU politics should be deprived of political legitimacy and prestige by pro-democratic EU actors as much as possible. Such a principle is justified along two lines: one internal and insensitive to political effects, and the other consequentialist and highly sensitive to context. As we shall see, these two justificatory grounds can pull in opposite directions, and one of the challenges of political containment is to try to balance these internal and consequentialist approaches.

The internal approach starts from the importance of the expressive commitment of pro-democratic actors to democratic values. It is valuable, this view, for democratic actors to not only support but to be seen to be supporting a democratic ethos. The opposite is also true: it is harmful for them to be seen to be undermining a democratic ethos. The harm consists in such actions being at odds with democratic values and thus calling into question both the actor's commitment to these values and even the validity of those values themselves. Depriving autocratic actors of symbolic legitimacy by denying them shared photo opportunities, press conferences and messages of congratulations is a felicitous venue for pro-democratic actors to mark their attachment to those values that are called into question by democratic backsliding (including the value of democracy, equality and the rule of law). In isolating and undermining autocratic actors in EU politics symbolically, pro-democratic actors can be seen to be declaring that, unlike the agent of democratic backsliding, they support and affirm fundamental values. The contrary also holds, that by tolerating agents of democratic backsliding who reject basic democratic commitments, EU actors can be plausibly seen as making light of these normative commitments themselves.

Notice that the value of this internal motivation for expressing democratic values and refraining from expressing support for anti-democratic values and actors is wholly independent of the putative effect of these sorts of expressive acts on the agents of democratic backsliding. It may well be the case that denying an anti-democratic leader a photo opportunity in a specific circumstance might not plausibly be expected to have a causal effect on undermining that leader's political support. And in any case, the empirical effects of each such individual act of symbolic resistance to authoritarian politics will be extremely difficult if not impossible to isolate. But that is beside the point. It is valuable for the supposedly pro-democratic actors themselves to act in a way that marks their support for democratic values, as it positively affirms the weight of these values as well as actors' commitment to them.

Let us take a look at some examples whereby EU actors fail in such political containment, instead supplying an agent of democratic backsliding with political legitimacy. This can function as an illustrative example of concretely determining what sort of activities this approach to political containment proscribes. In April 2022, Hungary held national parliamentary elections. While the elections were free from violence, coercion and egregious fraud, they took place in a context that was fundamentally skewed in favour of the incumbent Fidesz party led by Viktor Orbán. Not only were (and are) Fidesz using public media in a deeply partisan way bordering on blatant propaganda, but Fidesz allies have also consolidated broad control of private Hungarian media. The few independent voices that remain are starved of advertising, and harassed through tactics like strategic lawsuits against public participation (otherwise known as SLAPPs), denial of licensing, superfluous administrative and tax burdens, and surveillance (Media Freedom Rapid Response 2022: 46–9; Wójcik 2022: 10). These were among the many reasons that the elections were widely decried as unfair by international monitoring observers.[20]

Internationally, the initial response to the elections by political leaders split largely along ideological lines. Friends of the Orbán regime such as Matteo Salvini, Marine Le Pen, Nigel Farage and even Vladimir Putin were quick to congratulate him on Fidesz' performance in the elections. Salvini, for instance, leader of the far-right Lega and Deputy Prime Minister of Italy at the time of writing, posted a gushing message on Facebook hailing 'Viktor' (using only his first name) as a crusader against 'sinister fanatics' in the defence of 'family, security, merit, development, solidarity, sovereignty and freedom', having won the 'love and consent' of the 'free Hungarian people'.[21]

Because of the longstanding concerns with the state of Hungarian democracy, one might expect EU leaders to have a more muted public reaction to the Hungarian national election. But when Viktor Orbán was formally re-elected as Hungarian Prime Minister on 16 May, European Commission President Ursula von der Leyen posted the following message on Twitter:

> Dear Prime Minister Viktor Orbán, congratulations on your reelection today.
>
> The EU faces unprecedented challenges.
>
> I look forward to working together to ensure we can collectively address them successfully.

In a similar vein, European Council President Charles Michel posted the following:

PROTECTING DEMOCRACY IN EUROPE

> In these testing times, the EU's unity and sovereignty are our main strengths.
>
> Congratulations on your re-election dear Viktor Orban and looking forward to our continued cooperation at the European Council.

While their absence would have been notable, communicating concern with Hungarian democratic backsliding and with the Hungarian elections, congratulations from these EU leaders had the opposite effect. Hungarian democracy and the unfair elections were legitimized by von der Leyen and Michel, a 'huge gift for the Orban propaganda' in the words of one MEP (Freund 2022). And indeed, in the Hungarian press, the congratulations from the European Commission and European Presidents were widely reported.[22]

It also was not an inevitable courtesy to congratulate Orbán on his re-election. Take the President of the European Parliament, Roberta Metsola, for example. Though less well-known to the general public, Metsola is actually the EU's most senior dignitary according to diplomatic protocol (Council of the European Union 2015: 66). Her official Twitter/X account frequently posts congratulations to international and European leaders on their electoral victories, but was silent when it came to Orbán's 2022 re-election.[23] Indeed, the only congratulations Metsola has given from this account to date at the time of writing that had something to do Hungarian politics was a post on 14 October 2021 congratulating the reporters of the Forbidden Stories journalistic network for winning the Daphne Caruana Galizia Prize for their work on the Pegasus Project—exposing spyware surveillance of 50,000 human rights activists, journalists, opposition politicians and critical lawyers (Higgins 2022). What a difference of approach! Moreover, many other European leaders also stayed silent, such that a leading European news outlet wrote an article with the headline 'EU democratic leaders turn their back on Orbán' (Euractiv 2022). In hindsight, the link made here is clear and devastating: the EU's democratic leaders turned their back on Orbán's violations of fundamental values; by extension, after their 16 May congratulatory messages, von der Leyen and Michel do not count as members of this pro-democratic set.

At the same time, more consequentialist reasoning might lead in an opposite direction. Sometimes it may be justified to compromise on the purity how values are expressed, sullying democratic values in order to secure some greater good. This is sometimes called the problem of 'dirty hands' in politics. Is the cost really so high, for instance, of a simple congratulatory message on social media if the goodwill bought there can be later put to use in, say, pressuring Hungary not to block EU accession talks with Ukraine? These considerations are not without merit. Indeed, I have argued along these lines that a strategic approach to political containment would try to ensure the divisions between different actors undermining democracy and the rule of law are exploited (Jaraczewski and Theuns 2022). This builds on a characteristic vulnerability that we can see in many of the right-wing (radical conservative, far-right, radical right, right-wing populist, etc.) threats to democracy we see in contemporary European politics.

One defining feature of contemporary threats to democratic government in Europe and beyond is that there appears to be an element of coordination. From Javier Milei in Argentina, Jair Bolsonaro in Brazil and Donald Trump in the United States on the American continent to Santiago Abascal in Spain, Geert Wilders in the Netherlands and Aleksandar Vučić in Serbia on the European continent, these and many other recent challengers to liberal democratic norms share some key features. For all their many differences, they all use similar populist rhetoric and imagery: they promote nationalism and decry immigration; they come from the right wing of the ideological spectrum. However, while mutual expressions of public support and some transnational initiatives indeed show that right-wing populists pull together when they perceive this to be in their interest, it would be a mistake to conclude that their political strength draws primarily from such collaborative efforts. It is for more empirical research to try to parse the local and global indicators for support for radical right-wing challengers in democratic states, but the overall picture will resemble Adam Smith's famous 'invisible hand' metaphor, where smaller-scale uncoordinated activity and reactions to similar triggers at the national level result, at the macro-level, in something *resembling* a unified force.

Indeed, in EU politics, explicit efforts by radical right-wing populists to work together have often misfired, and as yet, they have been unable to form a united group in the European Parliament despite their growing strength. Instead, they represent a tangled network of shifting allegiances, spread over a number of different parliamentary groups.[24] A recent version of this controversy was that the Sweden Democrats and the Czech Civic Democrats threatened to quit the European Conservatives and Reformists Party if it admitted Fidesz.[25] Besides some substantive divisions on policy (for instance, on the Russian invasion of Ukraine), one of the reasons for this failure to cooperate in a stable way has been that, despite following a similar playbook and pursuing similar goals, the genetic character of the relevant parties is sometimes at odds. Some, like Marine Le Pen's Rassemblement National in France and Giorgia Meloni's Fratelli d'Italia, are the somewhat moderated incarnations of previously extreme right-wing or even neo-fascist parties. Others, like Viktor Orbán's Fidesz and Jarosław Kaczyćski's Law and Justice Party, have instead come rightward from more centre-right or—in the case of Fidesz—even from supposedly liberal roots. Another hurdle to cooperation is between government parties like Fidesz and Fratelli d'Italia and parties that have only ever been in the opposition. The need for Orbán and Meloni, for instance, to continue to strike deals with other EU leaders in the European Council is one reason why they may hesitate to associate too openly with more marginal or historically ostracized parties.

In sum, while the principled political containment of actors (mainly political parties and member state governments) is *prima facie* warranted when they openly violate EU fundamental values, including simply as an affirmation of the salience of these values, sometimes a more consequentialist tack may be justified. If selectively cooperating with some actors who may flaunt democratic values can exploit emerging rifts between anti-democratic forces in European politics, then it may be worth the normative cost—even at the risk of symbolically legitimating them. Strategies of political containment by pro-democratic actors should therefore be tailored to exploit such differences and, where feasible, exacerbate them. In this way, efforts to sideline and isolate more extreme threats to democracy can be combined with efforts to include and moderate less pressing threats.

CONTAINING AUTOCRACY IN THE EU

Conclusion

Far from containing democratic and rule of law backsliding in the EU, dialogue and monitoring mechanisms may have contributed to it by diverting scarce political resources and fuelling 'whataboutism', whereby autocratic actors justify their own actions by pointing to supposed deficiencies in others. In this chapter, I have offered principled arguments for more thoroughgoing strategies of containment of a non-democratic EU member state in violation of EU fundamental values. Hard legal containment of such a member state should *prima facie* follow the principle of maximum coherent exclusion. In other words, the primary normative principle that ought to shape legal containment is that EU actors should maximally exclude authoritarian governments from European political procedures, insofar as this is compatible with EU law and coherent with fundamental values. Trade-offs with this principle need to be justified explicitly on the grounds of some overall greater good or urgency. An example of such a measure of hard legal containment would be preventing a non-democratic member state from taking up the rotating presidency of the Council. Since Hungary has already taken up this role as of 1 July 2024, those authorized to prevent this outcome (the other members of the Council and the European Council) have failed in this duty.

In terms of political containment, I have argued that authoritarian actors in EU politics should be deprived of political legitimacy and prestige by pro-democratic EU actors as far as possible. It is wrong-headed and cynical for European Commission President Ursula von der Leyen to congratulate Orbán on his re-election under political conditions widely considered anti-democratic (unfair) by independent electoral observers, for example. However, continued cooperation with what is now generally considered by political scientists to be a competitive authoritarian regime (i.e. not a democracy) can be unavoidable. In the final chapter, I consider ways to dissociate from frankly autocratic regimes through much more extensive use of tools of differentiated integration and ultimately expulsion, but such responses require the coordinated action of a large number of EU member states. In the absence of broad political will to this end, pro-democratic actors in the EU should starve authoritarian politicians (be they of a governing or opposition party) of political oxygen.

The reasons for such political containment are not only premised on the supposed efficacy of this strategy. Indeed, the political theory methods that I bring to bear on this issue here preclude the sort of causal analysis of necessary and sufficient conditions for success that arguments on the efficacy of this strategy would require. The crux of my argument is simpler. If EU actors are committed to democratic values, then such political containment is *prima facie* justified simply as an expression of support for those values and for their salience. For example, the praise Charles Michel offers to 'dear Viktor Orban' in one social media post cheapens another where he praises the 'ultimate sacrifice' that Alexey Navalny made in his fight for the values of freedom and democracy (Michel 2024). Such inconsistency not only muddies the EU's moral and ethical stance but also calls into question its reliability as a champion of democratic values both internally and on the international stage. For pro-democratic actors in the EU to maintain their credibility and moral authority, they must reconcile their actions with their ideals. This is not a call for rigid dogmatism but for a coherent strategy that aligns with the foundational values the EU professes to uphold.

7

CULTIVATING PLURALIST DEMOCRACY IN EUROPE

It is justice, not charity, that is wanting in the world!
Mary Wollstonecraft, *A Vindication of the Rights of Woman*

Reading the previous two chapters may give the impression that the governments of European Union (EU) member states undergoing democratic backsliding are unitary actors and the sole relevant political representatives of their state. Looking through the lens of correcting complicity and containing autocracy focuses attention on overreaching executives in member states. But two things are crucial to note. First, while it has proven to be governments who have pursued policies of democratic decay in EU member states, those governments were generally first elected in elections that were both free and fair. Given this, challenges to democracy and the rule of law originate in political parties and political elites. Second, even though the pluralist contestation of government politics is suppressed in a state regressing on democracy (through chilling freedom of speech and government domination of media, for example), there remains domestic opposition. And any real hope for reversing democratic decline must ultimately come domestically—be that from pro-democratic actors such as civil society organizations, independent journalistic voices, human rights activists, critical academics, labour unions and/or opposition politicians. Such domestic actors are not only especially legitimate to resist democratic decay, but are also often the best placed to do so, provided they have adequate support (Grabowska-Moroz and Śniadach 2021; Pospieszna and Pietrzyk-Reeves 2022; cf. Gerő et al. 2023).

These two considerations invoke the need for European responses that focus on supporting pro-democratic actors, both in civil society and opposition politics. But this in turn requires that we pay careful attention to the sort of democratic ideal that EU actors should seek to protect. Correcting complicity and containing autocracy do not require a fully worked-out conception of democracy; it is enough to be able to identify cases of democratic backsliding and the primary and secondary wrongs associated with it. Judgements as to the illegitimacy of democratic backsliding can reach a shared conclusion on this from different starting points, following the model of 'incompletely theorized agreements' (Sunstein 1995).[1] This is one reason why different democracy indices track countries regressing on democratic values similarly, despite different conceptualizations and operationalizations of democracy. But direct support for pro-democratic actors requires a more worked-out conception of a democratic ideal. This is especially important in light of my critique of the legalistic and technocratic conception prominent in discourse by European Commissioners (see Chapter 3). Clearly, not just any conception of democracy will do when we are thinking through when and how to support pro-democratic actors.

The first substantive task of this chapter, then, lies in laying out the pluralist democratic ideal in a bit more detail. Once I have clarified the contours of pluralist democracy conceptually, we can move to application. Here, the key normative question is: should EU actors support pluralist democracy in EU member states where the space for civil society is shrinking? And if they should, what are the limits to the legitimacy of this type of response to democratic backsliding? In answer to these questions, I argue that a broad range of European political actors should offer direct support to pro-democratic actors in EU member states where democracy is under threat, including EU institutions and member states, but also European and national political parties. In terms of limits, I argue the pluralist ideal gives us the scope of legitimate intervention to cultivate pluralist democracy, and that such interventions are justified to the extent that they correct democratic distortions.

Cultivating pluralist democracy has some similarities to what is often called 'democracy support' in the context of international relations and development politics, but which is geared towards trying to counterbalance the prevailing anti-pluralistic bent of the relations of a backsliding state government with political and civil society actors resisting the processes of autocratization. It is not enough to cheer on critical journalists and academics, opposition political parties, and non-governmental organizations focused on minority and human rights protection, environmental and climate policies, and gender equality. There are strong reasons to support them directly. By this I mean that EU institutional actors like the European Commission and European political parties (as well as EU member states) should offer material support (such as direct funding, training resources, technical expertise, advocacy support, legal advice, policy guidance, communication tools, equipment, research and data analysis, networking opportunities, etc.) to pro-democratic actors in EU member states where democracy is under threat or indeed where the state has regressed on democratic norms to such an extent that it can no longer be called democratic.

The normative reasons for offering such support are overdetermined. In this chapter, I develop two independent justifications. First, following from my argument on the complicity of EU actors in democratic backsliding (in Chapter 5), such support can be construed as reparations for the harms of complicitous actions or omissions. Second, such support can be a way to counteract 'injustice externalities' (Theuns 2020) that arise from imposing economic conditionality or other financial sanctions on member states for violating democracy and the rule of law. These justifications would be strengthened by, but are independent from, the efficacy of such interventions in slowing down or reversing democratic backsliding.

Cultivating pluralist democracy through supporting pro-democratic actors in member states undergoing democratic backsliding, however, is not without risk. Even when motivated by convincing normative and political arguments, such support could backfire if the policies are not carefully designed. Indeed, the literature on EU responses to democratic backsliding warns us about possible so-called 'rally around the flag' effects, where an executive receives a short-term political boost due to a perceived international crisis. If the imposition of sanctions by EU actors feeds into a dynamic whereby anti-democratic actors are able to capitalize on 'playing the blame game on Brussels' (Schlipphak and Treib 2017; Sedelmeier 2017) or puts the domestic opposition in a 'traitor dilemma' of being forced to support sanctions against their own state (Wonka, Gastinger and Blauberger 2023), then the net impact of these responses may be negative. It may also be difficult to identify pro-democratic actors to support rigorously, especially given evidence that civil society organizations in backsliding states are often co-opted by the state (Gerö et al. 2023) or otherwise suffer 'GONGO-ization'.[2]

These challenges must be considered carefully when developing the precise scope and form of EU pro-democracy support. However, it is far from obvious that the empirical research weighs generally against cultivating pluralist democracy. The literature on international democracy support, closely related to the approach outlined in this chapter, makes clear links between international democracy support and democratic resilience in favourable conditions (Hyde, Lamb and Samet 2022; Samuels 2023). These effects hold especially where support is targeted (Leininger and Nowack 2022; Scott and Steele 2011) as opposed to broad development support, which may encourage rent-seeking and can thereby empower incumbents (Waldner and Lust 2018). Bypassing the government to provide support directly to opposition and civil society organizations is an established tactic in international democracy support where the risks of deliberate misallocation through corrupt officials is high (Dietrich 2013).

In any case, the complex interaction of the various conditions whereby democracy support is most likely to be successful is not directly applicable to the normative arguments over the principles justifying the support of pro-democratic actors in EU member states where democratic government is under threat. And, as a political theorist, what animates me most is the question of whether European political actors act legitimately in principle when they support pro-democratic actors. So, for the purposes of this chapter, I will largely park these empirical concerns, noting that policies of cultivating pluralist democracy must be carefully and contextually designed in cooperation with the relevant pro-democratic actors, who know their domestic social and political context far better than administrators in Brussels or in other member state capitals.

There is a different sort of counterargument to cultivating pluralist democracy in the EU that must be considered seriously and given a response. This is the worry that direct support of pro-democratic actors should be rejected as illegitimate partisan interference in the domestic politics in an EU member state. From the perspective of EU law, it might be argued to violate the obligation for the EU to respect the national identity as well as the constitutional and political structures of member states (Article 4.2 Treaty on European Union [TEU]). From the perspective of democratic theory, we might worry that such partisan interference would undermine the level playing field that is crucial for pluralist democracy.

The rest of the chapter proceeds as follows. First, I lay out the ideal of pluralist democracy and link this ideal to the various normative duties of EU actors to cultivate pluralist democracy, especially in the context of EU states backsliding on democracy by undermining pluralism in what is sometimes called the 'shrinking civil space'. Then, in the next section, I make two independent normative arguments about why EU actors should intervene in the domestic politics of backsliding member states to try to support pro-democratic actors. In the penultimate section, I consider an important objection to EU actors cultivating pluralist democracy—the charge that such support amounts to illegitimate partisan interference. Drawing on the conceptualization of pluralist democracy, I consider and reject this objection in the penultimate section. The last section concludes.

The pluralist democratic ideal

Before hashing out the principles that justify and shape the project of EU actors cultivating pluralist democracy in backsliding member states, I should first be clear on what sort of conception of democracy I think should be cultivated. In Chapter 4, I analysed the European Commission's approach to democracy, arguing that it was broadly legalistic and technocratic. The Commission is not alone in this approach. Thinking about democracy mostly in terms of the separation of powers, the cut and thrust of representative law and policy-making, and the drama of parliamentary elections—what is sometimes called the 'arena conception' of politics—is arguably the dominant perspective both by those working within this tightly demarcated political sphere and those outside of it.[3] But focusing only on such institutional aspects of the broadly liberal conception of democracy ignores much of what is valuable about democratic government. In particular, it sidelines the idea of democratic politics as a way to peacefully and equitably settle disagreements between people who hold very different ideas of the good life, be they religious, ideological, cultural or aesthetic.

This tension—between a technocratic conception of democracy and a pluralistic one—has a considerable backstory in the longstanding critique in the academic literature that the EU's conceptions of democracy and political dynamics have a tendency towards depoliticization and often miss a government-opposition logic (Mair 2007). Pluralist democracy, on the other hand, is able to capture the oppositional political dynamics that, under circumstances of democratic backsliding, can lead one political group (a leader, party or ideology) to try to dominate another. Given fundamental and ultimately incommensurable political conflicts within a democratic polity, there is an ever-present risk that the conflictual relation between democratic opponents (what Chantal Mouffe calls the 'agonistic' relation) degenerates into an antagonistic one. Indeed, we see empirically that European countries backsliding on democracy and the rule of law are also subject to trends of increasingly antagonistic polarization, as when, for example, Romanian parliamentarians increasingly refer to one another as 'criminals' (Mungiu-Pippidi 2018), or when judges in the United Kingdom are branded 'enemies of the people' in national newspapers (Breeze 2018).

The pluralist conception of democracy I want to defend is not a utopian dream of a perfect democratic system. Rather, it starts by recognizing that democracies do not arise from vacuums. Democratic states gain in democratic authority by constitutionalizing procedures whereby subjects gain a more formally equal share in sovereign power. As such, those previously subjected to arbitrary rule—the *populus*—progressively become a *demos* or democratic people. As this process unfolds, disagreements over policy and law are increasingly resolved through democratic contestation. Crucially, the pluralist democratic ideal holds that such disagreements can be settled in a procedurally fair manner; no member of the *demos* (citizen) should have any more formal weight in the democratic process than any other, and all should be eligible to be elected. Pluralist democracies are justified, normatively speaking, in that they constitute an advance towards the civic freedom and formal equality of citizens in a democratized polity, relative to the prior state of subjection to arbitrary rule (Theuns 2021: 41–3). This means that the democratic legitimacy of a particular political reform is contextual and comparative. A reform—for instance, the extension of the franchise to women over the age of 21—may constitute an advance in civic freedom and formal equality in one country, but be a regression in another. Advances towards fully equal civic freedom (when 'all those subjected'[4] to the law have equal democratic rights) thus constitute relative advances in democratic legitimacy, which is why pluralist democracy is 'non-ideal'.[5]

In this way, pluralist democracy is embedded into the contextual history of diverse democratic peoples' struggle for representation. It resists the formalism and dogmatism of a purely juridical perspective on democratic government, especially when these ideals conflict. Democracy is much more than a set of liberal constitutional principles, important as they are. Democracy is a normative and political response to the philosophical demands and political realities of pluralism. As such, it should nurture and protect this pluralism so that people from different walks of life can come to a democratic compromise about how to live together (Theuns 2021). One requirement of this process of political conciliation is the existence of a vibrant public sphere in which political alternatives are revealed, discussed and negotiated. And democracy is undermined when populists claim to speak for all the people as one, or when the government uses public resources to further partisan propaganda. In line with Gora and de Wilde (2022), I consider the degradation of this kind of pluralism in the public sphere of some EU member states to be an underrepresented feature of democratic backsliding in the EU.

PROTECTING DEMOCRACY IN EUROPE

I label this conception 'pluralist democracy' for two reasons. First, pluralist democracy will ordinarily result in a democratic polity characterized by competition between different political projects and ideologies (i.e. political pluralism). Indeed, an executive undermining of the possibility of such pluralist contestation by silencing critical academics, stifling the freedom of the press to hold the government to account, and co-opting civil society actors are direct attacks on this pluralist democratic ideal. Second, the foundational assumption of the pluralist conception of democracy is the pervasive possibility of 'value pluralism'. Value pluralism is the idea that good-faith disagreements between people about matters of value may not be resolvable in purely rational terms. Some value judgements may even lack a common evaluative metric (that is, they may be incommensurable). Artistic judgements can give a good illustration of this. Many people appreciate the music composed by Gustav Mahler; others are moved by the monumental paintings Rosa Bonheur made of animals. But a disagreement between someone arguing that Mahler's symphonies are superior to Bonheur's paintings and someone arguing the inverse may be impossible to adjudicate.[6]

To these two assumptions regarding pluralism—political pluralism and value pluralism—we need to add a philosophical commitment to treating each individual as an equal source of political value. This idea is related to value pluralism in that if we cannot always rationally resolve good-faith disagreements about the good life, we have no reason to prioritize one person's conception over another's. If people can conceivably and reasonably disagree about public affairs in ways that cannot be resolved rationally, democratic procedures facilitate the fair adjudication of these competing ideals.[7] Pluralist democracy requires we see people as equal sources of political value.[8] To use the formula attributed to Jeremy Bentham, everybody to count for one, and nobody for more than one. And while a demand to treat people as political equals underlies pluralist democracy's generally democratic conception of politics, the possibility of value pluralism demands majoritarian and iterative democratic procedures.

These are the empirical and philosophical underpinnings of pluralist democracy. The joint recognition of political pluralism and the pervasive possibility of value pluralism—that people as a matter of fact can and often do have divergent and sometimes deeply intransigent interests and ideals—sets up the terrain of democratic politics. But if we accept only these empirical claims, we are left without a normative justification for democratic rule; citizens' putative differences of opinion need not, in the absence of a *normative* standard of equality, be settled democratically. If we believe, for instance, that the right rules governing public affairs are religious rules in a holy book, then we may subscribe to the theocratic principle that God knows what is right, and if one disagrees, one should be forced onto the path of righteousness. Similarly, the philosophical claim regarding treating people as political equals is also insufficient. If we accept only the normative standard of treating citizens as equal sources of political value, but not value pluralism, then we may think that some political projects do not require neutral (democratic) adjudication. This may be especially tempting for political projects in which there seems to be a broad consensus. In EU studies, we can see an analogue to this idea in Giandomenico Majone's argument that the EU as a 'regulatory state' does not need democratic legitimation (Majone 1994). Why bother with contestatory democratic procedures if everybody agrees what should be done?

The idea that citizens in a democratic community ought to be recognized as equal sources of political value and the recognition of the fact of value pluralism (or, minimally, of its permanent latent possibility) are therefore jointly necessary to justify the pluralist democratic ideal. To put it differently, pluralist democracy takes as the starting point the possibility of value pluralism—deep and potentially incommensurable disagreements over the norms and values that ought to guide public policy and law—and channels this into a demand for political pluralism, characterized by free and fair competition between political parties that mobilize contrasting political ideologies. As Lise Esther Herman writes, 'The People is neither static nor monolithic. Plurality, contradiction and change characterize any free political community: the People debates, judges, changes its mind, and holds its leaders accountable' (Herman 2019). It is precisely the fact that citizens disagree with one another that motivates and guides the pluralist democratic project.

Understood this way, pluralist democracy shares some theoretical space with Chantal Mouffe's conception of 'agonistic democracy' as well as Jürgen Habermas' idea of the 'public sphere'.[9] Although Mouffe (2013) situates herself as opposed to the Habermassian understanding of democracy, they both follow a similar logic of democratic politics on this point. While Habermas conceptualized the public sphere as a space of struggle and 'political confrontation' (Habermas 1989: 27) where the executive power of governments is challenged, Mouffe (2005, 2013) has argued that passion and conflict are central to democracy:

> Belief in the possibility of a universal rational consensus has put democratic thinking on the wrong track. Instead of trying to design the institutions which, through supposedly 'impartial' procedures, would reconcile all conflicting interests and values, the task for democratic theorists and politicians should be to envisage the creation of a vibrant 'agonistic' public sphere of contestation. (Mouffe 2005: 3)

Mouffe argues that democracy cannot exist without a conflictual battle of ideas between political rivals. Such 'agonism' can be democratic—and politically productive—if and when rivals recognize each other's legitimate existence. Indeed, it is precisely this recognition that political opponents are rivals and not enemies that allows Mouffe's conception to be fundamentally democratic. This view, like pluralist democracy, rests on the normative assumption that the right way to settle disagreements in public life is through politics. But Mouffe's agonism is a useful lens through which to understand pluralist democracy for a second reason. Mouffe does not try to *resolve* political conflict, as if enough information or technical expertise, under the right deliberative conditions, would be likely to lead to consensus. Instead, she recognizes that individuals and groups have irreducibly different needs and wants. 'Agonistic democracy' is therefore a democratic political logic based on pluralism and ideological conflict, rather than the rational resolution of political disagreement (consensus-seeking). For Mouffe, pluralism can only exist if we recognize conflictual relations between actors holding fundamentally different and opposing views of how society should be. 'Plural' in this sense not only means that there are different political views in society, but that they are in conflict with each other and often cannot be reconciled.

We saw in Chapter 3 how far the conception of democracy that is dominant in European Commissioners' speeches is from this ideal.

It is also far from the practice of the Commission's response. Several illustrations suffice to sketch the broad differences. For instance, one option to address democratic backsliding while not taking a purely legalistic path would be to encourage transnational flows of communication that move away from EU intergovernmental decision-making processes. A more diverse range of actors (for example, political opposition, civil society and trade unions) could be called to the table, in such a way that a voice is given to non-executive democratic actors (cf. Beetz 2023). While this is especially urgent in member states where the executive has cemented control, this could also extend beyond backsliding countries such as Hungary and Poland to address the 'opposition deficit' of the EU (Rauh and de Wilde 2018). Beyond the proactive support for pro-democratic actors that is my main focus in this chapter, the pluralist ideal suggests the European Commission should be bolder in speaking out against the erosion of civil society and the public sphere of backsliding member states. In line with its legalist-technocratic conception of democracy, it does this (albeit to a limited degree) when it comes to concerns with judicial independence, checks and balances, and the rule of law. Extending such discursive pressure to more vocally resist the erosion of civil society and the public sphere could help undermine the political support for actors involved in backsliding. It would certainly be a powerful signal of the Commission's commitment to democratic values. And it may even encourage other actors in the multilevel EU political system (for example, national parliaments from other EU member states) to put further discursive pressure on backsliding governments and to support pluralist democracy in member states where this is under threat.

Why cultivate pluralist democracy in backsliding EU states?

What reasons do EU actors and other EU member states have for cultivating pluralist democracy in member states regressing on democracy and the rule of law? One straightforward reason is simply normative affinity. Partisans of pluralist democracy in EU member states undergoing democratic decline by definition share the values of democracy, pluralism, (political) freedom and equality with pro-democratic partners in EU institutions and other member states. However, there is considerable reticence amongst democrats regarding the political ideal of trying to further democratic government abroad. To some, it smacks of an imperial project, too close to the history of European colonialism with its self-serving and racist *mission civilisatrice* narrative used to so many evil ends for so long (cf. Paris 2002; Kundnani 2023). Others associate democracy promotion with the US neoconservative agenda of mixing militarism with a rhetoric of universalist ideals, a view put succinctly by neocon historian Michael Leeden, who claimed 'the best democracy program ever invented is the U.S. army' (cited in Bacevich 2013: 85). And even if we suppose that the EU is earnest in its intention to act as a 'normative power' in international affairs, criticisms of its own efforts at promoting democracy abound, running from blunt accusations of self-interest masquerading as idealism (Hyde-Price 2006; Seeberg 2009) to my own work arguing that the tools the EU uses to try to further these goals can be incompatible with democratic values (Theuns 2017, 2019). Whether or not such criticisms also stick to EU actors cultivating pluralist democracy in EU member states is debatable, but they do invite us to look beyond mere good intentions.

Instrumental reasons for supporting pro-democratic actors

There are several other instrumental reasons that could serve as strong motivation for cultivating pluralist democracy, depending on the particular actor we focus on. For example, pro-democratic member states could justify such a response as a way to protect democratic governance at home, given that their own domestic political freedoms are tied together with other member states. This is because the democratic character—and consequently the political legitimacy and authority of each member state government—has an impact on the democratic character, legitimacy and authority of each other member state, given the pooling of member state sovereignties in EU supranational integration (see Chapter 1).

A similar instrumental motivation takes seriously the risk of the 'diffusion' of democratic backsliding (Hyde 2020; Holesch and Kyriazi 2022). If proximity to states undergoing democratic backsliding increases the risks to democratic government at home, then it makes sense to try to reverse, stabilize and prevent it if you want to avoid a similar cycle of democratic regression taking root. This logic on authoritarian diffusion is buttressed by the fact that authoritarian political leaders in Europe act to try to boost their ideological partners in other member states. Not only do they campaign for one another, including in national elections (see Chapter 1), but there are also brazen examples of direct political interventions intended to influence electoral outcomes.

This sort of political activity was starkly illustrated by the February 2024 investigative report by Szabolcs Panyi about a video campaign vaunting the dangers of illegal migration on YouTube. This clip, commissioned by Viktor Orbán's Cabinet Office and paid for by the Hungarian government, ran as sponsored content in seven EU member states in autumn 2023, including in the blackout period directly before the Slovak election in September (Panyi 2024a). Or take another case reported by Panyi, linking Orbán directly to Slovak electoral politics. In the run-up to the February 2020 Slovak general election, then Prime Minister Peter Pellegrini asked Orbán to mediate between him and the Kremlin to try to get an invitation to Moscow (Panyi 2024b). Pellegrini's reasoning was that such a visit would boost him in the elections, which his pro-Russian Smer party was slated to lose following a wave of anti-government sentiment after the 2018 murder of investigative journalist Ján Kuciak and his fiancée Martina Kušnírová.[10] Orbán set up the invitation through his Foreign Minister Péter Szijjártó, and Pellegrini was received by Russian Prime Minister Mikhail Mishustin on 26 February, three days before the general election.[11] Supporting pro-democratic actors in Hungary would seem to be a fitting response for pro-democratic member states to try to resist such interventions in their own domestic politics. More generally, if cultivating pluralism helps buttress democratic government not only in the backsliding member state but also at home, then this would counter the worry that this amounts to some sort of neo-colonial interference in the domestic matters of foreign countries.

A different kind of instrumental reason for cultivating pluralist democracy in EU member states undergoing democratic backsliding links such support to the kinds of material sanctions I have argued are justified, like enforcing the conditionality of EU funding or seeking high fines as a consequence of systemic infringement actions (see Chapter 6). The idea here is that material sanctions come with risks that they have counterproductive effects, and providing material support to pro-democratic actors in a sanctioned state might undercut some of these risks (Schlipphak and Treib 2017; Sedelmeier 2017; Theuns 2020).

The relationship between economic development and democratization or democratic stability, however, is complex and disputed, although analysts agree that there is an important link. In this literature, there are broadly two positions: the original 'modernization theory' popularized by Seymour M. Lipset, and an alternative position critical of that view that has been called the 'exogenous' view. Lipset held that economic development—growth and wealth—were important causal factors driving democratization, and perhaps even prerequisites for the democratization of autocratic states (Lipset 1959; Boix and Stokes 2003). 'Exogenous' accounts, in contrast, argue that a better way to understand the link between economic development and democracy is that wealthy, vital democracies are more likely to remain democratic than democracies with weak economies (Przeworski and Limongi 1997: 157). Clearly, this is not the place to try to adjudicate between these two theories. Nor is it necessary for us to do so, as both ring the same warning bell: imposing thoroughgoing economic conditionality as a response to member states backsliding on democracy and the rule of law risks exacerbating democracy concerns in the state in question. Indeed, the worst-case scenario of imposing such conditionality is that it does not incentivize the relevant government(s) to reform their backsliding but rather sparks further processes of de-democratization. In this way, material sanctions, where they are profound enough to impact a member state's economic vitality, risk generating a negative feedback loop: imposed as a response to concerns over backsliding, the effects may include, indirectly and unintentionally, further backsliding, in turn leading to more stringent conditionality measures, further backsliding on the back of a still weaker economy, and so on.

Targeted investment in the backsliding state, through direct support to pro-democratic actors, is one way to mitigate the risks of such negative feedback loops and counterproductive effects of high fines and EU budget conditionality, and at the same time a way to mitigate injustice externalities. Channelling funding from the backsliding state's government to civil society actors—or directly to lower-level state entities, such as opposition-controlled regions and municipalities—would constitute a 'positive' arm of material sanctions. While the 'negative' arm would cut back or—in extreme cases—cut off EU funds and support to the backsliding government, cultivating plurality democracy would vitalize the remaining pro-democratic actors in the backsliding state and create new linkages for democracy support. At best, such alternative funding streams to pro-democratic actors in a backsliding state could contribute causally to reversing or slowing democratic and rule of law backsliding.

Yet, despite such independently motivated reasons for European democrats to want to stymie authoritarians on the European stage, there is still the question of whether cultivating pluralist democracy through direct support to pro-democratic actors in member states undergoing democratic backsliding is the right way to go about doing it. Because all of these self-interested reasons turn on the empirical question of whether and when cultivating pluralist democracy is likely to make a substantial contribution to slowing or reversing democratic backsliding where democracy is under threat. Is it in fact the case that cultivating pluralist democracy would strengthen—materially and symbolically—those domestic civil society and political actors resisting backsliding? Would the existence of broad pro-democracy support disincentivize democracy and rule of law backsliding and incentivize reform of such activities by backsliding governments? Confidence on this point would require not only identifying cases where similar democracy support was followed by a stabilization or reversal of democratic decline, but also controlling for a wide range of possible alternative explanations for such patterns. The empirical literature on democracy support in international affairs suggests that the conditions under which democracy support may be effective are narrow (Krasner and Weinstein 2014) and that the risks of unintended harms may be exacerbated when international organizations pursue democracy support ineptly (Meyerrose 2020). The absence of normative confidence on the legitimacy of democracy promotion abroad, combined with the lack of empirical confidence about the efficacy of democracy support, calls for more intrinsic and internal ('immanent') arguments.[12] To this end, two arguments provide, in my view, adequate justification for cultivating pluralist democracy in the EU: (1) reparations for the harm of democratic backsliding, and (2) counterbalancing unjust side effects of material sanctions.

Cultivating pluralist democracy to repair the harms of democratic backsliding

One way to ground a duty to cultivate pluralist democracy by supporting pro-democratic actors in EU member states where democracy is threatened is through the framework of the complicity argument I developed in Chapter 5. Recall that complicity can be understood as the secondary wrong of making a potentially causal contribution to a primary wrong, either through one's blameworthy action or omission. While previous studies of transnational complicity in EU democratic backsliding have focused on European political parties, especially the European People's Party (Kelemen 2020a; Meijers and van der Veer 2019; Wolkenstein 2020, 2021), I argued that a far broader range of EU actors were complicit, making the case specifically for the complicity of the European Commission and EU member state governments sitting in the Council and the European Council. Complicity with a secondary wrong grounds two sorts of normative duties. First, it grounds duties of redress. This means that the complicitous agent should, all other things being equal, desist from those actions or omissions that made it complicit in the primary wrong. Second, it grounds duties of reparation to those harmed by the primary wrong.[13]

The link between reparations for transnational complicity in EU democratic backsliding and cultivating pluralist democracy is clear when we recognize that pro-democratic actors in a backsliding state are often the ones harmed most directly by the sorts of developments that, when taken together, make up a pattern of democratic backsliding. Take for example the use of strategic lawsuits against public participation (SLAPPs), the intimidation lawsuits that are abusively filed, often against critical journalists and often by public officials. The case which put SLAPPs in the spotlight in European politics was the car bombing of Maltese anti-corruption journalist Daphne Caruana Galizia in October 2017. At the time of her assassination, Caruana Galizia was subject to 47 libel cases against her (Bonello Ghio, Nasreddin and The Daphne Caruana Galizia Foundation 2022: 63–4). In one of these cases, then Deputy Leader of the centre-left Partit Laburista and Minister for the Economy Chris Cardona sued Caruana Galizia for breaking a story about him visiting a brothel while on a work trip to Germany. In a move typical of SLAPP lawsuits, Cardona did not attend any of the hearings. He did, however, obtain a 'garnishee order' freezing Caruana Galizia's assets, including her bank accounts, in place at the time she was murdered (ibid.: 44–5). Another litigant against Caruana Galizia was Malta's then Prime Minister Joseph Muscat, who ultimately resigned in December 2019 in the aftermath of the scandal over the assassination. He sued Caruana Galizia over the allegation that his wife, Michelle Muscat, was the owner of Egrant, a secret company based in Panama. Incredibly, at the time of writing, Muscat's litigation against Daphne Caruana Galizia continues, with Muscat pursuing the claim against the heirs of the defendant (Brincat 2023).

Without getting into the legal details, let us suppose, *arguendo*, that the cases against Caruana Galizia were indeed unjustified SLAPP cases. The primary wrongdoers are the SLAPP litigants, including Muscat and Cardona. But others, certainly in the Maltese government but potentially also at the European level, might be complicit in the primary wrongdoing, for instance by failing to call out such abusive litigation against Maltese journalists. Those harmed by the primary wrong include, obviously, Daphne Caruana Galizia herself, who paid for her courage to call out Maltese public corruption with her life. But others were harmed too, notably her heirs who still have to face some of the SLAPP suits. Indeed, it is not a stretch to consider that the prevalence of such SLAPP suits in Malta, and the legal rules that allow litigants to continue frivolous suits against the heirs of murdered defendants, harms Maltese journalists as a collective body, for instance through a chilling effect on critical investigative journalism, particularly by freelance journalists.

If EU actors are complicit in such a wrong, for instance through a culpable failure to call out a pattern of abusive SLAPP litigation in a member state despite this violating EU fundamental values, a first step is to correct complicity through redress. And indeed, in the aftermath of Caruana Galizia's murder, we saw several EU actors step up in ways that can be interpreted in this light, with the European Parliament sending a series of rule of law fact-finding delegations to Malta (European Parliament 2019), and European Commission Vice-President Věra Jourová pushing for the Media Freedom Act, dubbed 'Daphne's Law', which was finally adopted by a large majority on 13 March 2024 (Resolution 2022/0277).[14] But, if EU actors are indeed complicit, then they also owe duties of reparation. Reparation cannot be given to Daphne Caruana Galizia directly because she has been killed, but celebrating her memory (for instance, through the European Parliament-endorsed Daphne Caruana Galizia Journalism Prize) may go some way to meet this duty. And if we suppose that freelance journalists in Malta were harmed collectively by the legal and political framework that allowed Caruana Galizia, amongst others, to be hounded by defamation suits, direct support for critical, pro-democratic journalism in Malta would be one other way to try to repair the wrong.

Cultivating pluralist democracy to counteract injustice externalities

A different justification of the normative duty for EU actors to offer direct support to pro-democratic actors in member states where democracy is under threat frames such support as a corrective for unfair adverse side effects of material sanctions. Some of the responses I have argued are necessary both to correct complicity and to contain autocratic politics are EU budget conditionality and hefty financial sanctions. But, as I have argued, such material sanctions are blunt tools, and can harm people who have no share in the blame for violations and in fact may be actively resisting such violations. Supporting pro-democracy actors can be a way to offset such 'injustice externalities' (Theuns 2020: 158).

In Chapter 5, I worked out the broad lines of the normative case for economic responses to democratic backsliding—namely, tying EU funds to democracy and the rule of law using, for instance, the

CULTIVATING PLURALIST DEMOCRACY IN EUROPE

Common Provisions Regulation and the Rule of Law Conditionality Regulation, as well as seeking fines for the violation of EU fundamental values as legal obligations through the use of infringement proceedings. There are several independent normative grounds for such responses. On the one hand, the European Commission and pro-democratic member states ought to use economic tools as a way to correct their complicity in democratic backsliding in EU member states. On the other, I argued in Chapter 6 that there are independent reasons to use economic measures to try to limit and constrain autocratic actors that centre on the value of democratic government, the spillover effects of autocratic participation in EU law and policy processes on the democratic legitimacy of EU law and policy for all EU citizens, and the threat of autocratic diffusion. But an important limitation of the use of economic tools to respond to democratic backsliding concerns the unequal distribution of the effects of economic conditionality mechanisms and large fines (one of the reasons the empirical literature on the efficacy of economic sanctions in international relations is generally bleak).

When the EU implements budget conditionality on states violating fundamental values (as I have argued it should), the consequent economic disadvantage will not be evenly distributed. Other things equal, those who are already poorly off are likely to be more strongly affected by disadvantages due to their vulnerability and to diminishing marginal returns on resources. Further, political elites (and the wealthy more generally) in backsliding states will usually have managed to secure their own material wellbeing (sometimes indeed on the back of the corruption and cronyism that are the mainstay of backsliding regimes). They will therefore have a relatively larger buffer with which to weather scanter periods. This seems remarkably unfair. Why should ordinary citizens collectively pay the price for the wrongs of their governments? While a few of them will be co-authors of that process of backsliding, and some complicit to it, many others unrelentingly resist and decry their state's backsliding towards illiberalism, populism and authoritarianism. Seen from their perspective, economic conditionality mechanisms seem a very blunt instrument, and any disadvantage they suffer is indeed unjust.

This problem is exacerbated by the fact that even targeted economic sanctions often have unintended 'spillover' effects, harming people who are not directly targeted. This is all the more true for the extensive and broadly applied financial conditionality that is needed—and indeed has recently been used—against EU member states violating fundamental values. The empirical literature on economic sanctions in international affairs even warns us that sometimes those opposed to an authoritarian government suffer *more* as a result of sanctions than pro-government actors (Peksen and Drury 2009; 2010). The reason for this is that although economic sanctions are likely to reduce the size of the economic 'pie' that can be divided in a sanctioned state, the sanctioned authoritarian governments still have a determinate role in how the pie is divided. They can use this role to insulate their supporters from the harmful effects of sanctions, which would mean those not insulated, including presumably those pro-democratic actors opposed to the authoritarian government, are all the more exposed.

Take a concrete example from European politics. The Hungarian-Fidesz government, who has pursued anti-democratic politics in Hungary now for over a decade, which has led to a huge decline in democratic government, has been the subject of economic conditionality since 2022. Despite an inexplicable concession of €10 billion in December 2023—seemingly given in exchange for Hungary's abstention on the start of Ukrainian accession talks and funding—a very significant sum is still being withheld under a combination of conditionality for structural and cohesion funds using the Common Provisions Regulation, NextGenEU COVID-19 recovery funds, and funds withheld using the general regime of conditionality for the protection of the Union budget, the so-called 'Rule of Law Conditionality Regulation at the time of writing (Kelemen 2023; see Chapter 5 for further details).

But cutting EU funding to Hungary also cuts EU funding to opposition-controlled municipalities such as Budapest, which are 'islands in the illiberal storm' of democratic decay.[15] To make matters worse, the Fidesz government has drastically reduced funding to opposition-led municipalities (including Budapest), for instance by simultaneously lowering the business tax raised by these municipalities and raising the 'solidarity tax' they must pay, ostensibly to redistribute wealth to poorer municipalities (Kovarek and Dobos 2023: 110).

CULTIVATING PLURALIST DEMOCRACY IN EUROPE

This partisan use of funding as a political tool also extends to the distribution of EU funds, which are used 'as a means of political punishment' (Gyévai and Jávor 2023: 22). The Hungarian government's propensity to use national and European funding and taxation policy as a way to harm opposition-controlled municipalities is a clear illustration of how EU funding conditionality can be weaponized.

Despite widespread reporting of the partisan misuse of EU funding when centralized and distributed through the national government in member states regressing on democracy,[16] direct support of pro-democratic actors in EU member states subject to budget conditionality is still rare. (At the time of writing, only Hungary was subject to budget conditionality, after the Commission announced the release of withheld funds to Poland in February 2024, though Slovakia may soon join Hungary).[17] The mayor of Budapest, Gergely Karácsony, of the opposition Green Dialogue party (Párbeszéd—A Zöldek Pártja), has been a key figure calling for direct (EU) funding of opposition cities. In a speech given in May 2023, Karácsony went as far as saying this was a 'matter of life and death' for the Budapest municipality, given how the Fidesz government was funnelling EU financing away from the city.[18] Consistent pressure from Karácsony and other pro-democratic mayors in countries where democracy is under threat (many united in the Pact of Free Cities; see Matthes 2023) has led to the European Parliament adopting a resolution in 2022 that includes the call 'for more direct EU funding to be made available to local and regional authorities' (Resolution 2021/2075, Articles 59–60). Then Hungarian Momentum MEP Katalin Cseh, the rapporteur for the report that led to this resolution being adopted, explained the link of this resolution to EU budget conditionality, saying it was 'extremely important that [EU] funds that may be withheld due to the irresponsibility of the government can reach the final beneficiaries directly'.[19] And indeed, subsequently, the EU has provided some direct funding to help Budapest, as well as opposition-controlled Miskolc and Pécs, in meeting the 2030 climate goals, as part of an envelope of €360 million from Horizon Europe to support 100 cities in the EU becoming 'climate-neutral and smart cities' (European Commission 2022). This (admittedly small) start illustrates how funnelling resources to pro-democratic actors can be a way to offset the unjust side effects of material sanctions for democratic backsliding.

PROTECTING DEMOCRACY IN EUROPE

The objection from illegitimate partisanship

So far, if the arguments I have given are convincing, I have established two reasons for pro-democratic actors in EU politics to offer direct support to pro-democratic actors in backsliding states to try to cultivate pluralist democracy there. But there is an important counter-argument that runs in the opposite direction. Is providing direct support for pro-democratic actors not illegitimate interference in the domestic democratic politics of another member state? How does it hold up to the Article 4 TEU obligation for the EU to respect the national identity as well as the constitutional and political structures of member states? Perhaps such partisanship even undermines pluralist democracy in that it undermines the ideal of an equal democratic playing field where each individual is treated as an equal source of political value. Another version of this objection worries that such partisanship breaks with the norm of liberal neutrality; especially where the actor in question is an EU actor like the European Commission, such pro-democracy support may run counter to norms (or rules) stipulating that the EU ought not to take sides in a party-political fashion. Let us take the two versions of this objection in turn.

The version of the objection that charges cultivating pluralist democracy with normative incoherence can be grasped well by using the idea of performative contradiction I elaborated in Chapter 4. If you recall, in philosophy a performative contradiction is when the content of a statement contradicts the act of stating it; for instance, if someone were to say 'I do not exist' or 'I never tell the truth'. My application of this idea in political theory extends to when a political act intended (in part) to express support for a certain value in practice undermines that same value. In the context of cultivating pluralist democracy, the critique would run as follows: direct support of pro-democratic actors in EU member states regressing on democratic government is one way to express support for democratic values. But intervening in the democratic politics of a member state in a partisan way tilts the political playing field. Pluralist democracy requires that each individual is treated as an equal source of political value. Direct partisan support of pro-democratic actors in EU member states by actors outside of that state (such as the European Commission or other member state governments) therefore undermines the very principle of pluralist democracy that it seeks to promote. While it would be odd to see the specific language of performative contradiction in political speech, the objection that 'outside interference' is 'anti-democratic'—a common reaction to EU responses to democratic backsliding[20]—runs on this kind of logic. How can an EU actor seeking to cultivate pluralist democracy respond to this charge?

The pluralist response to this counterargument focuses on cultivating pluralist democracy as a *corrective* to democratic backsliding. For the sake of argument, let us put to the side the question of whether in fact such interventions are partisan (I will return to this question below). While some direct support of pro-democratic actors may avoid partisanship—for instance, by focusing on human rights NGOs or organizations that seek to monitor the free and fair process of elections—the approach in this chapter extends beyond such support to include partisan actors such as the (pro-democratic) political opposition. However, in the context of a state regressing on democracy, these sorts of interventions serve rather than detract from pluralism. By definition, EU member states undergoing democratic backsliding have a political playing field that is increasingly tilted in favour of one party or coalition of parties against others. This is what the Organization for Security and Co-operation in Europe election observation mission meant when it charged the 2022 Hungarian general elections with being 'marred by the absence of a level playing field' (OSCE 2022: 1). Elections in Hungary are (largely) free, but they are not fair. So while perhaps direct support for an opposition party in an EU member state that is a full democracy might be considered an illegitimate anti-democratic intervention, this objection does not stick in a member state that is a flawed democracy or an electoral autocracy. To be more precise still, cultivating pluralist democracy by providing direct support to pro-democratic partisans is legitimate insofar as it offsets the distortions to democratic equality and the equal playing field observed in member states backsliding on democracy.

This principle of correcting democratic distortions also serves as a delimitation of cultivating pluralist democracy where direct support is given to politically partisan actors. The more distorted the democratic playing field, the more direct support can be given to political actors. For example, at the time of writing, interventions in Hungary—which has regressed on democratic indicators so far that it is no longer considered a democratic state—can legitimately be more partisan than interventions in Slovakia which, while regressing on democratic standards, is still a democratic state.[21] Where threats to democracy do not (yet) amount to distortions of political equality and electoral fairness, partisan interventions are more difficult to justify on democratic grounds. Take an example I discussed in detail in Chapter 2: the Austrian far-right FPÖ party joining the government as a coalition partner in February 2000. While coalition negotiations were ongoing, the other EU member states threatened to impose bilateral diplomatic sanctions on the Austrian government if the FPÖ were to join it. But one problem with this response was that the FPÖ had not yet materially violated EU fundamental values when the threat was made;[22] in other words, the response anticipated possible future violations. Furthermore, no one seriously doubted that the FPÖ's electoral performance was the result of free and fair elections. So the partisan intervention by the EU-14 seems to fall foul of the sort of performative contradiction laid out above.

A different version of this objection holds that cultivating pluralist democracy is problematic when pursued by actors who ought not to be political partisans.[23] The most difficult version of this critique targets EU institutional actors' direct support for party-political organizations in an EU member state (such as political parties, party-affiliated foundations and think tanks).[24] Let us take the example of the European Commission. First, we should note that one of the opening articles of the TEU demands that 'The Union shall respect the equality of Member States before the Treaties as well as their national identities, inherent in their fundamental structures, political and constitutional, inclusive of regional and local self-government' (Article 4.2 TEU). Were the Commission to intervene in the domestic politics of a member state in a party-political fashion, this could undermine this general principle. Second, as stated in the Code of Conduct for the Members of the European Commission, Commissioners themselves must work with 'complete independence, integrity, dignity, with loyalty and discretion' (European Commission 2018: Article 2.2) and must in particular give priority to their Commission commitments over 'party commitment' (ibid.: Articles 9.1 and 10.1). In particular, the demand of loyalty and the injunction to rise above party politics in their work as Commissioners might be read to support the view that the Commission should be politically impartial.

However, the argument that EU actors such as the European Commission should be politically impartial and must therefore refrain from cultivating pluralist democracy in member states where democratic government is under threat runs into several problems. First, reading impartiality in this way contradicts other obligations of the Commission. Article 17 TEU insists that the Commission must promote the 'general interest' of the EU and 'ensure the application of the Treaties' (Article 17.1). As has been covered at length in this book, adherence to EU fundamental values is not only a political ideal but also a legal duty (see also Scheppele, Kochenov and Grabowska-Moroz 2020). As a supranational union of countries united in principle around common values, the EU has the authority to act to protect democracy (Müller 2015). It also simply is not true that European norms require political neutrality from the Commission. While held to norms of loyalty and discretion, European Commissioners not only have explicit authorization to maintain roles in party political contexts at the national and European levels (European Commission 2018: Articles 9 and 10) but have the responsibility to 'maintain political contacts in view of the accountability of the Commission to the European Parliament and the European electorate' (ibid.: Article 2.3).

The critique of illegitimate partisanship from EU actors also makes an important conceptual mistake. Protecting democratic principles is partisan at the constitutional but not at the party-political level. The (political) commitment to democratic government is not only permissible from EU actors but is mandated by Article 2 TEU. Cultivating pluralist democracy may require supporting a pro-democratic political opposition, but such interventions are only incidentally party-political. The political party being supported would be selected not by ideological criteria differentiating democratic parties (right-wing versus left-wing, for example, or progressive versus conservative) but by a more fundamental pro-democratic orientation. And while the clearest examples of democratic decay in

Europe have been driven by radical right-wing populists, this is not always the case. When threats to democratic government come from the left side of the political spectrum, interventions should support pro-democratic centrists and right-wing parties. And indeed, in the case of Malta discussed above, cultivating pluralist democracy through support to investigative journalism may undermine the governing Partit Laburista, a long-term member of the Party of European Socialists (PES), quite like cultivating pluralist democracy in Slovakia may work against Robert Fico's left-nationalist Smer party—a member of PES prior to their suspension in October 2023.[25] That the most serious threats to democratic government in EU member states in recent years have come from Poland and Hungary should not distract us from the fact that cultivating pluralist democracy is not an ideologically partisan intervention.

Conclusion

This chapter has set out the third prong of protecting democracy in Europe: cultivating pluralist democracy. Providing direct support for pro-democratic actors in EU member states where democratic government is threatened is legitimate for a wide range of European political actors. This is also the case regarding direct support for politically partisan actors by EU supranational institutions. The objection that this would constitute illegitimate partisan interference fails as long as such support corrects democratic distortions. This implies that the less democratic an EU member state becomes, the more politically partisan direct support can legitimately be. I have also argued that where EU institutions or member states share in transnational complicity in democratic backsliding, or when they impose material sanctions likely to have unjust effects, direct support might even be a normative duty they owe to those harmed.

Where cultivating pluralist democracy is carefully designed and implemented to avoid a counterproductive backlash, we can hope that it contributes to slowing or reversing democratic decay. One way this could take shape is simply that such support buttresses pro-democratic actors in backsliding countries, playing a part in correcting democratic distortions. Another is that such targeted investments could neutralize possible counterproductive effects of the material sanctions that ought to be imposed on member states backsliding on EU fundamental values. Such sanctions may otherwise undermine the conditions for (re)democratization by undercutting economic growth. By slowing or reversing democratic decay in EU member states where democracy is threatened, pro-democratic actors may also act against 'autocratic diffusion' to other member states.

However, even if these ideal outcomes of reversing or slowing backsliding are not achieved, there are strong normative reasons for cultivating democracy in Europe based on duties to repair the harms of backsliding or as a counterbalance to the unjust effects of material sanctions. Such support would send a strong message that the EU is partisan when it comes to democratic equality and the rule of law. In other words, funding pro-democratic civil society actors, as well as local and regional governments opposed to democratic and rule of law backsliding by the national government of their state, would clearly convey the importance that the EU accords with the Article 2 values. Pro-democracy support in member states may even be owed, given the complicity of some EU political actors to those wronged by democratic backsliding (see Chapter 5). Complicity in democratic backsliding not only generates duties of redress but also of reparations; as such, cultivating pluralist democracy may be one way to make said reparations. Support is also owed to pro-democratic actors when they have unjustly suffered from material sanctions imposed on a member state for violating EU fundamental values. The nature of material sanctions is that their effects are blunt—not only do citizens bear the brunt of their economic effects (rather than the political elites that are the agents of democratic decline), but opposition figures resisting this decline may suffer more than most as they are more exposed.

Some small steps have already been taken by EU actors to provide direct support to pro-democratic actors. For example, I have discussed Horizon Europe funding that has been made available to Budapest, Miskolc and Pécs, three cities in Hungary administered by the opposition, to help them meet the 2030 climate goals. While this is not directly geared to supporting them in resisting autocratization, it is a small help in insulating them from Fidesz weaponizing funding to undercut their work. The €1.5 billion Citizens, Equality, Rights and Values programme, part of the 2021–7 MFF, is also a step in the right direction as it facilitates direct support of civil society organizations pushing for democratic inclusion and the rule of law. Such examples, however, are generally too few and far between. Pro-democratic actors ought to seek far greater opportunities for cultivating pluralist democracy alongside correcting complicity and containing autocracy in Europe.

Together, this chapter (on cultivating pluralist democracy) and the two previous chapters (on correcting transnational complicity for EU democratic backsliding [Chapter 5] and containing autocratic actors in EU legal and political processes [Chapter 6]) lay out the 'positive' EU responses to democratic backsliding in EU member states. The next and final chapter lays out the normative justification for two subsequent steps if these three responses fail: first, exclusion from further EU integration, and finally, the *ultima ratio* of democratic backsliding—expulsion from the EU.

8

QUO VADIS? DEMOCRACY PROTECTION OR DISSOCIATION

Le doute n'est pas un état bien agréable, mais l'assurance est un état ridicule.

Voltaire, letter to Frederick II of Prussia[1]

It is time to take stock of the overall argument of this book so far. In the first part, I critically engaged European responses to democratic backsliding in European Union (EU) member states. For over a decade since the first serious democratic regressions occurred in Hungary in 2010, the European response was meek and legalistic. Step by step, democratic checks and balances were undermined in Hungary, Poland and beyond. There was a prevailing attitude that there was little that EU actors could do outside of the framework of Article 7 of the Treaty on European Union (TEU) and that stronger responses could backfire. I have argued we should understand this in light of an increasingly fatalistic and depoliticized attitude to values conflicts after the failure of the bilateral sanctions that were briefly imposed on Austria in 2000, following the inclusion of the far-right Freedom Party of Austria in the Austrian government (Chapter 2). Examining more recent EU discourse shows how this depoliticized approach is a dominant frame in how democracy is conceptualized more generally. A framing analysis of 155 Commissioner speeches given between 2018 and 2023 reveals an approach I call 'democracy without politics', wherein democratic contestation and disagreement are largely displaced by a technocratic legalism which stands in stark contrast to a pluralistic understanding of democracy (Chapter 3). This tracks with the Commission's narrow and largely ineffective responses to democratic backsliding in EU member states in this period.

If the dominant approach to democratic backsliding by EU actors has been weak and ineffectual, it is not for the lack of stronger tools. These include stripping a member state of treaty rights such as their right to vote in the Council (Article 7 TEU), making access to EU funding conditional on democracy and the rule of law (such as the Rule of Law Conditionality Regulation 2020/2092 and Common Provisions Regulation 2021/1060), using infringement actions to pursue fines against member states violating their legal obligations to uphold EU fundamental values (Article 258–60 of the Treaty on the Functioning of the European Union [TFEU]), and deregistering European political parties and foundations that violate these values (Regulation 1141/2014). However, in Chapter 4 I argue that the Article 7 sanction and the deregistration of political parties are normatively incoherent in that they themselves undermine democratic values. That would seem to leave EU budget conditionality and infringement actions as the best of the sanctioning tools available to EU actors to respond to democratic backsliding in member states.

These philosophical reflections lay the groundwork for the first three chapters of the second part of the book, where I set out normative principles that ought to govern responses to EU democratic backsliding. An urgent normative priority for EU actors is to correct their complicity in the wrongs of democratic backsliding. By not using those normatively coherent tools available to them, or showing too much forbearance in the use of these tools, EU actors share in the normative responsibility in backsliding and owe duties of redress and reparation (Chapter 5). The next type of response that I analyse concerns the containment of autocratic actors in European politics. While disenfranchisement in the Council is incoherent with democratic values (in line with my argument in Chapter 4), autocratic actors should be maximally excluded from EU law and policymaking to the extent that such exclusion is itself coherent with EU fundamental values (Chapter 5). Correcting complicity and containing autocracy should be complemented, in my view, by more positive actions to cultivate pluralist democracy where it is threatened. The third prong of my approach argues that a wide range of actors should offer direct support to pro-democratic actors in EU member states where democracy is threatened. In the context of democratic backsliding, this is justified not only when it takes the form of supporting civil society organizations like human rights non-governmental organizations, but also when support is offered to more straightforwardly political partisans as long as such support works to correct democratic distortions (Chapter 6).

Perhaps a concerted effort by pro-democratic parties at the national and European level, along with member states, civil society organizations, and EU institutions, would be enough to reverse democratic backsliding in EU member states. I certainly hope so. But it is important to recognize that the responses I have defended may not be enough to protect democracy in Europe. A single-minded critique of what has been can be compared to hyperopia, where distant events seem clear but what is close by is obscured from view—a fault I may concede. But overconfidence about what could come to be is like myopia, focusing only on what is right in front of us and missing the uncertainties and contingencies of what is further away. What should be done if, after correcting complicity, containing autocracy and cultivating pluralist democracy (within the normative limits I have described), one or several member states continue to slip towards frankly autocratic governance? The possibility of the failure of normatively coherent responses to democratic backsliding forces us to consider: what next? Are stronger responses like disenfranchising a member state in the Council through the Article 7 procedure legitimate if nothing else has worked, even if they are normatively incoherent with EU fundamental values?[2]

Militant democratic theory offers a way of thinking through this paradox. In particular, militant democrats argue that democracies are sometimes justified in acting anti-democratically in order to protect their democratic character, much like it is sometimes argued that a commitment to tolerance requires us to be intolerant of the intolerant (Popper 2013). So far, I have argued against responses that undermine the values they purport to protect (Chapter 4). But in this chapter,

I take seriously the militant democratic challenge that such responses to anti-democratic extremism are sometimes justified. Militant democratic views are controversial (Invernizzi Accetti and Zuckerman 2017). What I try to show in this chapter is that regardless of where we stand in this debate, EU actors must not resort to anti-democratic politics. Militant democrats and non-militant democrats alike should convene on the conclusion that there is a coherent measure, which is not anti-democratic, to which the EU should turn in extreme circumstances—the expulsion of autocratic states from the EU. The existential dangers autocrats pose to democracy in Europe, coupled with EU actors' limited authority to intervene, necessitate dissociation with autocratic member states where other legitimate responses have failed.

The remainder of this concluding chapter is structured around making this argument. I first lay out the conception of militant democracy that I think is most useful for thinking through this issue. I weigh the normatively most compelling justification of militant democratic responses in light of two key criteria: (1) that they are responses to existential threats and (2) that they are necessary to neutralize these threats. Next, I argue against the use of the 'strong' responses to EU democratic backsliding, focusing in particular on disenfranchising a frankly autocratic state in the Council. Such militant democratic responses are illegitimate because a non-militant response exists to such dire straits. As such, expulsion from the EU is the appropriate and legitimate final sanction for democratic backsliding in the EU. To be clear: protecting democracy in Europe by expelling a frankly autocratic member state would come at grave democratic costs, especially to the citizens of that state. But not expelling such a state would have graver and broader costs still.

A narrow conception of militant democracy

The theory of militant democracy holds that, under exceptional circumstances, democratic states are justified in acting anti-democratically in order to preserve their democracy. Militant democratic theory is a particularly suitable theoretical terrain for exploring this paradox as it explicitly recognizes that there is a democratic cost to militant democratic policies. In this sense, militant democrats can accept the normative incoherence I have argued mar some of the tools the EU has to respond to democratic backsliding and yet maintain that their use may be justified. Militant democracy was formulated first in the 1930s by Karl Loewenstein, whose foil was European and especially German fascism. He noted that fascists had been eager to use the procedures and rights of the liberal-democratic state in Weimar Germany to their advantage (Lowenstein 1937a: 423–4). When powerful anti-democratic actors undermine and discredit democratic procedures and institutions in this fashion, Loewenstein held that democracy must fight back: 'If democracy believes in the superiority of its absolute values over the opportunistic platitudes of fascism, it must live up to the demands of the hour, and every possible effort must be made to rescue it, *even at the risk and cost of violating fundamental principles*', including the 'suspension of fundamental rights' (ibid.: 432, emphasis added). While it may appear paradoxical to undermine democratic principles to protect democracy, Loewenstein thought the opposite view—which he called 'democratic fundamentalism'—amounted to 'legalistic self-complacency and suicidal lethargy' (ibid.: 430–1).

The narrow conception of militant democracy I use here is centred around this 'militant democratic paradox'.[3] Militant democratic measures, on this conception, are different (i.e. paradoxical) from other responses to anti-democratic threats in that they pose *prima facie* challenges to core democratic values such as civil and political equality. The term militant democracy is sometimes used in a looser way to describe democratic self-defence more generally, including through ordinary criminal law or constitutional prohibitions of some kinds of anti-democratic activity. The narrow conception can be distinguished from the broader conception in that narrowly militant democratic responses target the equal participation in democratic politics of specific people, or groups of people, considered to threaten democratic government (Invernizzi Accetti and Zuckerman 2017). This actor-focused conception can be contrasted with broader action-focused responses that include, in general terms and via more standard sanctions (fines, prison sentences, etc.), the prohibition of certain actions perceived to threaten democracy. We can think here, for example, of prohibitions on Holocaust denial or of fascist symbols, which are sanctioned with fines and even prison terms in several European jurisdictions. The narrow conception of militant democracy is delimited to those types of democratic self-defence that target the equal civil and political rights of actors perceived to threaten democracy. Standard examples here include banning extremist parties and stripping extremists of their right to vote or to stand for election. The final definitional criteria I use are that militant measures must be suitable for responding to anti-democratic threats and that they must be measures of self-defence.[4]

Understanding militant democracy in this narrow way is useful as it identifies a set of responses to anti-democratic actors that raise a very particular normative question: when (if ever) is it justified to act against democratic values in self-defence? This is the general question that we must answer to determine whether and when it is legitimate for EU actors to undermine fundamental values in their protection of democracy in Europe, so 'fire is fought with fire' (Loewenstein 1937b: 656).

The definitional question—whether to define militant democracy in a narrow or broader sense—is separate from the justificatory questions of when and how different types of democratic defence can be justified. Many democratic theorists, including most militant democrats, consider that (narrowly) militant democratic responses warrant a higher threshold of justification than non-militant responses to anti-democratic threats. Because the values to which democrats are committed ordinarily require equal civil and political rights among members of the democratic polity, deviations from this norm require special justification. Further, while some democratic theorists consider narrowly militant democratic responses to be generally illegitimate or unwise, many others think that democracies are warranted in acting militantly in self-defence in extreme circumstances where the continued existence of the democratic polity is at stake (ibid.).[5] The challenge is clarifying the precise scope and justification for militant responses.

As well as being more useful to our purposes, the narrow sense of militant democracy is also faithful to the original exposition of militant democratic theory, as well as to major contemporary contributions such as the theories of Alexander Kirshner (2014) and Bastiaan Rijpkema (2018). In the first of Karl Loewenstein's two founding articles on militant democracy in the 1930s, he argues that when democracies face existential threats from extremists, democrats are 'at war' (Lowenstein 1937a: 423). In such exceptional circumstances, Loewenstein argues, democracies are not bound by the ordinary democratic rules guaranteeing their opponents' equal civil and political rights. Rather, they should 'no longer restrain from restrictions on democratic fundamentals, for the sake of ultimately preserving these very fundamentals' (ibid.: 432). In line with the narrow definition of militant democracy I have set out, Loewenstein's approach deliberately identifies militant responses as those that restrict what are ordinarily fundamental democratic rights.

Justifying militant democracy: The existential threat and necessity conditions

On the narrow view of militant democracy, militant (i.e. anti-democratic) responses are therefore ordinarily impermissible in democratic politics but are justified when they are necessary to stave off a grave threat. Militant democratic responses that target the equal civil and political rights of anti-democratic actors must have a higher justificatory threshold than non-militant responses that do not *prima facie* challenge democratic norms. Without developing a full-fledged theory of the justifiability of militant democratic action, we can identify two precise conditions that must minimally be met. First, the threats to democracy must be existential (the existential threat condition); second, militant action must be necessary to contain this threat (the necessity condition). I show these conditions to be normatively plausible and also show that they cohere with the influential contemporary militant democratic theories proposed by Kirshner and Rijpkema. Once this is done, we can look at whether the EU's democracy crisis meets these conditions and could therefore justify militant responses.

The 'existential threat condition' captures the intuition that anti-democratic activity does not warrant debasing democratic values unless it poses an existential threat to the democratic character of a polity. When faced with minor threats, democracies should wield the standard tools of criminal and constitutional prohibitions, sanctioning anti-democratic actions with fines or imprisonment rather than targeting the equal civil and political rights of anti-democratic actors.

While Kirshner's influential theory of militant democracy does not explicitly formulate an 'existential threat condition', something like it is implied in his 'principle of limited intervention', which holds that (narrowly) militant democratic tools like party bans are only permissible 'to block antidemocrats from violating the rights of others' (Kirshner 2014: 27). Like the existential threat condition, Kirshner's principle of limited intervention means the threats cannot be hypothetical—there needs to be a real and significant risk of harm to warrant a militant response. An existential threat, however, has a weightier threshold than rights violation. If democracies are permitted to act militantly every time there is a mere risk of an anti-democrat violating an individual's rights, we may still be using a sledgehammer to crack a nut: the bluntness of militant responses in such circumstances risks creating more democratic harm than not acting at all. Ordinary rights violations at the individual level can be addressed using ordinary criminal law sanctions, rather than via restrictions on the offender's political and civil freedoms (Invernizzi Accetti and Zuckerman 2017: 184; Capoccia 2013: 207; Bourne 2012: 196). For this reason, the strongest defences of militant democratic actions limit their legitimate use to those militant responses necessary to neutralize the risk of anti-democrats harming the democratic character of the polity. This picks up a suggestion from Bastiaan Rijpkema's theory of militant democracy as 'self-correction'. Rijpkema grounds militant democratic interventions in the need to maintain democracy's 'unique characteristic ... [that] decisions can always be reversed' (Rijpkema 2018: 134).[6] Militant interventions are thus justified, in Rijpkema's theory, only when 'the self-corrective capacity of the democracy is threatened'; in other words, when the continued existence of democracy is threatened.

The 'necessity condition' captures the intuition that militant democratic restrictions on the equal civil and political rights of anti-democratic actors are only justifiable if they are necessary to neutralize the threat these actors pose to the democratic order. Militant democratic actions are necessary in the requisite way if only militant democratic responses could plausibly contain the anti-democratic threat. If non-militant responses could succeed, then these should be preferred to militant responses. In a recent book, Gabriele Badano and Alasia Nuti make a similar point, arguing that militant responses 'are fully justified only if other less extreme strategies have been implemented before-hand and have failed' (Badano and Nuti 2024: 111). To be more precise still, the necessity condition is a matter of lexical priority rather than a question of proportionality. Any response that upholds democratic fundamentals must be preferred over any response that undermines them. To re-write Badano and Nuti's condition, militant responses are justified only if all non-militant responses that plausibly might work to contain an existential anti-democratic threat have been implemented and have failed. As Kirshner writes, militant democratic action must 'to the greatest degree possible, [be] consistent with our reasons for embracing self-government' (Kirshner 2014: 4).

Kirshner defends a principle similar to the necessity condition, which he refers to as the 'principle of democratic responsibility'. This principle focuses on the democratic costs of militant action and how they challenge fundamental democratic values (ibid.: 55–9). Because of these costs, Kirshner argues, militant interventions must be temporally limited and shaped by the goal of eventually reinstating anti-democrats' equal political standing. While Kirshner does not formulate the necessity demand explicitly, it is implicit in his insistence that democrats must minimize anti-democratic action (ibid.: 55). Furthermore, Kirshner insists that 'if a society restricts participation when a more democratic response is possible, its efforts will have been self-defeating, inflicting *unnecessary damage* on its political institutions' (ibid.: 66, emphasis added). It is to minimize such unnecessary damage that the strongest normative defences of militant democracy require that they are limited by a necessity condition.

The existential threat and necessity conditions are jointly necessary to justify militant democratic responses on these exacting standards. So, even supposing only militant democratic action would be effective to contain specific anti-democratic actions, the existential threat condition proscribes militant responses if the threat is not sufficiently serious. In such circumstances, a democratic polity must accept the existence of anti-democrats, in line with its commitment to equal civil and political rights for all. Similarly, if the threat to democracy is existential, but if non-militant democratic action would be ineffective to contain the anti-democratic threat, the necessity condition proscribes militant responses. It is better to remain true to democratic values than undermine them with no hope of success.

Can militant responses to democratic backsliding in the EU be justified?

I do not wish to tackle the justifications for militant democracy at the most fundamental level—whether or not militant democratic measures can ever be justified—here.[7] Rather, let us assume, for the sake of argument, that such measures can be justified democratically, but only when the existential threat and necessity conditions are met in democratic defence. If the risks to democracy in Europe are low, European actors should not debase their values when they come to its defence. If there are non-militant measures that could neutralize the autocratic enemy at democracy's gates, then the cost of sacrificing democratic fundamentals is too high in any case. To return to the normative dilemma specific to this chapter, we must therefore ask: a) whether EU member states backsliding on democratic values (could) constitute a fundamental threat to the EU's democratic character, and b) whether a militant response like disenfranchisement in the Council would be appropriate, or if there are non-militant alternatives.

To take the first question: surely backsliding *could* constitute an existential threat to the EU's nature as a political community of states sharing a commitment to democracy, equality, the rule of law, and so on. Indeed, it is easier to answer this question positively in the supranational case (regarding the democratic character of the EU) than it is at the national level. At the national level, the existence of an anti-democratic party does not in itself pose an anti-democratic threat, nor does the election of some anti-democratic representatives to the legislature. What matters is if and how they may gain power and whether they could use that power to dismantle democracy. But at the European level, a member state being in serious and persistent breach of democratic values would itself constitute an existential threat to the EU's democratic character and, in the absence of a reaction from the EU, its deep-seated commitment to fundamental values (Kelemen 2017). Further, it follows from the indirect democratic legitimation of Council and European Council decisions (whereby their democratic legitimation depends on the democratic authority of member state governments) that there is a threshold at which Council and European Council voting is no longer even a derivatively democratic procedure. The same is true, given the national administration of European elections, for the election of Members of the European Parliament. The legitimacy of the European Commission, proposed by the European Council and elected by a vote of the European Parliament, is similarly interwoven with the legitimacy of member states. Even one bad apple in this case spoils the whole barrel.

Democratic backsliding in an EU member state thus constitutes an existential threat to the democratic character of the Union, but that is not enough to warrant militant democratic responses. Two more elements are needed. First, would militant democratic responses in this context qualify as democratic self-defence? Militant democracy was theorized at the national level, yet something important may be lost in translation when applying it to transnational politics. Second, would militant responses meet the demands of the necessity condition, or would other non-militant responses plausibly meet the challenge? Let us take these in turn.

As a supranational union of countries pooling some of their sovereignty in myriad but limited ways, it is not immediately obvious that EU actors responding to democratic backsliding in an EU member state are acting in self-defence. Recall that the strongest defences of the legitimacy of militant democratic action require the anti-democratic challenge to pose a real threat to the continued existence of the polity as a democratic community. We must therefore reflect on the extent to which the EU's own constitutional identity matters in this context.

Although it is tempting to address the question of democratic self-defence by asking whether or not the EU is 'a democracy', I believe this is a mistake. In my view, whether or not one considers the EU to be a sort of democratic federation, a supranational confederation or something in between does not matter. Regardless of one's perspective on the EU's constitutional identity, the EU acts in self-defence when it seeks to contain anti-democratic threats for two reasons.

First, the EU is centrally organized and shaped by its member states, so their politics are in that sense internal to EU politics, even where a policy domain is the exclusive competence of the member state. The EU acting to protect democracy in a member state responds to threats to democracy that are in the EU, rather than elsewhere. Second, the EU's character as a polity committed to democracy is threatened by democratic backsliding. The EU's commitment to democracy is not merely an abstract ideal, but is implicated in its legal coherence and in the democratic legitimacy of EU law and governance. Ulrich Wagrandl makes this point simply: 'European citizens today are not only governed by themselves but, via European institutions, also by other states and their citizens, whom they and their state govern, in turn' (Wagrandl 2018: 157). If a member state's government is no longer democratic, its representative co-legislating in the Council has no legitimate standing to co-decide EU law and its head of government can no longer legitimately claim to represent its citizens in the European Council. The democratic authority of EU institutions whose mandate is delegated by member states (such as the European Commission, the Court of Justice of the European Union [CJEU] or the European Central Bank) would also be tarnished if an autocratic member were to be permitted to weigh in on this delegation. Even the democratic mandate of MEPs is tarnished when European elections take place in a member state with a political playing field tilted towards one party.

In sum, we do not need to settle the question of the ultimate constitutional character of the EU to assess whether it can act in democratic self-defence. Either way, the legitimacy of its institutional structure depends on direct and indirect democratic legitimation. It thus can be said to be acting in democratic self-defence when responding to internal anti-democratic threats. We must therefore conclude that the EU is acting in self-defence of its democratic legitimacy when it responds to try to combat democratic backsliding.

Are militant responses justified when there are existential threats to the democratic character of the EU?

Having determined that democratic backsliding by an EU member state can constitute an existential threat to the democratic character of the EU, we need to ask whether strong responses to EU democratic backsliding—like the sanction of stripping a member state government of their right to vote in the Council described in Article 7.3 TEU—could be an appropriate militant response. Or are there non-militant measures that could be invoked that would 'defend' democracy in such extreme circumstances? Because even if the threat posed by backsliding member states is sufficient to demand urgent action, militant democratic action would only be warranted (on the view I set out above) if there are no alternative avenues that do not undermine democratic values and could be reasonably expected to safeguard the democratic nature of the institution or procedures under threat.[8]

Jan-Werner Müller notes that those who argue against the use of militant democratic measures by the EU have generally 'taken to invoking constitutional identity as a kind of trump card against outside interference' (Müller 2018: 434). As must be clear by now, this is far from my view. EU member states have pooled their sovereignty such that if one member becomes autocratic, the democratic character of all others is tainted. I have argued that many different EU actors should impose wide-ranging sanctions against member state governments veering towards authoritarianism and massively scale up positive democracy protection measures, such as supporting free media, pro-democratic civil society actors, the independence of the judiciary and critical voices in academia. Specifically militant measures are impermissible in my view not because they are 'too strong', but because a more thoroughgoing response that does not challenge democratic values in the same way is possible: namely dissociation from autocratic member states.

Expulsion from the European Union

An EU expulsion mechanism has rarely been seriously considered amongst Europe's leading politicians, though it is becoming a more common question in recent academic work on Europe's democracy crisis (Athanassiou 2009: 32–6; Hausteiner 2020: 15–16; Sadurski 2009; Müller 2015: 145–50; Olsen 2019; Patberg 2020, 2021; Bellamy and Kröger 2021: 632; Scherz 2023). In 2016, Jean

Asselborn, Minister of Foreign Affairs for Luxembourg, caused a stir when he came out in favour of a potential recourse to expulsion:

> We cannot accept that the fundamental values of the European Union are flagrantly violated. Those who, like Hungary, build fences against refugees fleeing war or violate the freedom of the press and the independence of the judiciary, should be temporarily or, if necessary, permanently expelled from the EU. (Schiltz and Brüssel 2016, my translation)[9]

More recently, when discussing Hungarian and Polish opposition to a conditionality mechanism for the COVID-19 recovery fund in the Dutch Parliament, then Dutch Prime Minister Mark Rutte wondered 'Can you make a budget via an intergovernmental agreement, or can you found an EU without Hungary and Poland?' (Plenaire Verslagen 2020, my translation).[10] Besides these two rare exceptions, expulsion from the EU is rarely brought up in the context of European politics, however conflictual.[11]

One reason that the case for an EU expulsion mechanism is largely absent in normative theorizing may be that democratic theorists usually oppose the domestic analogues to expulsion: banishment and denaturalization. These actions, the argument goes, violate the fundamental rights of the banished by making them stateless. All citizens of democratic states have the right to remain in their state (albeit, for convicted inmates, in prison) and everyone has the right to a nationality. This is part of the 'right to have rights', to use Hannah Arendt's famous formulation (Arendt 1951: 294). Such a right is non-contingent. No individual, on this view, is utterly beyond the pale—at least in terms of their right to political membership.

However, in contrast to citizens' inalienable right to have rights, states do *not* have a fundamental right to trans-, inter- or supranational associations with other states (cf. Olsen 2023: 325). Such associations are voluntary.[12] States would not have their fundamental rights violated by being excluded from such associations. Thus, and consequently, a state's eventual expulsion from such an association is not at odds with their fundamental civic and political rights. Nor would the expulsion from the EU of a member state in serious and persistent breach of EU fundamental values violate their democratic rights, as long as the process of exclusion happened within an appropriate legal framework. If such breaches constitute an 'existential threat' to the democratic character and legitimacy of EU rules and Council decisions, expulsion is not only permissible but is the appropriate final sanction (cf. Hausteiner 2020: 59–62; Athanassiou 2009: 32–6; Olsen 2023; Scherz 2023).

Expelling a member state that had become frankly autocratic may be the only way to preserve the democratic character of the EU. While correcting complicity and containing autocracy limit the threat of autocratic politics, and cultivating pluralist democracy may slow or even reverse democratic backsliding, they may fail to prevent a member state becoming frankly autocratic. Expelling such a state from the EU would mean their government loses their say in law and policymaking in the Council. And, contrary to disenfranchising such a government in the Council, expulsion would not violate democratic norms by holding that country subject to laws that they do not have a proportionally equal say in deciding. Indeed, expulsion would prevent this autocratic state from tainting the democratic character of Union politics across the EU institutions. Their head of state or government would, for instance, no longer sit on the European Council. As a result, exclusion from the Council and the European Council would be a powerful way to neutralize the veto threat that autocratic actors are prone to use in these bodies whenever decision-making requires unanimity (Holesch and Kyriazi 2022). Nor would they nominate a European Commissioner or a judge to the European Court of Justice. The right to nominate a European Commissioner has been a particularly central tool of backsliding states to try to influence the dossiers on democracy and the rule of law (Kelemen 2024).[13] Finally, the thorny question of the legitimate mandate of Members of the European Parliament given elections held in an autocratic state would no longer arise were that state to be expelled (Mraz 2023). It may even be the case that political clarity about expulsion being the final sanction for democratic backsliding—i.e. that there are red lines that would-be autocrats cannot cross without risking their state's EU membership—may make recourse to expulsion unnecessary. The costs of expulsion may be too high for those elites pursuing antidemocratic politics, or the risk of expulsion may be enough to trigger their eviction.[14]

PROTECTING DEMOCRACY IN EUROPE

The costs of excluding autocratic members

I have argued for an important normative disanalogy between the banishment or denaturalization of an individual from a state and the expulsion of a state from an association. Yet, there is also an important point of similarity, at least in the context of the EU. Expelling a member state from the Union against its wishes (and the wishes of its citizenry) would have grave effects on the rights and freedoms of its citizens, and on the rights and freedoms of other citizens of the EU (Olsen and Rostbøll 2017). It ought never be considered lightly. However, the commitment to exclude seriously anti-democratic governments from the Union is vital to ensure that its democratic character and legitimacy can be preserved in the face of the all too persistent threat of autocratic politics.

Before we conclude in favour of an expulsion mechanism as the appropriate final response to a member state becoming frankly autocratic, we must consider the normative costs of expelling a backsliding member state—particularly with regard to the loss of rights and freedoms of the citizens of that state (Olsen and Rostbøll 2017; Patberg 2021; Scherz 2023). The citizens of such a state would be deprived, following expulsion, of their EU citizenship. Consequently, they would lose many important freedoms such as the freedom to work and travel in other member states. They would no longer be protected by the stringencies of EU labour, employment and competition law, nor could they have their trans-national interests represented in the European Parliament. These are just a smattering of examples of the deep and far-reaching ways in which citizens of an expelled state would be disadvantaged. Worse, many citizens in such a state would not have supported—and may have actively opposed—their government's autocratization. With them in mind, their state's expulsion from the EU seems harsh, lamentable, and unjust (Olsen 2019: 159–62; Olsen 2023; Patberg 2021; Scherz 2023). And even those citizens that supported their autocratic government (e.g. with their votes) cannot be held fully responsible for such choices given the unequal democratic playing field in a state backsliding on democracy and the rule of law (e.g. the absence of freedom of speech, a fully free press, independent courts, and so on).

DEMOCRACY PROTECTION OR DISSOCIATION

As a means of furthering the EU's commitment to the Article 2 values, the expulsion of an autocratic state may also raise questions. First, the values of democracy and equality do not apply only to the interaction of member states and EU processes and institutions, but also in relation to EU citizens. After all, Article 9 TEU states that the EU 'shall observe the principle of the equality of its citizens', while Article 10 TEU guarantees EU citizens the 'the right to participate in the democratic life of the Union'. Would the expulsion of a frankly autocratic member state not violate these rights, leading to a different sort of performative contradiction than the one outlined in Chapter 4? Second, there is currently no treaty mechanism to expel a member state; the only way for a member state to leave the Union that is laid out in the European treaties is through the Article 50 TEU procedure. Loewenstein argued for extra-legal militant responses in the context of his militant democratic theory, potentially opening the door for expulsion outside of the treaty framework. But if expulsion would undermine Article 2 values anyway, then there would be no reason to consider it as a better (*qua* non-militant) measure vis-à-vis disenfranchisement in the Council. Given that expulsion is not mentioned in the treaties, could an expulsion mechanism proceed in accordance with the rule of law?

The normative costs of expelling a state that has regressed too far on democracy and the rule of law cannot be taken lightly. Indeed, while an EU expulsion mechanism as a final political sanction of democratic and rule of law backsliding is necessary in the extreme case where a member state becomes frankly autocratic, the costs of expulsion are further reasons why responses centred on correcting complicity, containing autocracy and cultivating pluralist democracy are so urgent. Yet, contrasting the expulsion of an EU member state with the denaturalization or banishment of an individual citizen helps show that no fundamental rights are violated in the former case (in contrast to the latter). As argued above, the EU is a voluntarist association and (member) states have no unqualified right to membership.[15] By extension, and in keeping with European law[16] and CJEU jurisprudence,[17] EU citizens have a derivative and not a direct right to participation in Union democratic life. Their state's exit from the Union would not be undemocratic in itself and would not violate Articles 9 and 10 TEU (cf. Olsen and Rostbøll 2017).

An EU expulsion mechanism is also consistent with the rule of law. It is true that the EU treaties do not address the expulsion of a member state from the EU.[18] If the argument in this chapter is correct, then a proposal to add such a mechanism through a revision to the treaties would be warranted normatively. However, surely (at least) member states currently under review for democratic and rule of law backsliding would resist such changes, and their consent would be required. It seems that an expulsion mechanism may be desirable from the perspective of democratic theory, but is nevertheless unrealistic. There is another possibility though, evoked by Rutte (cited above): re-founding a new European Union with stronger democratic and rule of law protections and without recalcitrant members of the current EU (Chamon 2020; Chamon and Theuns 2021; Theuns 2022). This would require EU member states committed to democracy and the rule of law to collectively withdraw from the EU via the Article 50 procedure and re-found a new European Union. Autocratic member states would be left with a useless husk of the former EU. Such a procedure to withdraw and re-found requires no treaty change and violates no fundamental values.

While the eventual expulsion of an EU member state through a collective withdrawal and re-found procedure may seem outlandish, consider the alternative. If current trends of democratic backsliding continue, and a member state becomes frankly autocratic, could pro-democratic states and citizens countenance being bound to it through continued supranational union? No. Supranational union with an autocratic state would taint all EU law and governance.[19] Doing nothing about backsliding makes all EU member states committed to fundamental values complicit, as well as tainting the democratic character of the EU overall and of each of its member states (see Chapter 5). Being open to the eventual recourse to an expulsion mechanism is essential if the EU is to guarantee its commitment to the fundamental values of Article 2.

Conclusion

If the programme of correcting EU complicity in democratic backsliding, maximally containing autocracy within the limits of EU authority and cultivating pluralist democracy fail, more radical measures are needed. Accepting supranational integration with a frankly autocratic state degrades democracy in the whole Union. Expelling a frankly autocratic state is the only solution to the paradox of the illegitimacy of militant democratic measures such as disenfranchising a member state via Article 7 and the illegitimacy of having autocratic states continue to participate in EU law and policymaking. Moreover, Article 7 TEU is currently itself in conflict with the EU fundamental values of equality and democracy (see Chapter 4). This conflict cannot be justified via recourse to a militant measure such as disenfranchisement in the Council, since, even if we accept the hypothetical justifiability of militant measures, a democratically acceptable alternative exists that would safeguard the democratic character and legitimacy of the EU: expulsion from the Union. Militant democratic measures such as disenfranchisement in the Council should thus be replaced with expulsion from the Union as the ultimate political sanction for member states flagrantly violating EU fundamental values.

All this is not to say that the 'existential threat' threshold discussed above has now been met in the case of Hungary. The central message of this book is not that Hungary should be kicked out of the EU. However, serious reflection on what this threshold entails in practice, and on the need for an expulsion mechanism as a vital backstop to democratic backsliding, is made urgent especially by Hungary's descent towards autocracy. While Poland and the Czech Republic have shown the resilience of democratic institutions, the re-election of Robert Fico's Smer-led government in Slovakia in 2023 and the bold programme of illiberal reforms in the first months of Fico's fourth government warn that democratic recovery can be fragile (European Parliament 2024). Given the severity of these developments, it is no longer fanciful to imagine that European member states may be forced to choose between democratic values and maintaining their association with an autocratic member state. Prior to expulsion, if an autocratic member state or group of member states is blocking progress on important dossiers (such as by trying to blackmail others with their veto in a key area), EU member states should follow the principle of maximum coherent exclusion (see Chapter 6). Where further integration is envisaged, such autocratic member states ought to be sidelined aggressively by greatly scaling up the use of the mechanism of enhanced cooperation set out in Article 20 TEU and Article 326–34 TFEU (Chamon and Theuns 2021).

That the last resort in terms of a political response to democratic and rule of law backsliding must be the expulsion of a member state from the EU is undoubtedly a radical conclusion. However, its radical nature seems both tempered and justified when one considers that some EU member states may continue to sink into increasingly anti-democratic politics. Optimists hope that budding autocrats will be overturned at the ballot box. I share this hope. But what if they are not? Or what if they resist a peaceful transition of power? However unpalatable, EU member states cannot both permit a frankly autocratic state to continue to be a member of the Union and at the same time pretend to be committed to democracy.

NOTES

1. INTRODUCTION

1. For instance Bulgaria (Dimitrova 2022), Croatia (Čepo 2021), the Czech Republic (Hanley and Vachudova 2020), Malta (Veenendaal 2019), Romania (Iusmen 2015), Slovakia (European Parliament 2024) and Slovenia (Fink-Hafner 2022). Most recently, serious democratic concerns have emerged in Greece, where steady pressure on democracy since Kyriakos Mitsotakis' New Democracy government was elected in 2019 accelerated when it emerged the Greek National Intelligence Service was using spyware against journalists, politicians, prosecutors and public officials. Similar software has been used against journalists and opposition politicians in Hungary, Poland, and Spain, where Catalan politicians were put under spyware surveillance *en masse* between 2017 and 2020 (Deibert 2023; Higgins 2022).
2. Wilders' Freedom Party (the PVV) won the largest number of votes (23.5%) and seats (37/150), but fell well short of a majority. At the time of writing they govern with, in order of size, the right-wing People's Party for Freedom and Democracy (VVD), the centre-right New Social Contract (NSC) and the right-wing populist Farmer-Citizen Movement (BBB) parties.
3. Democratic backsliding is characterized when a government weakens or dismantles any of the political institutions required to sustain democracy (Bermeo 2016). Sometimes, the term is reserved for when a democratic state regresses on democracy, while autocratization is used to refer to the process whereby a non-democratic state becomes more autocratic. In this book, however, I use these terms interchangeably, along with democratic erosion, democratic decline and democratic decay. While I

will occasionally draw critical attention to 'bumpy, dynamic sequences of episodic crisis and confrontation' in member states that cannot be judged to be regression on democratic standards overall (Cianetti and Hanley 2021: 73), I generally focus on cases where there is a clear net regression of democratic norms. After the Cold War, the nature of typical cases of democratic backsliding shifted from overt actions like coups and election fraud to more incremental processes, with elites gradually undermining domestic checks and balances (Bermeo 2016; Waldner and Lust 2018). Scholars have identified different types of backsliding, distinguishing between the shift from liberal democracy to electoral democracy, from democracy to autocracy, and from institutionalized autocracy to personalist autocracy (Little and Meng 2024). Recently, the analytical focus has increasingly moved from examining the 'demand' side—political elites driving backsliding—to exploring the 'supply' side of democratic backsliding, specifically citizens' toleration of policies of democratic decline (Mazepus and Toshkov 2021; Wunsch and Gessler 2023).

4. Partisan used to mean 'party-political', although an influential recent account focuses more narrowly on partisans advancing principles 'that are generalizable, i.e. irreducible to the beliefs or interests of particular social groups' yet contestable (White and Ypi 2016). I use the term to indicate taking a clear position (take part) in favour of democratic government at the constitutional level. Far from undermining party-political and ideological partisanship, pro-democratic partisanship enables and sustains it.

5. While the clearest recent examples of democratic backsliding were pursued by populist radical right and far-right parties in government, there are democratic concerns from other ideological corners, as the examples of Bulgaria (Dimitrova 2022), Malta (Bonello Ghio et al. 2022; Veenendaal 2019), and Slovakia (European Parliament 2024) illustrate.

6. Regulation 1141/2014 on the Statute and Funding of European Political Parties and European Political Foundations.

7. For the sake of brevity, I will refer to the Council of the European Union as the Council throughout this book.

8. Stefan Auer's recent book, *European Disunion*, offers a sustained analysis on the structural problem inherent in EU integration formed by the combination of the EU having sufficient authority over member states to prevent much independent national action while member states retain the

authority—typically through such veto rights—to block collective solutions (2022).

2. MEMBERSHIP FATALISM AND DEPOLITICIZATION IN EU DEMOCRACY PROTECTION

1. The choices made by each person involved in deciding and implementing the EU response to each event of democratic backsliding in EU member states—from high officials in EU institutions to unknown policy advisors—are complex, multi-causal and contingent. For each relevant action or omission, these individuals may have acted otherwise not only if the circumstances were slightly different, but also if they had chosen to do so.
2. I do not claim that I am, strictly speaking, writing a genealogy here. But I have been inspired by genealogical approaches in important ways that I think should be acknowledged. In this chapter, I explore a perspective on European integration that I think is both largely overlooked and helps us to understand the long decade (2010–22) of particularly weak European responses to democratic decay in EU member states. To this end, I shape a narrative around the ideas of depoliticization and membership fatalism which is partial but rooted in fact. I do not argue along the formula that event A by actor B led to effect Y. Much less that the effects I am studying (the weak response of EU actors to democratic decay in member states) came about as the unavoidable consequence—the *telos*—of some prior mistakes or missed opportunities. Instead, I want to acknowledge the partial and contested character of my narrative, which recognizes history as 'a series of contingent even accidental appropriations, modifications, and transformations from the old to the new' (Bevir 2008: 267).
3. For those states already members of the EU. We will see the emergence of flagrant double standards between the intransigent violation of EU fundamental values by member states such as Hungary and Poland and the demanding conditions imposed on applicant states.
4. In this chapter, when the precise chronology of different treaties is important, I provide two dates: the first is the date a treaty was signed, the second—where relevant—is the date the treaty came into force after ratification.
5. Austria, who waited the longest of the three states in the fourth

enlargement, became a member six years after applying. In contrast, among the ten states who joined in 2004, the state who waited the least between formal application and membership was Slovenia, who waited eight years. Cyprus became a member fourteen years after making their formal application in July 1990. Romania and Bulgaria, despite applying in 1995 like Slovakia, Latvia, Estonia, and Lithuania, had to wait twelve years (until the sixth enlargement in 2007) to become EU members.

6. The latter opt-out was overturned in a referendum in June 2022, held in response to the 2022 expansion of the Russian war against Ukraine.
7. Elmar Brok et al. on behalf of the European People's Party Convention Group, 'Suggestion for amendment of Article I-59'. On file with the author, with thanks to Gráinne de Búrca.
8. See Markus Patberg's excellent work on the democratic legitimacy of leaving the EU (2020, 2021, but cf. Olsen and Rostboll 2017) and my own work on the importance of the reversibility of democratic decisions (Theuns 2021: 41).
9. The wording of this part of Article 7 in the Treaty of Lisbon is identical to the Treaty of Nice. The Treaty of Amsterdam has 'this Treaty' in the place of 'the Treaties' but is otherwise identical.
10. I critically evaluate the legitimacy of this sanction in Chapter 4.
11. As Sadurski notes, it is a curious sign of the blinkered perspective of EU officials at the time that they considered the Nice revision to strengthen the Article 7 procedure through the inclusion of the dialogue and monitoring mechanism (euphemistically referred to as the 'preventative arm' of Article 7, though it has proven to be the facilitating arm) rather than weakening it (2009, section 2).
12. For instance, Haider was forced to resign as governor of Corinthia in 1991 after he said 'in the Third Reich they had an orderly employment policy, which not even your government in Vienna can manage to bring about' during a debate in the Corinthian Parliament (BBC News 2000).
13. In exit polls, 49% of FPÖ voters cited the FPÖ's position on immigration as motivating their choice, but fully 66% cited the FPÖ's campaign against corruption and entrenched power (Mitten 2002).
14. This figure masks the true oligopolistic nature of Austrian politics in this period, as it goes up to 50 out of 54 years if we include the governments by ÖVP or SPÖ without the other in coalition, i.e. the 1966–70 'Klaus II' ÖVP government and the successive governments headed by Bruno Kreisky (SPÖ) between 1970 to 1983. And even in the short

years when Austrian politics seemed to be structured more agonistically, the reality was deeply consensual—72% of the laws passed in this period were adopted unanimously (Mitten 2002).
15. My translation. *Wir garantieren: STOP der Überfremdung!* appeared on posters used by the FPÖ in Vienna in the 1999 general elections.
16. The fourteen countries who were members prior to 2004: Austria, Belgium, Denmark, Finland, France, Germany, Greece, Republic of Ireland, Italy, Luxembourg, the Netherlands, Portugal, Spain, and Sweden.
17. I owe these examples to Gehler (2017: 210).
18. Orbán had taken Fidesz out of the Liberal International and joined the conservative European People's Party in 2000.
19. For instance, in 2021 Hungary repealed a law restricting funding for civil society organizations after the Court of Justice of the European Union ruled these were illegal and imposed penalty payments on Hungary before immediately introducing new restrictions (cf. Amnesty International 2021).

3. 'DEMOCRACY WITHOUT POLITICS': UNPACKING COMMISSION SPEECHES

1. This quote by Adam Michnik, former Polish dissident and founding editor of the *Gazeta Wyborcza*, was part of a lecture he gave in New York, reported in the *New Yorker* (9 December 1996: 52).
2. This resulted in a slightly smaller overall dataset of 136 speeches.
3. The remaining frames used in the corpus of von der Leyen's speeches are 'pluralism' (11 times), 'problem-solving', 'data protection and cyber security' (each used 6 times), 'elections', 'data protection', 'media freedom' and 'minorities' (each used 5 times).
4. In general, it is perhaps interesting to note that I found no significant difference in how Várhelyi conceptualized democracy compared to the other Commissioners whose speeches I examined.
5. Timmermans uses the rule of law frame much more often though—a total of 29 out of 41 coded references to democracy in the corpus of speeches analysed.
6. See Theuns (2017, 2019) and Sampson and Theuns (2023) about the link between promoting economic development and the 'normative' goals of EU foreign policy.

7. To be fair to the Commission, the member states as represented in the Council of the EU must take the lion's share of blame for the 'Sisyphean' ordeal the Article 7 procedure has become, not least for having sidelined the European Parliament in the Article 7 hearings against Hungary (for discussion see Pech 2020).

4. AN IMMANENT CRITIQUE OF EU TOOLS AGAINST DEMOCRATIC BACKSLIDING

1. This quality also serves to delimit its normative value: immanent critique is only persuasive if the legal or political norms emerging from a practice are considered worthwhile (for whatever reason). Where a legal or political environment is abhorrent, an immanent critique of its normative coherence is worthless. To be specific, the interest of my analysis in this chapter is premised on our broadly sharing a commitment to the fundamental values listed in Article 2 TEU, especially democracy, equality and the rule of law.
2. I do not look here at tools that do not include a possibility for sanctions, such as the Rule of Law Framework and the Rule of Law Review Cycle.
3. I do not consider the possibilities of using the Common Provisions Regulation (CPR) 2021/1060 to suspend payments (Article 97) or impose 'financial corrections' by withholding support from EU funds due (Article 104) when there is evidence of a 'serious deficiency' in the 'management and control system of a programme' using European Structural and Investment Funds (Article 2.32). Given their structural similarities, the status of this regulation in terms of its normative coherence will be substantially similar to the Rule of Law Conditionality Regulation 2020/2092. I discuss the CPR, used powerfully to withhold EU funds to Poland and Hungary, in Chapter 6.
4. This is regulated under EU Regulation 1141/2014 on the Statute and Funding of European Political Parties and European Political Foundations as amended by Regulation 2018/673 and Regulation 2019/493 (the deregistering sanctions mechanism is laid out specifically in Article 10).
5. It is possible to read Article 10.3 merely as the right to vote for representatives in the European Parliament, in which case it would not be directly relevant to democratic backsliding in EU member states.
6. The Article 7 procedure against Poland was initiated when the Commission submitted a reasoned proposal to the Council that there

was a clear risk of a serious breach of the rule of law in December 2017. The Article 7 procedure against Hungary was initiated when the European Parliament submitted a reasoned proposal to the Council in September 2018, paying special attention to the values of democracy, the rule of law, and human rights.

7. One interesting recent proposal seeks to extend the Article 7 sanction to full exclusion in the European Council and the Council via an operative reading of Article 10.2 TEU (Cotter 2022).
8. I have made a structurally similar critique of EU democracy promotion, arguing that certain anti-democratic measures in EU-negotiated free trade agreements undermine the democratic character of EU foreign policy *even if* they would have the eventual effect of democratizing the partner state (Theuns 2019; see also Theuns 2017).
9. I have used this logic elsewhere to argue that the EU foreign policy instruments such as the European Neighbourhood Policy are democratically illegitimate when they require states that are not EU members to adopt large swathes of the *acqui communautaire* to gain privileges (Theuns 2017).
10. Ascertaining where this threshold lies in practice is doubly difficult. First, different specifications of the normative standard of democratic legitimacy will result in differing standards of adequacy. Second, even where a standard has been settled, it is exceedingly difficult to measure the aggregate legitimacy of a particular state using 'checklists' due to the fact that such a standard will consist of a myriad of different constitutional, legal and political elements with complex interactions (Scheppele 2013).
11. Indeed, the idea that all political views are objectively equally valuable in the substantive sense, despite fundamental disagreement between them, is in essence an anti-pluralistic and therefore anti-democratic view (see Theuns 2021).
12. Whereas in national democracies this is ordinarily cast as 'one person one vote', that standard does not translate easily to a supranational polity such as the EU, where some member states are much more populous. The current EU treaties aim to neutrally settle respective voting weights through balancing majorities of member states and majorities of European citizens.
13. So, for instance, childless retired persons' judgements over appropriate standards for governing child-care are legitimately included in a

democratic decision-making procedure upholding the All-Subjected Principle. As are the judgements of blind persons on the appropriate limits to roadside advertising.

14. 'Ordinarily' given the possibility in some cases of opt-outs or exemptions, now a field of study in their own right as 'differentiated integration'; 'automatically' given the direct effect of EU law.
15. This is not to say that EU law does not constrain the choices of non-EU member states. Think, for instance, of those European Economic Area non-EU member states that are, in the parlance that has become popular in light of the Brexit debate, 'rule takers'. Or of those states in the EU's 'neighbourhood' who are encouraged to adopt large swathes of the EU *acquis communautaire* in order to enter into privileged trading relationships with the EU (Theuns 2019). Yet, while such dependencies may violate a prodemocratic ethos, they do not in themselves violate the EU's internal commitment to equality and democracy.
16. For a contrasting analysis of EU fundamental values that emphasizes their inherent ambiguity see Mos (2020).
17. I thank Nikolas Kirby for raising this objection and for discussion of this point.
18. Mechanisms that do not include a possibility for sanctions, such as the Rule of Law Framework and the Rule of Law Review Cycle, are not discussed. Since they do not involve a sanction, the question of the normative coherence of the sanction with the values the mechanisms purport to defend does not arise. This is not to say that the mechanisms are flawless, and I review some of their failings in Chapter 6.
19. ECJ 21 December 2019, Case C-808/18, *Commission v Hungary*.
20. ECJ 13 June 2024, Case C-123/22, *Commission v Hungary*.
21. Another example of a heavy fine imposed by the ECJ in the context of democratic backsliding was when the PiS-led Polish government was fined €1m a day for failing to suspend the activities of the Disciplinary Chamber of the Polish Supreme Court (ECJ 27 October 2021, Case C-204/21, *Commission v Poland*), a mechanism for sanctioning judges earlier ruled to undermine the principle of judicial independence and, consequently, the rule of law (ECJ 19 November 2019, joined cases C-585/18, C-624/18 and C-625/18, *A.K. and Others v Sąd Najwyższy*, *CP v Sąd Najwyższy* and *DO v Sąd Najwyższy*).
22. For discussion of Poland and Hungary's brazen (and successful) attempt to blackmail other member states and use the Council Conclusions to

try to delay the implementation and limit the scope of application of the Regulation, see Łacny (2021: 82) and Hillion (2021: 267).
23. Or indeed if budget conditionality can be imposed using other tools like the Common Provisions Regulation 2021/1060.
24. Hereafter referred to as the Authority.
25. The procedure has been started several times but has never led to a Europarty being substantively evaluated for violating European fundamental values, let alone being sanctioned (see Wolfs 2022: 215–21). Alberto Alemanno and Laurent Pech (2019) complain the Authority has been characterized by 'permanent inaction' and that one can 'reasonably doubt' its claim to be committed to discharging its mandate.
26. In Theuns (2021: 41), I argue for a distinction between descriptively democratic procedures (as, in this case, when a group of democratic states make a collective agreement) and democratically legitimate procedures, which must meet a further demand in that they do not undermine core procedural requirements of democratic government. Such a distinction allows us to identify anti- or undemocratic decisions that are nevertheless descriptively democratic in terms of the procedures of their adoption.
27. I take no position on the justifiability of such 'militant democratic' measures in truly extreme circumstances: where they are both necessary to contain anti-democratic extremists and where they threaten the continued existence of the democratic order. I return to the issue of militant democracy in Chapter 8.

5. CORRECTING EU COMPLICITY IN DEMOCRATIC BACKSLIDING

1. This argument applies equally to democratic governance in EU member states as in external affairs (Richter and Wunsch 2020; Theuns 2019).
2. This is not an exhaustive list. I focus on these three institutions as they are the most salient ones for my argument. For example, I have chosen not to analyse separately the complicity of members of the Council, member state governments, the Court of Justice of the European Union, the European Parliament overall, European parliamentary groups, parties and foundations, and more obscure institutions such as the Authority for European Political Parties and European Political Foundations, which is authorized to sanction violations of EU fundamental values such as democracy and the rule of law by European political parties and founda-

tions (see Norman 2021; Theuns 2023). Needless to say, their preclusion does not imply that I think these actors are *not* complicit in EU democratic backsliding. Specifically, the complicity of member state governments (and, by extension, the Council) is implicated in the complicity of the European Council. The case of the European Parliament is more complex. While for each of the above institutions the 'unitary actor assumption' (whereby one treats the institution as if it is a sole agent) is a useful fiction at best, analysing the European Parliament as if it were a singular actor would obscure the deep ideological divisions between Members of the European Parliament in an unhelpful way. Though I will not rehearse their arguments here, I agree with existing analyses on the complicity of certain parties in the European Parliament, especially the European People's Party (Kelemen 2020a; Meijers and van der Veer 2019; Wolkenstein 2020, 2021).

3. It may even sometimes be the case, if we consider the problem from all angles, that it is understandable—even justifiable—for an actor to continue to act or omit in ways that make them complicit in democratic backsliding. This may be the case for example if some more weighty reason like geopolitical security or interstate dependence makes the costs of intervening in democratic or rule of law backsliding too high. Where this is the case, remedial duties of reparation will outweigh duties of redress.

4. It is an important caveat that I am not writing about the legal notion of complicity and accomplices to crimes. While legal theory is useful and relevant when researching moral complicity (and I draw on legal examples in this chapter), some important aspects of legal complicity such as matters of evidence or criminal procedure have little direct bearing on moral complicity. To mark this difference, I use the term 'complicit agent' rather than 'accomplice' to denote those who bear moral complicity in wrongdoing.

5. Here I depart somewhat from Lepora and Goodin (2013); I agree with them that the 'badness of the principal wrongdoing' (104) and the 'extent of contribution' (106–08) are relevant criteria, as captured in my first two axes. However, I think it is a mistake in their otherwise very carefully argued book not to adequately weigh the cost of acting otherwise, and indeed when they discuss specific examples, they do mention the cost of acting (e.g. 116, 129). They also develop the criteria 'responsibility for the contributory act' (104–06) and 'the extent of shared

purpose' (108–09) as relevant aspects of the wrongness of complicity, but these will not feature in my analysis.

6. Nothing rests on whether my readers agree that this specific example is immoral, but for an interesting discussion of the morality of sex between professors and undergraduates, see Srinivasan (2022, Ch. 5).
7. Furthermore, it is plausible to say that I did something wrong by providing them with the keys to my apartment with the reasonable expectation that they would go there to have sex with one of their undergraduate students even in cases where they subsequently did *not* go through with the act. But that takes us away from the territory of complicity *stricto sensu*, as in such circumstances there is no primary wrong.
8. Sometimes the primary agent of wrongdoing will be less blameworthy than the complicit actor, because they have a justification or excuse that alleviates them of some or all of the responsibility for the wrongdoing. However, the primary wrong itself will always be greater than the wrong of complicity (see Lepora and Goodin 2013: 102).
9. I follow the Commission in using this nomenclature, and 'Conditionality Regulation' in short. However, the full name of the Regulation (tellingly) does not refer to the rule of law at all in its title, which describes it as a Regulation 'on a general regime of conditionality for the protection of the Union budget' (Regulation 2020/2029).
10. To use the technical philosophical term, the complicit act or omission is a *pro tanto* wrong. This means the wrongness of the complicit act or omission is not erased but may be outweighed by other considerations. This philosophical notion is often compared with *prima facie* wrongs—things that appear wrong but are in fact right all things considered. The difference is important because it is reasonable to consider that *pro tanto* wrongs still generate duties of reparation to those harmed, whereas *prima facie* wrongs do not.
11. The literature on moral responsibility is much wider still, including circumstances in which an agent may have responsibilities for alleviating a harm even where they are indirectly connected to a wrongful act that generates that harm, for instance because of an anterior promise of assistance, as in the case of military alliances, or where an agent has a remedial responsibility even though there is no identifiable wrongful act, such as may be the case if we ascribe an agent with a humanitarian duty to assist victims of a natural disaster merely because of their capacity to do so. These forms of moral responsibility fall outside of the scope of my study, however.

12. Of course, moral responsibility might not track culpability in the sense of criminal law nor liability in the sense of civil law. For a fine-grained discussion of this type of responsibility, see Miller (2004: 249–50).
13. For a more detailed analysis about different types of primary contribution to a wrong as co-principal, see Lepora and Goodin, who distinguish full joint wrongdoing, conspiracy, cooperation and collusion (2013: 37–41).
14. I do not separate out actions or omissions that may have materially contributed to democratic and rule of law regression but may have been excusable or justified. This is because, following my definition of complicity, such contributions are still *pro tanto* harms that can generate duties of reparation to those wronged by democratic backsliding, even if the complicit actions or omissions are morally acceptable all things considered.
15. The Court of Justice of the European Union is the judicial branch of the EU, comprising both the European Court of Justice, the highest court of the EU, and the General Court, which hears cases brought against EU institutions.
16. Of course, the core treaty mechanism for responding to violations of EU fundamental values, as with democratic and rule of law backsliding, is not Article 258 TFEU but Article 7 TEU. However, the Commission's roles in Article 7 sanction proceedings are more limited, it being one of three actors (alongside member states and the European Parliament) who can make 'reasoned proposals' to the Council that a member state risks violating EU fundamental values, and being one of two actors (alongside member states) who can propose to the European Council that a member state is indeed in 'serious and persistent breach' of these values (Articles 7.1 and 7.2 TEU).
17. Notice that Article 258 TFEU follows Article 17 TEU in narrowly using the term 'shall' when instructing the Commission to write a considered opinion on the perceived violation of EU law, but does subsequently give leeway to not bring the matter to Court ('may'), even in cases where a member state fails to comply with the Commission's opinion.
18. I share the deep scepticism about these instruments with many academic and legal experts. The key here, as Sonja Priebus has argued recently (2022), is that these sorts of mechanisms, which focus on trying to avoid value conflicts from arising through monitoring, dialogue and negotia-

tion, are appropriate only where noncompliance is involuntary and occasional; where noncompliance is deliberate and extensive, as has been the case with Hungary and Poland, further monitoring and dialogue will be ineffective at best.
19. Infamously, in the 2022 general election, the leading opposition candidate for Prime Minister, Péter Márki-Zay, got only five minutes to present his platform on public television.
20. I hope it is clear by this point in the book that this metaphor ought not be extended to the role of the Commission, whose efforts have been anything but Herculean and have largely failed.
21. The ECJ decision was actually pre-empted by a decision of the Hungarian Constitutional Court in July 2012, which led to Orbán referring to the decision as 'a dead dog being beaten in his head' (quoted in Kelemen 2017: 40).
22. The 'pre-Article 7' procedure the Commission created in 2014 to add steps of monitoring and dialogue before launching Article 7 proceedings against member states violating fundamental values.
23. For this reason, John Cotter has argued that Article 10 can be 'instrumentalized' to exclude antidemocratic member states from the European Council and the Council (2022).
25. Regulation 2018/0136.
24. The reason why the Regulation focused on these financial aspects, rather than democratic or rule of law deficiencies in general, was that the prevailing legal view in the Commission was that a sanctions-mechanism properly speaking—to discipline member states for violating EU fundamental sanctions—was reserved to the Article 7 procedure.
26. In full, 'The European Council shall provide the Union with the necessary impetus for its development and shall define the general political directions and priorities thereof. It shall not exercise legislative functions' (Article 15.1 TEU).
27. This could follow a similar dynamic as has been argued to galvanize member state support for budget conditionality (Blauberger and Sedelmeier 2024: 14–19).
28. It is extremely difficult to get precise figures for these suspensions as neither they nor the legal rationales are systematically provided by the Commission (Scheppele and Morijn 2023: 43–4).
29. The cases are pending at the time of writing as *T-530/22, T-531/22, T-532/22 and T-533/22 European association of judges v Council and*

T-116/23 MEDEL and others v Commission. I owe the references to Scheppele and Morijn (2023: 42).

30. I borrow the idiom of 'horse-trading' in this context from a quote by MEP Daniel Freund, reported by Reuters. The full line is 'this kind of horse-trading—EU money in exchange for a veto—must not be allowed in the EU' (Noestlinger 2024).

6. CONTAINING AUTOCRACY IN THE EU

1. This aphorism is generally attributed to Charles Martin of Burgundy (1433–77) but sometimes to Willem Frederik van Oranje-Nassau (1772–1843). In English it reads, 'there is no need to hope in order to act nor to succeed in order to persevere' (my translation).
2. Of course, ultimately, the United States was involved in many so-called 'proxy wars' with the USSR over the course of the Cold War, as well as more direct confrontations, such as the Cuban Missile Crisis in 1962. However, the strategy of containment was generally understood to be avoiding direct military conflict with communist states.
3. These are neither exhaustive nor mutually exclusive categories.
4. This concern has become all the more urgent with the Dutch coalition that was sworn in on 2 July 2024, led by the far-right Freedom Party (PVV), whose programme included anti-constitutional measures such as banning mosques and the Qur'an, although to persuade the three other parties in government to form this coalition, the PVV stepped away from their baldest anti-constitutional proposals, putting them 'on ice' ('in de ijskast').
5. It also plays into the hands of the discursive strategy of 'whataboutism' whereby violators of fundamental values try to point to supposedly analogous examples in other member states. This is framed in the context of specific piecemeal regressions, each in themselves arguably not sufficient cause for panic, that when put together in a collection of worst practices amount to the wholesale and systemic degradation of democratic government, a technique that has been called 'salami slicing' (Haggard and Kaufmann 2021).
6. I variously refer to such a state as a 'competitive authoritarian' state, an 'authoritarian' state, and an 'autocratic' state. Clearly, determining threshold conditions of precisely when a backsliding state switches from being a democracy to no longer being a democracy is going to be difficult

7. Both Article 7.1 and 7.2 TEU require consent of the European Parliament, defined in Article 354 of the Treaty on the Functioning of the European Union as two-thirds of votes cast representing at least an absolute majority of members.
8. These are the best-known tools developed as forms of soft legal containment, but they are not the only ones, though they all suffer from similar flaws. For completeness, the interested reader can look up the Justice Scoreboard created by the Commission in 2013 (Jakab and Kirschmair 2021), the Council's Annual Rule of Law Dialogue set up in 2014 (Oliver and Stefanelli 2016), and the expanded European Semester, revised by the Commission in 2018 (Pech 2021).
9. The only time the Rule of Law Framework has been invoked was against Poland in January 2016 (Kochenov and Pech 2016).
10. Before one accuses Kelemen of hyperbole, note that one of the motivations for the creation of the Council's Annual Rule of Law Dialogue was to try to dissuade the Commission from pursuing the new 'pre-Article 7' Rule of Law Framework (Kochenov and Pech 2015). As such, things are even worse than he puts it, in that there is a dialogue (the Annual Rule of Law Dialogue) to prevent a dialogue (the Rule of Law Framework) before the dialogue (set out in Article 7.1 TEU) before the dialogue (set out in Article 7.2 TEU) before sanctions might be imposed (in Article 7.3 TEU).
11. Denmark's score is 0.90 in the 2023 World Justice Project Rule of Law Index (1.0 is theoretically the top score) while Hungary's is 0.51.
12. Denmark's score is 0.883 in the 2024 V-Dem Liberal Democracy Index (1.0 is theoretically the top score) while Hungary's is 0.325.
13. What is essential in pursuing such 'creative' application of the current legal framework is that EU actors remain within the letter and the ultimate spirit of the relevant legal provisions. The letter of the law frequently provides room for interpretation. Provisions can be interpreted in a narrow way or more broadly. When deciding between such narrow and broad interpretations, I advocate that one must pay attention to the ultimate *ratio juris* of the provision, which must include, first and foremost, respect for the EU's fundamental values as listed in Article 2 TEU. This is why, for instance, I judge the sanction listed in Article

7 TEU to be illegitimate (qua in conflict with democratic values) while I argue below for the exclusion of an autocratic government from the rotating presidency of the Council. It is vital in such considerations that hard legal containment stays within the letter of the law, else the EU itself can be accused of 'undemocratic liberalism' (Mudde 2021). For related critiques on the anti-democratic nature of the EU's recent use of emergency politics, see Kreuder-Sonnen (2018), White (2019) and Auer (2022).

14. Admittedly there is quite a bit of argumentative lifting done by the 'other things equal' condition. In the messy real world, other things are rarely equal. It may be that sometimes compromises with the principle of maximal coherent exclusion are justified on the grounds that they are necessary to secure some other greater good. One might reasonably ask, to take a recent controversy as a concrete example, what sorts of compromises might be sought with Hungary to secure EU aid to Ukraine. We should be wary of overly concessive or self-defeating attitudes to such compromises, however. In the case of aid to Ukraine, a multilateral agreement of member states excluding Hungary could have achieved the same level of funding support as that agreed in the 'Ukraine Facility' at the European Council meeting in February 2024, without requiring any concessions to Viktor Orbán.

15. Compatibility with EU law is of course one of the tests of compliance with Article 2 fundamental values given the inclusion in that article of the value of the rule of law (see van den Brink 2023).

16. Even these specific concerns about a Hungarian presidency of the Council are not new. Some have argued that the previous Hungarian presidency of the Council, in the first half of 2011, gave it political cover with the Barroso Commission in the crucial early stage of democratic regression where Fidesz brought Hungarian media to heel and rewrote the Hungarian basic law (Batory 2013: 237).

17. Council Decision (EU) 2016/1316 of 26 July 2016 set out this agenda, with the Hungarian presidency (July–December 2024) cooperating with the Belgian and Spanish presidencies before it.

18. See Council Decision (EU) 2016/1316 of 26 July 2016 (van den Brink 2023: 14).

19. A court case that is relevant to cite is the French Constitutional Court's 1978 decision which held that the individualization of criminal law penalties was compatible with Article 6 of the Declaration of the Rights of

Man and of the Citizen, the foundational human rights document and—in French law—constitutional provision codifying equality before the law (*Décision n° 78–97 DC du 27 juillet 1978*).

20. 'Numerous shortcomings already became clear in the period running up to the vote, from the biased media through to the all-pervasive linkage of state and party' (quoted in OSCE 2022).
21. My translation. The original post, in Italian, reads as follows: 'Bravo Viktor! Da solo contro tutti, attaccato dai sinistri fanatici del pensiero unico, minacciato da chi vorrebbe cancellare le radici giudaico-cristiane dell'Europa, denigrato da chi vorrebbe sradicare i valori legati a famiglia, sicurezza, merito, sviluppo, solidarietà, sovranità e libertà, hai vinto anche stavolta grazie a quello che manca agli altri: l'amore e il consenso della gente. Forza Viktor, onore al libero Popolo ungherese'. Available at: https://www.facebook.com/salviniofficial/posts/507424820951772
22. For example, to take only some of the main anglophone Hungarian news outlets, see About Hungary 2022, Daily News 2022, Hungary Today 2022.
23. For instance, she used her official Twitter/X account (@EP_President) to congratulate Joe Biden in January 2021, Alexander Stubb in February 2023, and Petteri Orpo in April 2023. These and other congratulatory tweets could be accessed at the time of writing by searching 'congratulations (from: EP_President)' in the Twitter/X search bar.
24. At the time I am writing this in early July 2024, it is unclear how many groups this will be in the tenth European Parliament (2024–9). The most recent reporting is that Fidesz has succeeded in forming a group called 'Patriots for Europe' with Czech populists Action of Dissatisfied Citizens and the Austrian far-right Freedom Party of Austria. By the time this book is published, it will be clear if this group has managed to consolidate populist radical right-wing MEPs or if it has added yet another group to the mix, thereby furthering populist radical-right fragmentation in the European Parliament.
25. Given the lack of opposition to the admission of Reconquête!—the far-right party of French firebrand Eric Zemmour—in February 2023, this opposition seems to be more a matter of grandstanding and, in the case of Sweden, Hungarian foot-dragging on Sweden's NATO prospects, than a matter of principle.

7. CULTIVATING PLURALIST DEMOCRACY IN EUROPE

1. More generally, these sorts of judgements fall into the non-ideal approach that has been called 'real-world political philosophy' (Wolff 2015), which is particularly useful for addressing normative questions regarding EU institutions (Zala et al. 2020).
2. 'GONGO-ization' refers to the process whereby a non-governmental organization (NGO) becomes a 'government-organized' non-governmental organization (GONGO; Hasmath, Hildebrandt and Hsu 2019).
3. This conception of politics as an arena is not only 'mainstream' but also 'malestream': 'to insist that the political is synonymous with the public sphere is to exclude from political analysis the private arena within which much of women's oppression, subordination and, indeed, resistance occurs' (Hay 2002: 71).
4. In democratic theory, this standard is known as the 'All-Subjected Principle' (Beckman 2022).
5. The term 'non-ideal theory' is used here to denote a normativity focused on addressing injustices incrementally rather than theorizing a utopian end-state. Non-ideal theory is introduced in Chapter 1 (see also Zala et al. 2020).
6. This is different from the idea that aesthetic judgements are relative, which is sometimes invoked to argue that disagreements on the relative merit of, say, Rosa Bonheur and Alfred Sisley cannot be settled—*de gustibus et coloribus non est disputandum* ('in matters of taste and colour, there can be no dispute'). Actually, the argument I make here for pluralist democracy is at odds with relativism in that the philosophical commitment to treating people as equal sources of political value is ultimately a universalist claim (for an argument that philosophical relativism can ground a commitment to democracy, see Invernizzi Accetti 2015).
7. I am deliberately agnostic here about whether this would be best realized through direct democracy, representative democracy, or some other procedure like selection by lottery.
8. This demand of political equality ought not be confused with what one might call an 'equal value claim'—the idea that different and contrasting political and ideological views have, as a matter of normative fact, equal value.
9. To be clear, I do not think it is necessary to endorse either Habermas' or Mouffe's democratic political theory to subscribe to the pluralist

conception of democracy. Indeed, pluralism—while occasionally sidelined by democratic actors (cf. Chapter 3 for an argument as to the conception of democracy used by EU Commissioners)—is a feature of most approaches to democratic theory, from Robert Dahl's (1969) emphasis on the importance of political opposition for democracy to John Dryzek's (2002) insistence that democratic deliberation is 'authentic' only when it includes oppositional public spheres which foster pluralistic and critical democratic processes.

10. Pellegrini was Prime Minister at the time of these events, and at the time of writing is President of Slovakia. He founded Hlas after splitting from Smer in 2020, which now governs in a coalition with Smer and the far-right Slovak National Party (SNS).
11. Though they did outperform the last pre-election polls by a couple of percentage points, the Moscow visit was not enough to change the outcome of the election, with Smer losing 10% of their vote-share compared with the 2016 general election.
12. The empirical data and methods that have become standard in the political science and international relations literature that attempt these sorts of research questions seriously also fall well outside of the scope of the political theory methods used in this book.
13. Using the language of normative duties and reparations does not mean I commit to the ideal-theoretical notion that the demands of justice are objective or that they 'trump' political considerations. I rather use these terms in line with my non-ideal and practice-dependent approach to normativity. In other words, I do not claim here that duties (of redress and reparation) for complicity in the harms of democratic backsliding are owed to those harmed through the application of some abstract external moral calculation, but rather that they are political consequences of European actors' own stated commitment to *inter alia* democracy and the rule of law.
14. The law was adopted by 464 votes in favour to 92 against and 65 abstentions. It prohibits member states from pressuring journalists to reveal their sources, sets new standards of transparency for the financing of public and private media, introduces proportionality standards in public media advertising expenditure, and restricts large social media platforms' freedom to restrict or delete content posted by independent media sources.
15. This was part of the headline of an article reporting on the 'Pact of Free

Cities', which was signed by the opposition mayors of Budapest, Warsaw, Prague and Bratislava in 2019 (Walker 2019). In a 2023 media interview, Gergely Karácsony, the opposition mayor of Budapest, makes the link between EU budget conditionality and reduced funding for the municipality clear: 'We have a large stake in the operational programmes that are affected by the EU's freezing of funds to Hungary [due to the rule of law situation and corruption issues]' (Karácsony and Lakner 2023).

16. This was a common theme between investigative journalists, NGOs, civil society representatives and opposition politicians meeting with the European Parliament's Committee on Budget Control, for example, which sent a delegation to Budapest to review the application of the Rule of Law Conditionality Regulation and Hungary's capacity to appropriately manage funding currently withheld under the Resilience and Recovery Facility (see Hohlmeier et al. 2023).

17. On 18 December 2023, the European Chief Prosecutor highlighted concerns over legal changes proposed by Fico's government, affecting laws ranging from the Criminal Procedure Code to whistleblower protection, which could undermine the EU budget's protection. Citing the Conditionality Regulation, the European Chief Prosecutor indicated these amendments would disrupt the European Public Prosecutor's Office operations, reducing its ability to tackle fraud against the EU's financial interests (European Public Prosecutor's Office 2023).

18. According to calculations by the municipality, the money Budapest receives from EU resources has dropped by over 40%, from around 340 billion forints (approximately €920 million) in the 2014–22 financial cycle to around 200 billion forints in the 2021–7 cycle (Leitner 2023).

19. The original phrase, from a social media post posted on 15 February 2022, reads 'kiemelkedően fontos, hogy a kormány felelőtlensége miatt esetlegesen visszatartott források közvetlenül megérkezhessenek a végső kedvezményezettekhez' (Cseh 2022). Thanks to Miklós Zala for his help with the translation.

20. In an evocative example of such rhetoric, Viktor Orbán accused Brussels of being a 'bad contemporary parody' of the Soviet Union during a 2023 speech commemorating the 1956 Hungarian insurrection against Soviet dominance (Hülsemann 2023).

21. The 2023 Regimes of the World classification, based on V-Dem data, for example, has Slovakia as one of the least democratic electoral democracies, hovering just four places above the grey zone between the electoral democracy and electoral autocracy regime types (Nord et al. 2024: 17).
22. At least, not in terms of their governance; the rhetoric of FPÖ leaders like Jörg Haider was in conflict with fundamental values.
23. There is a separate question as to the legal rules surrounding direct support of civil society actors and political parties, at least by EU actors. An important obstacle is the proportion of direct management of EU funds by the European Commission. This is currently around a fifth, with the rest being co-administered with member states in accordance with a principle of partnership. Increasing this figure substantially would require changes to the Common Provisions Regulation and the Multiannual Financial Framework. One way to approach direct support for pro-democratic actors would be via EU-wide funding instruments such as the €1.5 billion Citizens, Equality, Rights and Values programme, which is part of the 2021–7 Multiannual Financial Framework (MFF). This does mean negotiating with backsliding states, as the MFF requires unanimity (Article 312 TFEU). A different route would be to use enhanced cooperation under Article 20 TEU and Articles 326–34 TFEU to create instruments that member states backsliding on democracy and the rule of law have no say in.
24. It is less controversial—though no less urgent—for a European political party to provide direct support to a member party in a backsliding state at the national level, or for a national government to provide grant support to a human rights organization, to give two examples.
25. Along with Pellegrini's Hlas, Smer was suspended for forming a coalition with the far-right Slovak National Party led by Andrej Danko (see Jochecová, Wax and Barigazzi 2023).

8. *QUO VADIS?* DEMOCRACY PROTECTION OR DISSOCIATION

1. This phrase can be found in a letter dated 28 November 1770, written by Voltaire to Frederick II, who was styled King in Prussia (König in Preußen) at the time. In English it reads 'doubt is not pleasant, but certainty is ridiculous' (my translation).
2. Disenfranchisement in the Council via the sanction described in Article

7 TEU is the main legal response to values violations that arose from my analysis in Chapter 4, so I focus on it here. However, the argument I make also applies to other existing militant sanctions such as the deregistration of European political parties and foundations. It also applies to militant proposals, such as the recent proposal by John Cotter to exclude autocratic member states from both the European Council and the Council of the European Union through an 'operative' interpretation of Article 10 TEU (Cotter 2022).

3. The terms militant democratic 'paradox' or 'democratic paradox' are used in different ways. Most importantly, they are also used to refer to the possibility of democratic polities abandoning democratic politics via democratic procedures. I limit myself here to the values conflict between militant measures and democratic values.
4. The relevant question here is the justification of democracy promotion and democracy support in international affairs.
5. I will not further address the question of the 'all things considered' justifiability of militant democracy. My core claim in this chapter is that militant democrats supporting militant responses when the existential threat and necessity conditions are met should nevertheless oppose the EU's use of militant democratic tools. Those like Invernizzi Accetti and Zuckerman (2017), who oppose militant democratic tools even in those contexts, have even stronger reasons to reject the EU's use of militant measures like Article 7 disenfranchisement in the Council.
6. In previous work, I have referred to this as the demand that democratic processes are 'iterative' (Theuns 2021: 41). I differ from Rijpkema, though, in that I think decisions by democratic majorities to undermine this iterative character (i.e. by abolishing democratic government), while they cannot be democratically legitimate, may be descriptively democratic.
7. In other words, I am not endorsing the militant democratic position. Rather, the aim is to show that even if militant democracy is correct, and anti-democratic measures are justifiable under 'existential' circumstances, militant measures like Article 7 are still illegitimate. If we were to take a more principled position against the justifiability of anti-democratic actions to defend democracy, then my argument is all the stronger. Expulsion would be warranted when faced with a frankly autocratic state simply because it would be the only response coherent with democratic values that would neutralize the threat. In other words, the

question of whether stronger militant measures could be justified in exceptional circumstances would not even arise.

8. Militant democratic theory takes democratic legitimacy and democratic equality as fundamental *pro tanto* values that can only be thwarted for their own sake—to ensure that a polity maintains its character as democratic in light of an existential threat. Theorists who prioritize a different fundamental value such as, for instance, egalitarian distributive justice or republican non-domination, might baulk at the normative costs of expelling an autocratic member state. I cannot resolve disagreement on such bed-rock normative principles here, but note that my key claim—that guaranteeing the democratic legitimacy of the EU requires the possibility of recourse to an expulsion mechanism—is not vulnerable to such disagreements.

9. Original: 'Wir können nicht akzeptieren, dass die Grundwerte der Europäischen Union massiv verletzt werden. Wer wie Ungarn Zäune gegen Kriegsflüchtlinge baut oder wer die Pressefreiheit und die Unabhängigkeit der Justiz verletzt, der sollte vorübergehend oder notfalls für immer aus der EU ausgeschlossen werden'.

10. Original: 'Kun je een begroting maken via een intergouvernementeel verdrag of kun je nu een Europese Unie oprichten zonder Hongarije en Polen?'

11. I discuss an interesting though marginal exception that arose in debates over the European Convention in Chapter 2.

12. This view presupposes a vision of the EU polity focused more on the voluntarism of Articles 49 and 50 regarding, respectively, accession to and withdrawal from the Union, than on the EU as an 'ever closer union' from the preamble to the TEU and Article 1. In other words, it presupposes that it is currently descriptively more accurate to consider the EU to be a somewhat more intergovernmental Union than a federalist or post-national one (Bellamy 2019: 83–9).

13. The Orbán-nominated Commissioner for Neighbourhood and Enlargement, Olivér Várhelyi, was accused of deliberately trying to circumvent and undermine democratic and rule of law reforms in EU accession countries allied to Hungary, particularly Serbia, leading the European Parliament to call for an independent investigation into possible breaches of the Code of Conduct for the Members of the Commission (European Parliament 2023: clause 124).

14. Whether and when this may be the case is for more empirically tooled

colleagues to try to ascertain, but the high levels of support for EU membership in countries that are undergoing or have recently gone through cycles of democratic decline would speak to the plausibility of an effect of this kind (Clancy 2022; cf. De Búrca 2022: 30).

15. Given this view of the EU, it could be asked whether member states could not volunteer to be subjected without representation. For instance, one may wonder whether a member state sanctioned under Article 7 but deciding not to trigger Article 50 does not 'voluntarily' remain subject to the treaties given their Article 50 option to withdraw. However, the voluntarism of the EU as an association (i.e. member states are members voluntarily and can leave) does not mean they could legitimately disenfranchise themselves, or accept their subjection. Just as vote-selling may be voluntary but cannot be democratic, so too for subjection to EU law without the right to vote in the Council (cf. Olsen 2023: 325).

16. See, centrally, Article 20 TFEU which makes EU citizenship derivative to the citizenship of a member state. For discussion, see van den Brink and Kochenov (2019).

17. In, for example, the *Kaur*, *Grzelczyk* and *Zambrano* decisions of the European Court of Justice (see van den Brink and Kochenov 2019: 1372–3).

18. Notwithstanding Christophe Hillion's controversial suggestion that the 'continued and deliberate defiance of the core principles of [EU] membership' by backsliding states *amounts* to those states notifying the Council of its intention to withdraw from the EU under Article 50 TEU (Hillion 2020; cf. Scholtes 2020; see also Athanassiou 2009).

19. This extends beyond Council law-making to, for instance, the appointment of European Commissioners (though the fact these must be approved by the European Parliament acts as a check, as we saw with the rejection of Hungarian nominee László Trócsányi in September 2019).

BIBLIOGRAPHY

Abizadeh, A. (2008). 'Democratic theory and border coercion: No right to unilaterally control your own borders'. *Political Theory*, 36(1), 37–65.

About Hungary (2022). 'Ursula von der Leyen congratulates PM Orbán on re-election'. Available at: https://abouthungary.hu/news-in-brief/ursula-von-der-leyen-congratulates-pm-orban-on-re-election (last accessed 17/05/2024)

Ahtisaari, M., Frowein, J., & Oreja, M. (2001). 'Report on the Austrian government's commitment to the common European values, in particular concerning the rights of minorities, refugees and immigrants, and the evolution of the political nature of the FPÖ', *International Legal Materials*, 40(1), 102–23.

Akcja Demokracja & aHang Hungary (2020). 'There is nothing to cheer about today'. Available at: https://www.akcjademokracja.pl/akcja-demokracja-ahang-hungary-there-is-nothing-to-cheer-about-today/ (last accessed 17/05/2024)

Alemanno, A. & Chamon, M. (2020). 'To save the rule of law you must apparently break it'. *Verfassungsblog*. Available at: https://verfassungsblog.de/to-save-the-rule-of-law-you-must-apparently-break-it/ (last accessed 17/05/2024)

Alemanno, A. & Pech, L. (2019). 'Holding European political parties accountable: Testing the horizontal EU values compliance mechanism'. *Verfassungsblog*. Available at: https://verfassungsblog.de/holding-european-political-parties-accountable-testing-the-horizontal-eu-values-compliance-mechanism/ (last accessed 17/05/2024)

Amnesty International (2021). 'Hungary repeals controversial laws restricting the right to association but concerns remain'. Available at: http://www.amnesty.org/en/documents/eur27/4526/2021/en/ (last accessed 17/05/2024)

BIBLIOGRAPHY

Andor, L. (2019). 'Fifteen years of convergence: East-West imbalance and what the EU should do about it'. *Intereconomics*, 54(1), 18–23.

Arendt, H. (1951). *The Burden of Our Time*. London: Secker & Warburg.

Athanassiou, P. (2009). 'Withdrawal and expulsion from the EU and EMU: Some reflections'. *ECB Legal Working Paper Series* (No. 10). Available at: www.ecb.europa.eu/pub/pdf/scplps/ecblwp10.pdf (last accessed 17/05/2024)

Auer, S. (2022). *European Disunion: Democracy, Sovereignty and the Politics of Emergency*. London & Oxford: Hurst Publishers and Oxford University Press.

Bacevich, A.J. (2013). *The New American Militarism: How Americans are Seduced by War*. Oxford: Oxford University Press.

Badano, G. & Nuti, A. (2024). *Politicizing Political Liberalism: On the Containment of Illiberal and Antidemocratic Views*. Oxford: Oxford University Press.

Bánkuti, M., Halmai, G., & Scheppele, K.L. (2012). 'Disabling the constitution'. *Journal of Democracy*, 23(3), 138–46.

Bapat, N.A., Heinrich, T., Kobayashi, Y., & Morgan, T.C. (2013). 'Determinants of sanctions effectiveness: Sensitivity analysis using new data'. *International Interactions*, 39(1), 79–98.

Bárd, P. (2018). 'The rule of law and academic freedom or the lack of it in Hungary'. *European Political Science*, 19(1), 87–96.

Bárd, P. & Kochenov, D.V. (2021). 'War as a pretext to wave the rule of law goodbye? The case for an EU constitutional awakening'. *European Law Journal*, 27(1–3), 39–49.

Bátorfy, A. & Urbán, Á. (2020). 'State advertising as an instrument of transformation of the media market in Hungary'. *East European Politics*, 36(1), 44–65.

Batory, A. (2013). 'Uploading as political strategy: The European Parliament and the Hungarian media law debate'. *East European Politics*, 30(2), 230–45.

——— (2016). 'Defying the Commission: Creative compliance and respect for the rule of law in the EU'. *Public Administration*, 94(3), 685–99.

BBC News (2000). 'Haider in context: Nazi employment policies'. Available at: http://news.bbc.co.uk/1/hi/639385.stm (last accessed 02/08/2024)

Beckman, L. (2009). *The Frontiers of Democracy: The Right to Vote and Its Limits*. Basingstoke: Springer.

——— (2014). 'The subjects of collectively binding decisions: Democratic inclusion and extraterritorial law'. *Ratio Juris*, 27(2), 252–70.

——— (2022). *The Boundaries of Democracy: A Theory of Inclusion*. Abingdon: Routledge.

BIBLIOGRAPHY

Beetz, J.P. (2023). 'Saving popular sovereignty from a slow death in the European Union'. *JCMS: Journal of Common Market Studies*, 62(2), 508–24.

Bélanger, M-È. & Wunsch, N. (2022). 'From cohesion to contagion? Populist radical right contestation of EU enlargement'. *JCMS: Journal of Common Market Studies*, 60(3), 653–72.

Bellamy, R. (2019). *A Republican Europe of States: Cosmopolitanism, Intergovernmentalism and Democracy in the EU*. Oxford: Oxford University Press.

Bellamy, R. & Kröger, S. (2021). 'Countering democratic backsliding by EU member states: Constitutional pluralism and "value" differentiated integration'. *Swiss Political Science Review*, 27(3), 619–36.

Bennett, C. (2016). 'Penal disenfranchisement'. *Criminal Law and Philosophy*, 10(3), 411–25.

Bermeo, N. (2016). 'On democratic backsliding'. *Journal of Democracy*, 27(1), 5–19.

Bevir, M. (2008). 'What is genealogy?' *Journal of the Philosophy of History*, 2(3), 263–75.

Blauberger, M. & Kelemen, R.D. (2017). 'Can courts rescue national democracy? Judicial safeguards against democratic backsliding in the EU'. *Journal of European Public Policy*, 24(3), 321–36.

Blauberger, M. & Sedelmeier, U. (2024). 'Sanctioning democratic backsliding in the European Union: Transnational salience, negative intergovernmental spillover, and policy change'. *Journal of European Public Policy*, 1–27, online first.

Boix, C. & Stokes, S.C. (2003). 'Endogenous democratization'. *World Politics*, 55(4), 517–49.

Bonello Ghio, R., Nasreddin, D., & The Daphne Caruana Galizia Foundation. (2022). 'Shutting out criticism: How SLAPPs pose a threat to European democracy'. In: *The Coalition Against SLAPPs in Europe (CASE)*. Available at: https://www.the-case.eu/wp-content/uploads/2023/04/CASEreportSLAPPsEurope.pdf (last accessed 17/05/2024)

Bourne, A.K. (2012). 'The proscription of political parties and militant democracy'. *Journal of Comparative Law*, 7, 196–213.

Boyce, B. (1993). 'The democratic deficit in the European Community'. *Parliamentary Affairs*, 46(4), 458–78.

Breeze, R. (2018). '"Enemies of the people": Populist performances in the Daily Mail reporting of the Article 50 case'. *Discourse, Context & Media*, 25, 60–7.

Brincat, E. (2023). '"We need a miracle": Matthew Caruana Galizia on defending libel case against mum'. *Times of Malta*. Available at: https://timesofmalta.com/article/we-need-miracle-matthew-caruana-galizia-defending-libel-case-mum.1027396 (last accessed 17/05/2024)

Buchanan, A. (2002). 'Political legitimacy and democracy'. *Ethics*, 112(4), 689–719.

BIBLIOGRAPHY

Burnham, P. (2001). 'New Labour and the politics of depoliticisation'. *The British Journal of Politics & International Relations*, 3(2), 127–49.

Capoccia, G. (2013). 'Militant democracy: The institutional bases of democratic self-preservation'. *Annual Review of Law and Social Science*, 9, 207–26.

Čepo, D. (2021). 'Structural weaknesses and the role of the dominant political party: Democratic backsliding in Croatia since EU accession'. In: Kapidžić, D. & Stojarová, V. (eds). *Illiberal Politics in Southeast Europe*. Abingdon: Routledge, 137–55.

Chamon, M. (2020). 'Re-establishing the EU: Dissolution, withdrawal or succession'. *EU Law Live*, 32, 2–6.

Chamon, M. & Theuns, T. (2021). 'Dissociation through enhanced cooperation or collective withdrawal'. *Verfassungsblog*. Available at: https://verfassungsblog.de/resisting-membership-fatalism/ (last accessed 17/05/2024)

Chiru, M. & Wunsch, N. (2021). 'Democratic backsliding as a catalyst for polity-based contestation? Populist radical right cooperation in the European Parliament'. *Journal of European Public Policy*, 30(1), 64–83.

Cholbi, M.J. (2002). 'A felon's right to vote'. *Law and Philosophy*, 21(4–5), 543–65.

Christiano, T. (2008). *The Constitution of Equality*. Oxford: Oxford University Press.

Cianetti, L. & Hanley, S. (2021). 'The end of the backsliding paradigm'. *Journal of Democracy*, 32(1), 66–80.

Clancy L. (2022). 'Despite recent political clashes, most people in Poland and Hungary see the EU favourably'. *Pew Research Center*. Available at: https://www.pewresearch.org/short-reads/2022/10/18/despite-recent-political-clashes-most-people-in-poland-and-hungary-see-the-eu-favorably/ (last accessed 17/05/2024)

Commissie Rechtsstatelijkheid in Verkiezingsprogramma's (2023). 'De Partijprogramma's voor de Verkiezingen 2023 Rechtsstatelijk?' Available at: https://www.advocatenorde.nl/document/20231106-nova-rapport-cie-rechtsstatelijkheid-in-verkiezingsprogrammas-website (last accessed 17/05/2024)

Constitutional Council (n.d.). 'Decision No. 78–97 DC of July 27, 1978'. Available at: https://www.conseil-constitutionnel.fr/decision/1978/7897DC.htm (last accessed 17/05/2024)

Cotter, J. (2022). 'To everything there is a season: Instrumentalising Article 10 TEU to exclude undemocratic member state representatives from the European Council and the Council'. *European Law Review*, 47(1), 69–84.

Council of the European Union (2015). *Handbook of the Presidency of the*

Council of the European Union. Available at: https://ecer.minbuza.nl/documents/20142/1066448/Presidencyhandbook+en.pdf/ca923b28-8553-33cd-1d97-f7b1e854356e?t=1545240508252 (last accessed 17/05/2024)

——— (2018). *Proposal for a Regulation of the European Parliament and of the Council on the Protection of the Union's Budget in Case of Generalised Deficiencies as Regards the Rule of Law in the Member States 2018/0136*. Available at: https://data.consilium.europa.eu/doc/document/ST-13593-2018-INIT/en/pdf (last accessed 17/05/2024)

Crespy, A. (2010). 'When "Bolkestein" is trapped by the French anti-liberal discourse: A discursive-institutionalist account of preference formation in the realm of European Union multi-level politics'. *Journal of European Public Policy*, 17(8), 1253–70.

Cseh, K. (2022). 'Az Európai Parlament elfogadta a Cseh-jelentést, magyar kezdeményezésre juthatnak a városok közvetlenül európai uniós pénzekhez'. *Facebook*. Available at: https://www.facebook.com/csehkatalin.momentum/posts/493411358816661 (last accessed 17/05/2024)

Dahl, R.A. (1969). 'Political opposition in western democracies'. In: Blondel, J. (ed.). *Comparative Government: A Reader*. London: Macmillan Education, 229–34.

——— (1994). 'A democratic dilemma: System effectiveness versus citizen participation'. *Political Science Quarterly*, 109(1), 23–34.

Daily News (2022). 'Congratulations to Orbán from Moscow and Brussels'. Available at: https://dailynewshungary.com/congratulations-to-orban-from-moscow-and-brussels/ (last accessed 17/05/2024)

Deibert, R.J. (2023). 'The autocrat in your iPhone: How mercenary spyware threatens democracy'. *Foreign Affairs*, 102, 72–88.

De Jongh, M. & Theuns, T. (2017). 'Democratic legitimacy, desirability and deficit in EU governance'. *Journal of Contemporary European Research*, 13(3), 1284–300.

Deibert, R.J. (2023). 'The autocrat in your iPhone: How mercenary spyware threatens democracy'. *Foreign Affairs*, 102, 72–88.

De Ville, F. & Orbie, J. (2014). 'The European Commission's neoliberal trade discourse since the crisis: Legitimizing continuity through subtle discursive change'. *The British Journal of Politics and International Relations*, 16(1), 149–67.

Dietrich, S. (2013). 'Bypass or engage? Explaining donor delivery tactics in foreign aid allocation'. *International Studies Quarterly*, 57(4), 698–712.

Dimitrova, A.L. (2022). 'Battered by geopolitical winds, Bulgaria struggles to restart much needed reforms'. *JCMS: Journal of Common Market Studies*, 60(1), 88–100.

Dryzek, J.S. (2002). *Deliberative Democracy and Beyond: Liberals, Critics, Contestations*. Oxford: Oxford University Press.

BIBLIOGRAPHY

Enyedi, Z. (2018). 'Democratic backsliding and academic freedom in Hungary'. *Perspectives on Politics*, 16(4), 1067–74.

Erman, E. & Möller, N. (2015). 'What distinguishes the practice-dependent approach to justice? *Philosophy & Social Criticism*, 42(1), 3–23.

Euractiv (2022). 'EU democratic leaders turn their back on Orbán'. Available at: https://www.euractiv.com/section/politics/news/eu-democratic-leaders-turn-their-back-on-orban/ (last accessed 17/05/2024)

Euronews (2021). '"There will be no Polexit": Kaczynski says Poland's future is in the EU'. Available at: https://www.euronews.com/2021/09/15/there-will-be-no-polexit-kaczynski-says-poland-s-future-is-in-eu (last accessed 17/05/2024)

European Commission (2013). 'European Commission closes infringement procedure on forced retirement of Hungarian judges'. Available at: https://ec.europa.eu/commission/presscorner/detail/EL/IP_13_1112 (last accessed 17/05/2024)

——— (2014). 'European Commission presents a framework to safeguard the rule of law in the European Union'. Available at: https://ec.europa.eu/commission/presscorner/detail/en/IP_14_237 (last accessed 17/05/2024)

——— (2015). 'Hungary: No systemic threat to democracy, says Commission, but concerns remain'. Available at: https://www.europarl.europa.eu/news/en/press-room/20151201IPR05554/hungary-no-systemic-threat-to-democracy-says-commission-but-concerns-remain (last accessed 17/05/2024)

——— (2018). *Code of Conduct for the Members of the European Commission*. Available at: https://eur-lex.europa.eu/legal-content/EN/TXT/PDF/?uri=CELEX:32018D0221(02) (last accessed 17/05/2024)

——— (2022). 'The Commission announces 100 cities participating in the EU Mission for climate-neutral and smart cities by 2030'. Available at: https://ec.europa.eu/commission/presscorner/detail/en/IP_22_2591 (last accessed 17/05/2024)

——— (2024a). *Communication from the Commission to the European Parliament, the Council, the European Economic and Social Committee and the Committee of the Regions: 2023 Rule of Law Report*. Available at: https://eur-lex.europa.eu/legal-content/EN/TXT/HTML/?uri=CELEX:52023DC0800 (last access 02/08/2024)

——— (2024b). 'Poland's efforts to restore rule of law pave the way for accessing up to €137 billion in EU funds'. Available at: https://ec.europa.eu/commission/presscorner/detail/en/ip_24_1222 (last accessed 17/05/2024)

European Council (2020). 'European Council meeting (10 and 11 December

BIBLIOGRAPHY

2020)—Conclusions'. Available at: https://www.consilium.europa.eu/media/47296/1011-12-20-euco-conclusions-en.pdf (last accessed 17/05/2024)

European Parliament (2000). *Charter of Fundamental Rights of the European Union (2000/C 364/01)*. Available at: https://www.europarl.europa.eu/charter/pdf/text_en.pdf (last accessed 17/05/2024)

——— (2019). *Mission Report Following the Ad-Hoc Delegation to Malta 2–4 December 2019. Committee on Civil Liberties, Justice and Home Affairs*. Available at: https://www.europarl.europa.eu/cmsdata/272237/Mission%20Report_Malta%20December%202019.pdf (last accessed 17/05/2024)

——— (2022). *European Parliament resolution of 19 May 2022 on the Commission's 2021 Rule of Law Report (2021/2180(INI))*. Available at: https://eur-lex.europa.eu/legal-content/EN/TXT/?uri=CELEX:52022IP0212 (last accessed 17/05/2024)

——— (2023). *European Parliament Resolution of 1 June 2023 on the Breaches of the Rule of Law and Fundamental Rights in Hungary and Frozen EU Funds*. Available at: https://www.europarl.europa.eu/doceo/document/TA-9-2023-0216_EN.html (last accessed 17/05/2024)

——— (2024). *European Parliament Resolution of 17 January 2024 on the Planned Dissolution of Key Anti-corruption Structures in Slovakia and its Implications for the Rule of Law*. Available at: https://www.europarl.europa.eu/doceo/document/TA-9-2024-0021_EN.html (last accessed 17/05/2024)

European Parliamentary Assembly (1959). *Official Report of Debates, Sixth Joint Meeting of the Members of the Consultative Assembly of the Council of Europe and the Members of the European Parliamentary Assembly*. Available at: https://aei.pitt.edu/34145/ (last accessed 17/05/2024)

European Public Prosecutor's Office (2023). 'Statement regarding the legislative amendments proposed by the Slovak government'. Available at: https://www.eppo.europa.eu/en/news/statement-regarding-legislative-amendments-proposed-slovak-government (last accessed 17/05/2024)

Ewald, A. (2002). 'Civil death: The ideological paradox of criminal disenfranchisement law in the United States'. *Wisconsin Law Review*, 5, 1045–132.

Fairbrass, J. (2011). 'Exploring corporate social responsibility policy in the European Union: A discursive institutionalist analysis'. *JCMS: Journal of Common Market Studies*, 49(5), 949–70.

Falkner, G. & Plattner, G. (2020). 'EU policies and populist radical right parties' programmatic claims: Foreign policy, anti-discrimination and the single market'. *JCMS: Journal of Common Market Studies*, 58(3), 723–39.

BIBLIOGRAPHY

Featherstone, K. (1994). 'Jean Monnet and the "democratic deficit" in the European Union'. *JCMS: Journal of Common Market Studies*, 32(2), 149–70.

Fink-Hafner, D. (2022). 'Slovenia: Ripe for autocratisation'. In: Lynggaard, K., Jensen, M.D., & Kluth, M. (eds). *Governments' Responses to the Covid-19 Pandemic in Europe: Navigating the Perfect Storm*. Cham: Springer, 209–21.

Freund, D. [@daniel_freund] (2022). 'Both Ursula von der Leyen AND Charles Michel sent their congratulations to Viktor Orban today'. *Twitter/X*. Available at: https://twitter.com/daniel_freund/status/1526205198892417025?s=20&t=UlukZkWZ3YH2tZEv_93pdA (last accessed 17/05/2024)

Gaddis, J.L. (2005). *Strategies of Containment: A Critical Appraisal of American National Security Policy during the Cold War*. Oxford: Oxford University Press.

Gaedeke, D. (2016). 'The domination of states: Towards an inclusive republican law of peoples'. *Global Justice: Theory Practice Rhetoric*, 9(1), 1–27.

Gajda-Roszczynialska, K. & Markiewicz, K. (2020). 'Disciplinary proceedings as an instrument for breaking the rule of law in Poland'. *Hague Journal on the Rule of Law*, 12(3), 451–83.

Gehler, M. (2017). '"Preventive hammer blow" or boomerang? The EU "sanction" measures against Austria 2000'. In: Pelinka, A. (ed.). *Austria in the European Union*. London: Routledge, 180–222.

Gerő, M., Fejős, A., Kerényi, S., & Szikra, D. (2023). 'From exclusion to co-optation: Political opportunity structures and civil society responses in de-democratising Hungary'. *Politics and Governance*, 11(1), 16–27.

Gofas, A. & Hay, C. (2010). *The Role of Ideas in Political Analysis: A Portrait of Contemporary Debates*. London: Routledge.

Goodin, R. (2007). 'Enfranchising all affected interests, and its alternatives'. *Philosophy and Public Affairs*, 35(1), 40–68.

Gora, A. & de Wilde, P. (2022). 'The essence of democratic backsliding in the European Union: Deliberation and rule of law'. *Journal of European Public Policy*, 29(3), 342–62.

Grabowska-Moroz, B. & Śniadach, O. (2021). 'The role of civil society in protecting judicial independence in times of rule of law backsliding in Poland'. *Utrecht Law Review*, 17(2), 56–69.

Greenberg, M. (2021). 'Legal interpretation'. *Stanford Encyclopedia of Philosophy*. Available at: https://plato.stanford.edu/archives/fall2021/entries/legal-interpretation (last accessed 17/05/2024)

Gyévai, Z. & Jávor, B. (2023). 'Seizing an unparalleled opportunity to meet the EU strategic objectives'. Available at: https://politicalcapital.hu/

BIBLIOGRAPHY

pc-admin/source/documents/PC_OSF_DirectEUFunding_Cities_Study_2023.pdf (last accessed 17/05/2024)

Haapala, T. & Oleart, A. (2022). *Tracing the Politicisation of the EU: The Future of Europe Debates Before and After the 2019 Elections*. Cham: Palgrave.

Habermas, J. (1989). *The Structural Transformation of the Public Sphere: An Inquiry into a Category of Bourgeois Society*. Cambridge, MA: MIT Press.

Haggard, S. & Kaufman, R. (2021). 'The anatomy of democratic backsliding'. *Journal of Democracy*, 32(4), 27–41.

Hahn, J. (2018). 'Speech of Commissioner Johannes Hahn at the Majalat Civil Society Forum'. Available at: https://ec.europa.eu/commission/presscorner/detail/en/speech_18_4077 (last accessed 17/05/2024)

——— (2019). 'Opening remarks by Commissioner Hahn at the "EU Med means business—Shaping the future of entrepreneurship in the South"'. Available at: https://ec.europa.eu/commission/presscorner/detail/en/speech_19_7109 (last accessed 17/05/2024)

Halmai, G. (2017). 'The early retirement age of the Hungarian judges'. In: Nicola, F. & Davies, B. (eds). *EU Law Stories*. Cambridge: Cambridge University Press, 471–88.

Hanley, S. & Vachudova, M. A. (2020). 'Understanding the illiberal turn: Democratic backsliding in the Czech Republic'. In: Cianetti, L., Dawson, J., & Hanley, S. (eds). *Rethinking 'Democratic Backsliding' in Central and Eastern Europe*. Abingdon & New York: Routledge, 34–54.

Hart, H.M., Eskridge, W.N., Frickey, P.P., & Sacks, A.M. (1994). *The Legal Process: Basic Problems in the Making and Application of Law*. Santa Barbara: Foundation Press.

Hasmath, R., Hildebrandt, T., & Hsu, J.Y. (2019). 'Conceptualizing government-organized non-governmental organizations'. *Journal of Civil Society*, 15(3), 267–84.

Hausteiner, E.M. (2020). 'Can federations expel member states? On the political theory of expulsion'. *Journal of International Political Theory*, 16(1), 47–67.

Hay, C. (2002). *Political Analysis*. Basingstoke: Palgrave.

Hay, C. & Rosamond, B. (2002). 'Globalization, European integration and the discursive construction of economic imperatives'. *Journal of European Public Policy*, 9(2), 147–67.

Herman, L.E. (2019). 'The slow death of Hungarian popular sovereignty'. *EUROPP*. Available at: https://blogs.lse.ac.uk/europpblog/2019/01/16/the-slow-death-of-hungarian-popular-sovereignty/ (last accessed 17/05/2024)

Higgins, J. (2022). 'Spying scandal further increases the worries of Hungarian journalists'. *Media Freedom Rapid Response*. Available at: https://www.mfrr.eu/spying-scandal-further-increases-worries-of-hungarian-journalists/ (last accessed 17/05/2024)

BIBLIOGRAPHY

High Authority of the European Coal and Steel Community (1953). 'The establishment of the common market for steel, Special Report of the High Authority'. *Supplement to the General Report on the Activities of the Community*. Available at: https://core.ac.uk/download/pdf/148848521.pdf (last accessed 17/05/2024)

Hillion, C. (2020). 'Poland and Hungary are withdrawing from the EU'. *Verfassungsblog*. Available at: https://verfassungsblog.de/poland-and-hungary-are-withdrawing-from-the-eu/ (last accessed 17/05/2024)

——— (2021). 'Compromising (on) the general conditionality mechanism and the rule of law'. *Common Market Law Review*, 58(2), 267–84.

Hintikka, J. (1962). 'Cogito, ergo sum: Inference or performance?' *The Philosophical Review*, 71(1), 3–32.

Hix, S. & Bartolini, S. (2006). 'Politics: The right or the wrong sort of medicine for the EU?' *Notre Europe Policy Papers* No. 19.

Hohlmeier, M., Sarvamaa, P., Wolters, L., Freund, D., Rónai, S., & Cseh, K. (2023). 'Draft mission report following the mission to Hungary, 15–17 May 2023'. *Committee on Budgetary Control*. Available at: https://www.europarl.europa.eu/meetdocs/2014_2019/plmrep/COMMITTEES/CONT/DV/2023/09-04/HUCONT_MISSION-REPORTclean_EN.pdf (last accessed 17/05/2024)

Holesch, A. & Kyriazi, A. (2022). 'Democratic backsliding in the European Union: The role of the Hungarian-Polish coalition'. *East European Politics*, 38(1), 1–20.

Hooghe, L. & Marks, G. (2009). 'A postfunctionalist theory of European integration: From permissive consensus to constraining dissensus'. *British Journal of Political Science*, 39(1), 1–23.

Hülsemann, L. (2023). 'Orbán slams Brussels as a "bad contemporary parody" of Soviet Union'. *POLITICO*. Available at: https://www.politico.eu/article/hungary-viktor-orban-brussels-is-a-bad-contemporary-parody-of-soviet-union/ (last accessed 17/05/2024)

Hungary Today (2022). 'EC President von der Leyen congratulates Orbán'. Available at: https://hungarytoday.hu/ec-president-von-der-leyen-congratulates-orban/ (last accessed 17/05/2024)

Hyde, S.D. (2020). 'Democracy's backsliding in the international environment'. *Science*, 369(6508), 1192–6.

Hyde, S.D., Lamb, E., & Samet, O. (2022). 'Promoting democracy under electoral authoritarianism: Evidence from Cambodia'. *Comparative Political Studies*, 56(7), 1029–71.

Hyde-Price, A. (2006). '"Normative" power Europe: A realist critique'. *Journal of European Public Policy*, 13(2), 217–34.

Invernizzi Accetti, C. (2015). *Relativism and Religion: Why Democratic Societies Do Not Need Moral Absolutes*. New York: Columbia University Press.

BIBLIOGRAPHY

Invernizzi Accetti, C. & Zuckerman, I. (2017). 'What's wrong with militant democracy?' *Political Studies* 65(1), 182–99.

Iusmen, I. (2015). 'EU leverage and democratic backsliding in Central and Eastern Europe: The case of Romania'. *JCMS: Journal of Common Market Studies*, 53(3), 593–608.

Jakab, A. & Kirchmair, L. (2021). 'How to develop the EU justice scoreboard into a rule of law index: Using an existing tool in the EU rule of law crisis in a more efficient way'. *German Law Journal*, 22(6), 936–55.

Jałoszewski, M. & Szczygieł, K. (2020). 'EU funding fraud in Poland we know little about'. *Vsquare*. Available at: https://vsquare.org/eu-funding-fraud-in-poland-we-know-little-about/ (last accessed 17/05/2024)

Jaraczewski, J. & Theuns, T. (2022). 'Splitting up Europe's authoritarian alliance'. *Euractiv*. Available at: https://www.euractiv.com/section/politics/opinion/splitting-up-europes-authoritarian-alliance/ (last accessed 17/05/2024)

Jenne, E.K. & Mudde, C. (2012). 'Can outsiders help?' *Journal of Democracy*, 23(3), 147–55.

Jochecová, K., Wax, E., & Barigazzi, J. (2023). 'European socialists suspend Robert Fico's Smer party and its ally Hlas'. *POLITICO*. Available at: https://www.politico.eu/article/european-socialists-suspent-robert-fico-smer-hlas-party/ (last accessed 17/05/2024)

Jourová, V. (2018). 'Speech by Commissioner Jourová on values in times of rising nationalism opening the Fundamental Rights Forum'. Available at: https://ec.europa.eu/commission/presscorner/detail/en/speech_18_5883 (last accessed 17/05/2024)

——— (2020). 'Equipping Europe with better tools to defend the rule of law and democratic values'. Available at: https://ec.europa.eu/commission/presscorner/detail/ro/speech_20_1313 (last accessed 17/05/2024)

——— (2021). 'Opening remarks by Vice-President Jourová at the European Parliament Plenary debate on "Government attempts to silence free media in Poland, Hungary and Slovenia"'. Available at: https://ec.europa.eu/commission/presscorner/detail/en/SPEECH_21_1116 (last accessed 17/05/2024)

——— (2022). 'Speech by Vice-President Jourová at EU DisinfoLab Conference: Fighting disinformation amid Russia's aggression against Ukraine'. Available at: https://ec.europa.eu/commission/presscorner/detail/en/speech_22_6442 (last accessed 17/05/2024)

——— (2023). 'Vice-President Jourová speech on defending EU values in the time of the war'. Available at: https://ec.europa.eu/commission/presscorner/detail/en/speech_23_417 (last accessed 17/05/2024)

Juncker, J.-C. (2018). 'President Jean-Claude Juncker's State of the Union address 2018'. Available at: https://ec.europa.eu/commission/presscorner/detail/en/speech_18_5808 (last accessed 17/05/2024)

——— (2019). 'Speech by President Juncker in the Plenary of the European Parliament at the debate on the conclusions of the European Council meeting of 17 and 18 October 2019'. Available at: https://ec.europa.eu/commission/presscorner/detail/en/speech_19_6143 (last accessed 17/05/2024)

Karácsony, G. & Lakner, Z. (2023). 'To change politics in Hungary, we need to find the switch'. *Green European Journal*. Available at: https://www.greeneuropeanjournal.eu/to-change-politics-in-hungary-we-need-to-find-the-switch/ (last accessed 17/05/2024)

Kelemen, R.D. (2017). 'Europe's other democratic deficit: National authoritarianism in Europe's democratic union'. *Government and Opposition*, 52(2), 211–38.

——— (2020a). 'The European Union's authoritarian equilibrium'. *Journal of European Public Policy*, 27(3), 481–99.

——— (2020b). 'You can't fight autocracy with toothless reports'. *EU Law Live*. Available at: https://eulawlive.com/op-ed-you-cant-fight-autocracy-with-toothless-reports-by-roger-daniel-kelemen/ (last accessed 17/05/2024)

——— (2023). 'The European Union's failure to address the autocracy crisis: MacGyver, Rube Goldberg, and Europe's unused tools'. *Journal of European Integration*, 45(2), 223–38.

——— (2024). 'Will the European Union escape its autocracy trap?' *Journal of European Public Policy*, 1–24 (early view).

Kelemen, R.D. & Pavone, T. (2023). 'Where have the guardians gone? Law enforcement and the politics of supranational forbearance in the European Union'. *World Politics*, 75(4), 779–825.

Kelemen, R.D. & Scheppele, K.L. (2018). 'How to stop funding autocracy in the EU'. *Verfassungsblog*. Available at: https://verfassungsblog.de/how-to-stop-funding-autocracy-in-the-eu/ (last accessed 17/05/2024)

Kirshner, A. (2014). *A Theory of Militant Democracy: The Ethics of Combatting Political Extremism*. New Haven: Yale University Press.

Kochenov, D. (2015). 'Biting intergovernmentalism: The case for the reinvention of article 259 TFEU to make it a viable rule of law enforcement tool'. *Hague Journal on the Rule of Law*, 7, 153–74.

——— (2017). 'Busting the myths nuclear: A commentary on Article 7 TEU', *EUI Working Paper No. LAW 2017/10*. Available at: https://papers.ssrn.com/sol3/papers.cfm?abstract_id=2965087 (last accessed 17/05/2024)

Kochenov, D. & Bárd, P. (2020). 'The last soldier standing? Courts versus politicians and the rule of law crisis in the new member states of the EU'.

In: Ballin, E.H., van der Schyff, G., & Stremler, M. (eds). *European Yearbook of Constitutional Law 2019*. The Hague: TMC Asser Press, 243–87.

Kochenov, D. & Pech, L. (2015). 'Monitoring and enforcement of the rule of law in the EU: Rhetoric and reality'. *European Constitutional Law Review*, 11(3), 512–40.

—— (2016). 'Better late than never? On the European Commission's Rule of Law Framework and its first activation'. *JCMS: Journal of Common Market Studies*, 54(5), 1062–74.

Körösényi, A., Illés, G., & Gyulai, A. (2020). *The Orbán Regime: Plebiscitary Leader Democracy in the Making*. London & New York: Routledge.

Kovács, K. & Scheppele, K.L. (2018). 'The fragility of an independent judiciary: Lessons from Hungary and Poland—and the European Union'. *Communist and Post-Communist Studies*, 51(3), 189–200.

Kovarek, D. & Dobos, G. (2023). 'Masking the strangulation of opposition parties as pandemic response: Austerity measures targeting the local level in Hungary'. *Cambridge Journal of Regions, Economy and Society*, 16(1), 105–17.

Krasner, S.D. & Weinstein, J.M. (2014). 'Improving governance from the outside'. *Annual Review of Political Science*, 17(1), 123–45.

Kreuder-Sonnen, C. (2018). 'An authoritarian turn in Europe and European studies?' *Journal of European Public Policy*, 25(3), 452–64.

Kundnani, H. (2023). *Eurowhiteness: Culture, Empire and Race in the European Project*. London & Oxford: Hurst Publishers & Oxford University Press.

Łacny, J. (2021). 'The Rule of Law Conditionality under regulation no 2092/2020 – Is it all about the money?' *The Hague Journal on the Rule of Law*, 13(1), 79–105.

Leininger, J. & Nowack, D. (2022). 'Protection against autocratisation: How international democracy promotion helped preserve presidential term limits in Malawi and Senegal'. *Third World Quarterly*, 43(2), 309–31.

Leitner, A. (2023). 'Budapest mayor: Access to EU funds "matter of life or death" for Budapest'. *The Budapest Times*. Available at: https://www.budapesttimes.hu/hungary/budapest-mayor-access-to-eu-funds-matter-of-life-or-death-for-budapest/ (last accessed 17/05/2024)

Lepora, C. & Goodin, R.E. (2013). *On Complicity and Compromise*. Oxford: Oxford University Press.

Levitsky, S. & Ziblatt, D. (2019). *How Democracies Die*. London: Crown.

Liboreiro, J. (2024). 'EU Parliament sues Commission over release of frozen funds to Hungary'. *Euronews*. Available at: https://www.euronews.com/my-europe/2024/03/14/european-parliament-sues-commission-over-the-release-of-102-billion-in-frozen-funds-to-hun (last accessed 17/05/2024)

BIBLIOGRAPHY

Lipset, S.M. (1959). 'Some social requisites of democracy: Economic development and political legitimacy', *American Political Science Review*, 53(1), 69–105.

Little, A.T. & Meng, A. (2024). 'Measuring democratic backsliding'. *PS: Political Science & Politics*, 57(2), 1–13.

Lodge, J. (1994). 'Transparency and democratic legitimacy'. *JCMS: Journal of Common Market Studies*, 32(3), 343–68.

Loewenstein, K. (1937a). 'Militant democracy and fundamental rights, I'. *American Political Science Review*, 31(3), 417–32.

——— (1937b). 'Militant democracy and fundamental rights, II'. *American Political Science Review*, 31(4), 638–58.

López-Guerra C. (2005). 'Should expatriates vote?' *The Journal of Political Philosophy*, 13(2), 216–34.

——— (2014). *Democracy and Disenfranchisement: The Morality of Electoral Exclusions*. Oxford: Oxford University Press.

Mair, P. (2007). 'Political opposition and the European Union'. *Government and Opposition*, 42(1), 1–17.

Majone, G. (1994). 'The rise of the regulatory state in Europe'. *West European Politics*, 17(3), 77–101.

Manfredi, C.P. (1998). 'Judicial review and criminal disenfranchisement in the United States and Canada'. *The Review of Politics*, 60(2), 277–306.

Matthes, C. (2023). 'The pact of free cities: Addressing rule of law problems from a local perspective'. *Polish Political Science Yearbook*, 52, 27–40.

Mazepus, H. & Toshkov, D. (2021). 'Standing up for democracy? Explaining citizens' support for democratic checks and balances'. *Comparative Political Studies*, 55(8), 1271–97.

Media Freedom Rapid Response (2022). 'SLAPPs against journalists across Europe'. *Article 19*. Available at: https://www.article19.org/wp-content/uploads/2022/03/A19-SLAPPs-against-journalists-across-Europe-Regional-Report.pdf (last accessed 17/05/2024)

Meijers Committee (2023). 'Comment on the exercise and order of the Presidency of the Council of the EU'. Available at: https://www.commissie-meijers.nl/comment/comment-on-the-exercise-and-order-of-the-presidency-of-the-council-of-the-eu/ (last accessed 17/05/2024)

Meijers, M.J. & van der Veer, H. (2019). 'MEP responses to democratic backsliding in Hungary and Poland. An analysis of agenda-setting and voting behaviour'. *JCMS: Journal of Common Market Studies*, 57(4), 838–56.

Merlingen, M., Mudde, C., & Sedelmeier, U. (2001). 'The right and the righteous? European norms, domestic politics and the sanctions against Austria'. *JCMS: Journal of Common Market Studies*, 39(1), 59–77.

Meyerrose, A.M. (2020). 'The unintended consequences of democracy

promotion: International organizations and democratic backsliding'. *Comparative Political Studies*, 53(10–11), 1547–81.
Michel, C. [@CharlesMichel] (2024). 'Alexei Navalny fought for the values of freedom and democracy'. *Twitter*. Available at: https://twitter.com/CharlesMichel/status/1758461749747966150 (last accessed 17/05/2024)
Miller, D. (2004). 'Holding nations responsible'. *Ethics*, 114(2), 240–68.
Mitten, R. (2002). 'Austria all black and blue: Jörg Haider, the European sanctions, and the political crisis in Austria.' In: Wodak, R. & Pelinka, A. (eds). *The Haider Phenomenon in Austria*. Abingdon & New York: Routledge, 179–212.
Morgan, G. (2020). 'Is the European Union imperialist?' *Journal of European Public Policy*, 27(9), 1424–40.
Morijn, J. (2019). 'Responding to "populist" politics at EU level: Regulation 1141/2014 and beyond'. *International Journal of Constitutional Law*, 17(2), 617–40.
Mos, M. (2020). 'Ambiguity and interpretive politics in the crisis of European values: Evidence from Hungary'. *East European Politics*, 36(2), 267–87.
Mouffe, C. (2005). *On the Political*. Abingdon: Routledge.
——— (2013). *Agonistics: Thinking the World Politically*. London: Verso Books.
Mounk, Y. (2018). *The People vs. Democracy*. Cambridge, MA: Harvard University Press.
Mraz, A. (2023). 'Undemocratic parts in a democratic whole? Normative challenges of EP elections in backsliding EU member states'. Paper presentation at ENROL Workshop on Theoretical Perspectives on Democratic Backsliding in the EU. Oslo, Norway.
Mudde, C. (2021). 'Populism in Europe: An illiberal democratic response to undemocratic liberalism (The Government and Opposition/Leonard Schapiro Lecture 2019)'. *Government and Opposition*, 56(4), 577–97.
Müller, J.W. (2015). 'Should the EU protect democracy and the rule of law inside member states? *European Law Journal*, 21(2), 141–60.
——— (2018). 'Militant democracy and constitutional identity'. In: Jacobsohn, G. & Schor, M. (eds). *Comparative Constitutional Theory*. Cheltenham: Edward Elgar Publishing, 415–35.
Mungiu-Pippidi, A. (2018). 'Romania's Italian-style anticorruption populism'. *Journal of Democracy*, 29(3), 104–16.
Nicolaïdis, K. (2013). 'European democracy and its crisis'. *JCMS: Journal of Common Market Studies*, 51(2), 351–69.
Niklewicz, K. (2017). 'Safeguarding the rule of law within the EU: Lessons from the Polish experience'. *European View*, 16(2), 281–91.

BIBLIOGRAPHY

Noestlinger, N. (2024). 'Lawmakers set to sue EU leaders for "horse-trading" with funds to Hungary'. *Reuters*. Available at: https://www.reuters.com/world/europe/lawmakers-set-sue-eu-leaders-horse-trading-with-funds-hungary-2024-03-12/ (last accessed 17/05/2024).

Nord, M., Lundstedt, M., Altman, D., Angiolillo, F., Borella, C., Fernandes, T., Gastaldi, L., God, A.G., Natsika, N., & Lindberg, S.I. (2024). 'Democracy report 2024'. *University of Gothenburg: V-Dem Institute*. Available at: https://v-dem.net/documents/43/v-dem_dr2024_lowres.pdf (last accessed 17/05/2024)

Norman, L. (2021). 'To democratize or to protect? How the response to anti-system parties reshapes the EU's transnational party system'. *JCMS: Journal of Common Market Studies*, 59(3), 721–37.

Oleart, A. & Theuns, T. (2023). '"Democracy without politics" in the European Commission's response to democratic backsliding: From technocratic legalism to democratic pluralism'. *JCMS: Journal of Common Market Studies*, 61(4), 882–99.

Oliver, P. & Stefanelli, J. (2016). 'Strengthening the rule of law in the EU: The Council's inaction'. *JCMS: Journal of Common Market Studies*, 54(5), 1075–84.

Olsen, T.V. (2019). 'Liberal democratic sanctions in the EU'. In: Malkopoulou, A. & Kirshner, A.S. (eds)/ *Militant Democracy and Its Critics: Populism, Parties, Extremism*. Edinburgh: Edinburgh University Press, 150–68.

——— (2023). 'Ejection for democracy protection: On the expulsion of EU member states. *Res Publica*, 29(2), 321–30.

Olsen, T.V. & Rostboll, C.F. (2017). 'Why withdrawal from the European Union is undemocratic'. *International Theory*, 9(3), 436–65.

Organization for Security and Co-operation in Europe (OSCE) (2022). 'Hungary's parliamentary elections well-run and offered distinct alternatives but undermined by absence of level playing field, international observers say'. Available at: https://www.osce.org/odihr/elections/hungary/515135 (last accessed 17/05/2024)

Owen, D. (2005). 'On genealogy and political theory'. *Political Theory*, 33(1), 110–20.

Pan, Z. & Kosicki, G.M. (2005). 'Framing and the understanding of citizenship'. In: Dunwoody, S., Becker, L.B., McLeod, D.M., & Kosicki, G.M. (eds). *The Evolution of Key Mass Communication Concepts*. New York: Hampton Press, 165–204.

Panyi, S. (2024a). 'How Orbán flooded Central Europe with millions of online ads during election season'. *VSquare*. Available at: https://vsquare.org/orban-central-europe-online-ads-election-season/ (last accessed 17/05/2024)

——— (2024b). 'How the Slovak leader asked for the Kremlin and Orbán's help (and got it)'. *VSquare*. Available at: https://vsquare.org/slovakia-elections-peter-pellegrini-russia-hungary-orban-szijjarto/ (last accessed 17/05/2024)

Pap, A.L. (2017). *Democratic Decline in Hungary: Law and Society in an Illiberal Democracy*. Abingdon & New York: Routledge.

Paris, R. (2002). 'International peacebuilding and the "mission civilisatrice"'. *Review of International Studies*, 28(4), 637–56.

Patberg, M. (2020). 'Can disintegration be democratic? The European Union between legitimate change and regression'. *Political Studies*, 68(3), 582–99.

——— (2021). 'The democratic ambivalence of EU disintegration: A mapping of costs and benefits'. *Swiss Political Science Review*, 27(3), 601–18.

Pech, L. (2020). 'Article 7 TEU: from "nuclear option" to "Sisyphean procedure"?' In: Belavusau, U. & Gliszczyńska-Grabias, A. (eds). *Constitutionalism Under Stress: Essays in Honour of Wojciech Sadurski*. Oxford: Oxford University Press, 157–74.

——— (2021). 'The rule of law'. In: Craig, P. & De Búrca, G. (eds). *The Evolution of EU Law*. Oxford: Oxford University Press, 307–38.

——— (2023). 'The future of the rule of law in the EU'. *Verfassungsblog*. Available at: https://verfassungsblog.de/the-future-of-the-rule-of-law-in-the-eu/ (last accessed 17/05/2024)

Pech, L. & Bárd, P. (2022). 'The Commission 2021 Rule of Law Report and the EU monitoring and enforcement of Article 2 TEU values'. *Policy Department for Citizens' Rights and Constitutional Affairs*. Available at: https://www.europarl.europa.eu/thinktank/en/document/IPOL_STU(2022)727551 (last accessed 17/05/2024)

Pech, L. & Scheppele, K.L. (2017). 'Illiberalism within: Rule of law backsliding in the EU'. *Cambridge Yearbook of European Legal Studies*, 19, 3–47.

Peksen, D. (2019). 'When do imposed economic sanctions work? A critical review of the sanctions effectiveness literature'. *Defence and Peace Economics*, 30(6), 635–47.

Peksen, D. & Drury, A.C. (2009). 'Economic sanctions and political repression: Assessing the impact of coercive diplomacy on political freedoms'. *Human Rights Review*, 10(3), 393–411.

——— (2010). 'Coercive or corrosive: The negative impact of economic sanctions on democracy'. *International Interactions*, 36(3), 240–64.

Pelinka, A. (2001). 'The Haider phenomenon in Austria: Examining the FPO in European context'. *Journal of the International Institute*, 9(1).

Platon, S. (2021). 'Bringing a knife to a gunfight: The European Parliament, the Rule of Law Conditionality, and the action for failure to act'.

BIBLIOGRAPHY

Verfassungsblog. Available at: https://verfassungsblog.de/bringing-a-knife-to-a-gunfight/ (last accessed 17/05/2024)

Plenaire Verslagen (2020). 'Tweede Kamer Der Staten-Generaal'. Available at: https://www.tweedekamer.nl/kamerstukken/plenaire_verslagen/detail/2019–2020/99 (last accessed 17/05/2024)

Poama, A. & Theuns, T. (2019). 'Making offenders vote: Democratic expressivism and compulsory criminal voting'. *American Political Science Review*, 113(3), 796–809.

Popper, K.R. (2013). *The Open Society and Its Enemies: New One-volume Edition*. Princeton: Princeton University Press.

Posner, R.A. (1985). *The Federal Courts: Crisis and Reform*. Cambridge, MA: Harvard University Press.

Pospieszna, P. & Pietrzyk-Reeves, D. (2022). 'Responses of Polish NGOs engaged in democracy promotion to shrinking civic space'. *Cambridge Review of International Affairs*, 35(4), 523–44.

Priebus, S. (2022). 'The Commission's approach to rule of law backsliding: Managing instead of enforcing democratic values?' *JCMS: Journal of Common Market Studies*, 60(6), 1684–700.

Przeworski, A. & Limongi, F. (1997). 'Modernization: Theories and facts'. *World Politics*, 49(2), 155–83.

Puddington, A. (2011). 'Freedom in the world 2011: The authoritarian challenge to democracy'. *Freedom House*. Available at: https://freedomhouse.org/sites/default/files/2020–02/Freedom_in_the_World_2011_complete_book.pdf (last accessed 17/05/2024)

Rafaela, S. & Theuns, T. (2023). 'Why Hungary cannot be permitted to hold the EU presidency'. *EUobserver*. Available at: https://euobserver.com/news/arf56a4fcc (last accessed 17/05/2024)

Raik, K. (2004). 'EU accession of Central and Eastern European countries: Democracy and integration as conflicting logics'. *East European Politics and Societies*, 18(04), 567–94.

Rauh, C. & de Wilde, P. (2018). 'The opposition deficit in EU accountability: Evidence from over 20 years of plenary debate in four member states'. *European Journal of Political Research*, 57(1), 194–216.

Raz, J. (1992). 'The relevance of coherence'. *Boston University Law Review*, 72(2), 273–321.

Regulation 2017/1939 (2017). *Council Regulation (EU) 2017/1939 of 12 October 2017 Implementing Enhanced Cooperation on the Establishment of the European Public Prosecutor's Office*. Available at: https://eur-lex.europa.eu/eli/reg/2017/1939/oj (last accessed 17/05/2024)

Regulation 2018/0136 (2018). *Regulation of the European Parliament and of the Council on the Protection of the Union's Budget in Case of Generalised Deficiencies as Regards the Rule of Law in the Member States*. Available at:

https://eur-lex.europa.eu/legal-content/EN/TXT/?uri=CELEX%3A52018PC0324 (last accessed 17/05/2024)

Regulation 2020/2092 (2020). *Regulation (EU, Euratom) 2020/2092 of the European Parliament and of the Council of 16 December 2020 on a General Regime of Conditionality for the Protection of the Union Budget*. Available at: https://eur-lex.europa.eu/eli/reg/2020/2092/oj (last accessed 17/05/2024)

Reiman, Jeffrey. (2005). 'Liberal and republican arguments against the disenfranchisement of felons'. *Criminal Justice Ethics*, 24(1), 3–18.

Resolution 2021/2075 (2021). 'European Parliament resolution of 15 February 2022 on the challenges for urban areas in the post-COVID-19 era'. Available at: https://www.europarl.europa.eu/doceo/document/TA-9-2022-0022_EN.html (last accessed 17/05/2024)

Resolution 2022/0277 (2022). 'European Parliament legislative resolution of 13 March 2024 on the proposal for a regulation of the European Parliament and of the Council establishing a common framework for media services in the internal market (European Media Freedom Act) and amending Directive 2010/13/EU (COM(2022)0457—C9–0309/2022—2022/0277(COD))'. Available at: https://www.europarl.europa.eu/doceo/document/TA-9-2024-0137_EN.pdf (last accessed 17/05/2024)

Reynders, D. (2020). 'Keynote speech by Commissioner Reynders at the webinar with the Institute of International and European Affairs, Dublin'. Available at: https://ec.europa.eu/commission/presscorner/detail/en/speech_20_2761 (last accessed 17/05/2024)

Richter, S. & Wunsch, N. (2020). 'Money, power, glory: The linkages between EU conditionality and state capture in the Western Balkans'. *Journal of European Public Policy*, 27(1), 41–62.

Rijpkema, B. (2018). *Militant Democracy: The Limits of Democratic Tolerance*. Abingdon & New York: Routledge.

Rippon, S., Zala, M., Theuns, T., de Maagt, S., & van den Brink, B. (2020). 'Thinking about justice: A traditional philosophical framework'. In: Knijn, T. & Lepianka, D. (eds). *Justice and Vulnerability in Europe*. Cheltenham: Edward Elgar Publishing, 16–36.

Runciman, D. (2018). *How Democracy Ends*. London: Profile Books.

Sadurski, W. (2009). 'Adding bite to a bark: The story of Article 7, EU enlargement, and Jorg Haider'. *Columbia Journal of European Law*, 16(3), 385–426.

Sampson, M. & Theuns, T. (2023). 'Comparing Chinese and EU trade agreement strategies: Lessons for normative power Europe?' *International Relations*, 1–24, online first.

Samuels, D. J. (2023). 'The international context of democratic backsliding:

Rethinking the role of third wave "prodemocracy" global actors'. *Perspectives on Politics*, 21(3), 1001–12.

Sangiovanni, A. (2007). 'Justice and the priority of politics to morality'. *The Journal of Political Philosophy*, 16(2), 137–64.

——— (2015). 'How practices matter'. *The Journal of Political Philosophy*, 24(1), 3–23.

Schall, J. (2006). 'The consistency of felon disenfranchisement with citizenship theory. *Harvard Black Letter Law Journal*, (22), 53–93.

Scheiring, G. (2020). *The Retreat of Liberal Democracy: Authoritarian Capitalism and the Accumulative State in Hungary*. Cham: Springer Nature.

Scheppele, K.L. (2012). 'The unconstitutional constitution'. *The New York Times*. Available at: https://archive.nytimes.com/krugman.blogs.nytimes.com/2012/01/02/the-unconstitutional-constitution/ (last accessed 17/05/2024)

——— (2013a). 'The rule of law and the Frankenstate: Why governance checklists do not work'. *Governance*, 26(4), 559–62.

——— (2013b). 'What can the European Commission do when member states violate basic principles of the European Union? The case for systemic infringement actions'. *Verfassungsblog*. Available at: https://verfassungsblog.de/wp-content/uploads/2013/11/scheppele-systemic-infringement-action-brussels-version (last accessed 17/05/2024)

——— (2016). 'Enforcing the basic principles of EU law through systemic infringement actions'. In: Closa, C. & Kochenov, D. (eds). *Reinforcing Rule of Law Oversight in the European Union*. Cambridge: Cambridge University Press, 105–32.

Scheppele, K.L., Kochenov, D.V., & Grabowska-Moroz, B. (2020). 'EU values are law, after all: Enforcing EU values through systemic infringement actions by the European Commission and the member states of the European Union'. *Yearbook of European Law*, 39, 3–121.

Scheppele, K.L. & Morijn, J. (2023). 'What price rule of law?' In: *The Rule of Law in the EU: Crisis and Solutions. Swedish Institute for European Policy Studies*. Available at: https://sieps.se/en/publications/2023/the-rule-of-law-in-the-eu-crisis-and-solutions/ (last accessed 17/05/2024)

Scheppele, K.L. & Pech, L. (2018). 'Didn't the EU learn that these rule-of-law interventions don't work?' *Verfassungsblog*. Available at: https://verfassungsblog.de/didnt-the-eu-learn-that-these-rule-of-law-interventions-dont-work/ (last accessed 17/05/2024)

Scheppele, K.L., Pech, L., & Kelemen, R.D. (2018). 'Never missing an opportunity to miss an opportunity: The Council Legal Service opinion on the Commission's EU budget-related rule of law mechanism'. *Verfassungsblog*. Available at: https://verfassungsblog.de/never-missing-an-opportunity-to-miss-an-opportunity-the-council-legal-service-opinion-on-the-commissions-eu-budget-related-rule-of-law-mechanism/ (last accessed 17/05/2024)

Scheppele, K.L., Pech, L., & Platon, S. (2020). 'Compromising the rule of law while compromising on the rule of law'. *Verfassungsblog*. Available at: https://verfassungsblog.de/compromising-the-rule-of-law-while-compromising-on-the-rule-of-law/ (last accessed 17/05/2024)

Scherz, A. (2013). 'The legitimacy of the demos: Who should be included in the demos and on what grounds?' *Living Reviews in Democracy*, 4, 1–14.

——— (2023). 'How should the EU respond to democratic backsliding? A normative assessment of expulsion and suspension of voting rights from the perspective of multilateral democracy'. Paper presentation at ENROL Workshop on Theoretical Perspectives on Democratic Backsliding in the EU. Oslo, Norway.

Schiltz, C.B. & Brüssel. (2016). 'Jean Asselborn fordert Ausschluss Ungarns aus der EU'. *Die Welt*. Available at: https://www.welt.de/politik/ausland/article158094135/Asselborn-fordert-Ausschluss-Ungarns-aus-der-EU.html (last accessed 17/05/2024)

Schlipphak, B. & Treib, O. (2017). 'Playing the blame game on Brussels: The domestic political effects of EU interventions against democratic backsliding'. *Journal of European Public Policy*, 24(3), 352–65.

Schmidt, V.A. (2010). 'Taking ideas and discourse seriously: Explaining change through discursive institutionalism as the fourth "new institutionalism"'. *European Political Science Review*, 2(1), 1–25.

Scholtes, J. (2020). 'On doctrinal contortions and legal fetishes: A sceptical response to Christophe Hillion'. *Verfassungsblog*. Available at: https://verfassungsblog.de/on-doctrinal-contortions-and-legal-fetishes/ (last accessed 17/05/2024)

Scott, J.M. & Steele, C.A. (2011). 'Sponsoring democracy: The United States and democracy aid to the developing world, 1988–2001'. *International Studies Quarterly*, 55(1), 47–69.

Sedelmeier, U. (2017). 'Political safeguards against democratic backsliding in the EU: The limits of material sanctions and the scope of social pressure'. *Journal of European Public Policy*, 24(3), 337–51.

Seeberg, P. (2009). 'The EU as a realist actor in normative clothes: EU democracy promotion in Lebanon and the European Neighbourhood Policy'. *Democratization*, 16(1), 81–99.

Sen, A. (2006). 'What do we want from a theory of justice?' *The Journal of Philosophy*, 103(5), 215–38.

Sigler, M. (2014). 'Defensible disenfranchisement'. *Iowa Law Review* (99), 1725–44.

Song, S. (2012). 'The boundary problem in democratic theory: Why the demos should be bounded by the state'. *International Theory*, 4(1), 39–68.

BIBLIOGRAPHY

Srinivasan, A. (2022). *The Right to Sex*. London: Bloomsbury Publishing.

Sunstein, C.R. (1995). 'Incompletely theorized agreements'. *Harvard Law Review*, 108(7), 1733–72.

Tangentopoli (2022). 'Fidesz campaigns in schools may be funded by EU money'. *K-Blog*. Available at: https://k.blog.hu/2022/03/11/fidesz_campaigns_in_schools_may_be_funded_by_eu_money (last accessed: 17/05/2024)

Theuns, T. (2017). 'Promoting democracy through economic conditionality in the ENP: A normative critique'. *Journal of European Integration*, 39(3), 287–302.

——— (2019). 'The legitimacy of free trade agreements as tools of EU democracy promotion'. *Cambridge Review of International Affairs*, 32(1), 3–21.

——— (2020). 'Containing populism at the cost of democracy? Political vs. economic responses to democratic backsliding in the EU'. *Global Justice: Theory Practice Rhetoric*, 12(2), 141–60.

——— (2021). 'Pluralist democracy and non-ideal democratic legitimacy: Against functional and global solutions to the boundary problem in democratic theory'. *Democratic Theory*, 8(1), 23–49.

——— (2022). 'The need for an EU expulsion mechanism: Democratic backsliding and the failure of Article 7'. *Res Publica*, 28(4), 693–713.

——— (2023). 'Is the European Union a militant democracy? Democratic backsliding and EU disintegration'. *Global Constitutionalism*, 13(1) 104–25.

Theuns, T. & Daemen, J. (2021). 'The Latvian ban on unvaccinated MPs should be a wake-up call: View'. *Euronews*. Available at: https://www.euronews.com/2021/11/18/the-latvian-ban-on-unvaccinated-mps-should-be-a-wake-up-call-view (last accessed 17/05/2024)

Timmermans, F. (2015). 'The European Union and the rule of law'. Keynote speech at Conference on the Rule of Law, Tilburg University, 31 August 2015.

——— (2019a). 'Speech by First Vice–President Frans Timmermans at the Committee of the Regions' plenary session on fundamental rights and EU values'. Available at: https://ec.europa.eu/commission/presscorner/detail/en/speech_19_7048 (last accessed 17/05/2024)

——— (2019b). 'Speech by First Vice-President Frans Timmermans at "The State of the Union" conference (European University Institute)'. Florence, Italy. Available at: https://ec.europa.eu/commission/presscorner/detail/en/speech_19_7085 (last accessed 17/05/2024)

Uitz, R. (2019). 'The perils of defending the rule of law through dialogue'. *European Constitutional Law Review*, 15(1), 1–16.

van den Brink, M. (2023). 'Taking the gamble? A legal and political analysis of the possible suspension of the Hungarian Council Presidency'. *CEU*

BIBLIOGRAPHY

Democracy Institute. Available at: https://democracyinstitute.ceu.edu/articles/martijn-van-den-brink-taking-gamble-legal-and-political-analysis-possible-suspension (last accessed 17/05/2024)

van den Brink, M. & Kochenov, D. (2019). 'Against associate EU citizenship'. *JCMS: Journal of Common Market Studies*, 57(6), 1366–82.

Várhelyi, O. (2022). 'Western Balkans Summit—New Directions 2022, Sofia'. Available at: https://ec.europa.eu/commission/presscorner/detail/en/speech_22_8318 (last accessed 17/05/2024)

Veenendaal, W. (2019). 'How smallness fosters clientelism: A case study of Malta'. *Political Studies*, 67(4), 1034–52.

Venice Commission (2013). 'Opinion on the Fourth Amendment to the Fundamental Law of Hungary'. CDL-AD(2013)012. Available at: https://www.venice.coe.int/webforms/documents/default.aspx?pdffile=cdl-ad(2013)012-e (last accessed 17/05/2024)

Vinocur, N. (2023). 'Brussels playbook: Germany in recession—Cancel Hungary's presidency?—EU, NATO support grows'. *POLITICO*. Available at: https://www.politico.eu/newsletter/brussels-playbook/germany-in-recession-cancel-hungarys-presidency-eu-nato-support-grows/ (last accessed 17/04/2024)

von Bogdandy, A. & Spieker, L.D. (2019). 'Countering the judicial silencing of critics: Article 2 TEU values, reverse Solange, and the responsibilities of national judges'. *European Constitutional Law Review*, 15(3), 391–426.

von der Leyen, U. (2021a). 'Special address by President von der Leyen at the Davos Agenda Week'. Available at: https://ec.europa.eu/commission/presscorner/detail/en/speech_21_221 (last accessed 17/05/2024)

——— (2021b). 'Speech by President von der Leyen at the opening of the Catholic University's academic year'. Available at: https://ec.europa.eu/commission/presscorner/detail/en/speech_21_7001 (last accessed 17/05/2024)

——— (2021c). 'Speech by President von der Leyen at the EU Ambassadors Conference 2021 via videoconference'. Available at: https://ec.europa.eu/commission/presscorner/detail/en/speech_21_6666 (last accessed 17/05/2024)

——— (2022). 'Keynote address by President von der Leyen at Princeton University'. Available at: https://ec.europa.eu/commission/presscorner/detail/en/speech_22_5723 (last accessed 17/05/2024)

——— (2023). 'Keynote address by President von der Leyen at the high-level "Future of Europe" business event'. Available at: https://ec.europa.eu/commission/presscorner/detail/en/SPEECH_23_381 (last accessed 17/05/2024)

Wagrandl, U. (2018). 'Transnational militant democracy'. *Global Constitutionalism*, 7(2), 143–72.

BIBLIOGRAPHY

Waldner, D. & Lust, E. (2018). 'Unwelcome change: Coming to terms with democratic backsliding'. *Annual Review of Political Science*, 21(1), 93–113.

Walker, S. (2019). 'Islands in the illiberal storm: Central European cities vow to stand together'. *The Guardian*. Available at: https://www.theguardian.com/world/2019/dec/16/islands-in-the-illiberal-storm-central-european-cities-vow-to-stand-together (last accessed 17/05/2024)

White, J. (2019). *Politics of Last Resort: Governing by Emergency in the European Union*. Oxford: Oxford University Press.

White, J. & Ypi, L. (2016). *The Meaning of Partisanship*. Oxford: Oxford University Press.

Wójcik, A. (2022). 'How the EU can defend media freedom and pluralism in Hungary and Poland'. *German Marshall Fund*. Available at: https://www.gmfus.org/sites/default/files/2022-11/Wojcik%20-%20Media%20Hungary%20Poland%20-%20paper.pdf (last accessed 17/05/2024)

Wolff, J. (2015). 'Social equality, relative poverty and marginalised groups'. In: Hull, G. (ed.). *The Equal Society: Essays on Equality in Theory and Practice*. Lanham, MD: Lexington Books, 21–41.

Wolfs, W. (2022). *European Political Parties and Party Finance Reform*. Cham: Palgrave Macmillan.

Wolkenstein, F. (2020). 'Partisan complicity in democratic backsliding'. *Global Justice: Theory Practice Rhetoric*, 12(2), 117–40.

——— (2021). 'European political parties' complicity in democratic backsliding'. *Global Constitutionalism*, 11(1), 55–82.

Wonka, A., Gastinger, M., & Blauberger, M. (2023). 'The domestic politics of EU action against democratic backsliding: public debates in Hungarian and Polish newspapers'. *Journal of European Public Policy*, 1–24 (early view).

Wunsch, N. & Gessler, T. (2023). 'Who tolerates democratic backsliding? A mosaic approach to voters' responses to authoritarian leadership in Hungary'. *Democratization*, 30(5), 914–37.

Zala, M., Rippon, S., Theuns, T., de Maagt, S., & van den Brink, B. (2020). 'From political philosophy to messy empirical reality'. In: Knijn, T. & Lepianka, D. (eds). *Justice and Vulnerability in Europe*. Cheltenham: Edward Elgar Publishing, 37–53.

Zgut, E. (2022). 'Informal exercise of power: Undermining democracy under the EU's radar in Hungary and Poland'. *Hague Journal on the Rule of Law*, 14(2–3), 287–308.

Żuk, P. (2020). 'One leader, one party, one truth: Public television under the rule of the populist right in Poland in the Pre-election period in 2019'. *Javnost–The Public*, 27(3), 287–307.

INDEX

Note: Page numbers followed by "*f*" refer to figures.

Abascal, Santiago, 7, 147
Adamowicz, Paweł, 41
agonism, 160
agonistic, 63, 156
agonistic democracy, 159–60
aHang (The Voice), 121
Ahtisaari, Martti, 33
Akcja Demokracja (Democracy Action), 121
Alemanno, Alberto, 120, 141
'All Subjected Principle', 76–7, 82
Amsterdam, Treaty of, 23, 24, 25, 28, 31, 33
Arendt, Hannah, 192
Aristotle, 142
Article 2 (TEU), 11, 13, 25–6, 71–2, 74, 80, 81, 86, 88, 89, 96, 116, 123, 133, 143, 175, 195
Article 7 (TEU), 4, 12, 13, 38–9, 43, 47, 57–8, 65–6, 70, 72–8, 84, 90, 91, 95, 111, 116, 131, 132–4, 137, 141, 142, 179, 180, 197
Asselborn, Jean, 191–2

asylum seekers, 85
Austria, 23, 43, 174, 179
    parliamentary election (1990), 29–30
    sanctions, 28–35, 133
Austrian People's Party (ÖVP), 28, 30–1, 32, 34–5
Authority for European Political Parties and European Political Foundations, 87–90
autocracy, containing, 98, 127–50
    Cold War containment, 128, 129
    'containment', term, 128–30
    economic measures of containment, 130
    hard legal containment (maximal coherent exclusion), 132, 137–43, 149
    legal containment, 129–30, 132–43
    normative incoherence, 131
    political containment, 129, 130, 143–8, 149, 150
    pre-Article 7 procedure, 134
    soft legal containment (social

247

INDEX

pressure, dialogue and monitoring), 132, 133–7

Badano, Gabriele, 187
Bárd, Petra, 135
Batory, Agnes, 114
Bentham, Jeremy, 158
Biden, Joe, 54
Bolsonaro, Jair, 147
Bonheur, Rosa, 158
Brussels, 42, 154–5
budget conditionality, 70, 86–7, 169, 180
    Rule of Law Conditionality Regulation, 13, 14, 42, 44, 58, 70, 84, 86–7, 91, 107, 117–22, 123, 130, 169, 170, 180
BZÖ, 34

Cardona, Chris, 167
Caruana Galizia, Daphne, 167–168
Central European University, 37
Chamon, Merijn, 120
Charter of Fundamental Rights, 124
Citizens, Equality, Rights and Values programme, 178
civic freedom, 157
Civic Platform (PO), 39
civil society, 37, 49, 61, 151, 158
climate goals (2030), 177
Clinton, Hillary, 113
Cohesion Fund, 118
collective responsibility, 108
Committee of the Regions, 31
Common Provisions Regulation, 124, 130, 169
communism, 128
complicity. *See* EU complicity, correcting

containment. *See* autocracy, containing
Constitutional Treaty, 25, 26, 28
Council Legal Services (2018), 12, 39
Council of the European Union, 14, 16, 96, 98, 127, 166, 187, 193
'Council of Wise Men', 32–3, 35
COVID-19 pandemic, 42, 131
    recovery funds, 118–20, 170
Cseh, Katalin, 171
Czech Civic Democrats, 148
Czech Republic, 24, 197

'Daphne's Law', 168
Delors, Jacques, 25
democratic contestation, 60, 61, 62
democratic deficit, 25
democratic fundamentalism, 183
Denmark, 24–5, 35, 136
depoliticization, 19, 22, 23, 25, 28–42, 56–61, 66
disinformation, 52, 57

EU complicity, correcting, 97–8, 101–25, 166
    capitulation on conditionality in the European Council, 115–22
    collective responsibility, 108
    complicity, notion of, 104–8
    transnational complicity, 110–15
    conciliatory Commission, 110–15
    'EU transnational complicity', 104
    redress and reparations, 99, 106–8, 122–5, 166
EU democracy protection tools, 65–91

INDEX

Article 2 (TEU), 11, 13, 25–6, 71–2, 74, 80, 81, 86, 88, 89, 96, 116, 123, 133, 143, 175, 195

Article 7 (TEU), 4, 12, 13, 38–9, 43, 47, 57–8, 65–6, 70, 72–8, 84, 90, 91, 95, 111, 116, 131, 132–4, 137, 141, 142, 179, 180, 197

Article 7 as a performative contradiction, 78–83, 168

Article 7 sanction, normative incoherence of, 75–8

deregistration of European political parties and foundations, 70, 87–90

disenfranchising an autocratic state, 83

EU budget conditionality, 70, 86–7, 169, 180

infringement actions, 70, 84–6

EU funds, 86–7, 107, 111, 117–19, 122, 123, 164, 170–1

recovery funds, 118–19, 170

for Ukraine, 124

EU Justice Scoreboard/Scorecard, 58, 111

EU Regulation 1141/2014, 13, 15, 70, 87–90, 91, 131

EU-14, 31, 32, 33, 34–5, 174

European Central Bank, 118, 190

European Coal and Steel Community, 24, 112

European Commission, 4, 12, 13, 14, 25, 35, 41, 98, 103, 107, 109, 123, 127, 134

appointment of Commissioners, 141

conceptualization of democracy, 45–63, 51f, 95, 155–6

'data protection and cyber security' frame, 54–5

democracy without politics, 49–50, 56–61, 179–80

'geopolitical threat' frame, 52, 53

'Guardian of the [European] Treaties', 111–12, 115

infringement actions, 84–6, 180

'international cooperation' frame, 54

'media freedom' frame, 53–4, 57, 60

'pluralism' frame, 55

'problem-solving' and 'minority protection' frames, 55–6

'quality of information' frame, 52–3, 57, 60, 61

rule of law as a prerequisite for democracy, 49–56, 57

Rule of Law Report, 11, 58, 111, 134–6

'rule of law/HR frame', 50–1

'technical' view of problems, 58–9, 63

European Council, 14, 16, 24, 26, 42, 57, 72, 96, 103, 109, 127, 166, 189, 193

capitulation on conditionality in, 115–22

COVID-19 recovery funds, 118–20, 170

decision-making, 78, 81

key actor in Article 7, 116

principle of 'equal rotation', 142–3

rotating presidency, 139–40, 142–3

summit (Dec 2023), 124

European Court of Human Rights, 135

European Court of Justice (ECJ), 31, 41, 42, 47, 79, 85, 86, 111, 114–15, 120, 124, 135, 190

249

INDEX

European Law Journal, 132
European People's Party (EPP), 74, 102, 104
European Peoples' Party Convention Group, 25–6
European Public Prosecutor's Office, 58
European Regional Development Fund (ERDF), 118
European Social Fund (ESF), 118
European Union (EU)
  membership fatalism, 12, 16, 19, 21–2, 23–8, 35–44, 66, 95
  membership, 4–5
  withdrawal procedure, 25–6
Euroscepticism, 21, 24, 29, 35
expressive consistency, 69–70, 78–83
expulsion mechanism, 99, 191–3
costs of excluding autocratic members, 194–6

Farage, Nigel, 145
Fico, Robert, 57, 176, 197
Fidesz (Fiatal Demokraták Szövetsége), 6, 8, 36–8, 42, 73, 74, 102, 104, 107, 113–14, 145, 148, 170–1, 177–8
  Fidesz-Christian Democratic People's Party alliance, 113
financial crisis (2008), 45
Finland, 23
Forbidden Stories, 146
Foucault, Michel, 20
Fratelli d'Italia, 148
Freedom House, 113
Freedom Party of Austria (FPÖ), 28–35, 43, 174
Frowein, Jochen, 33
Fundamental Rights Forum, 52

'GONGO-ization', 154

Goodin, Robert, 102, 107
Gora, Anna, 62
Greece, 24
Guterres, António, 30

Habermas, Jürgen, 160
Hahn, Johannes, 47, 54–5, 56
Haider, Jörg, 29, 30–1, 32, 43
Hallstein, Walter, 112
hard legal containment. *See* autocracy, containing
Herman, Lise Esther, 159
Hillion, Christophe, 16
Hungarian Constitutional Court, 37
Hungarian Media Authority, 114
Hungary, 3, 5, 8, 12, 14, 15, 23, 24, 57, 100, 117, 121, 122, 123, 161, 170–1, 174, 179
  Article 7 proceedings, 12, 38–9, 43, 57, 73–4, 113
  budget conditionality, 44
  cohesion funds, 118, 124
  constitutional reforms, 113–15
  European Regional Development Fund (ERDF), 118
  EU-level COVID-19 recovery funding, 119, 192
  GDP, 118
  immigration policy, 85
  judiciary reforms, 114–15, 124
  justice system, 37
  media freedom, 54, 114, 145
  media laws, restructuring, 114
  parliamentary elections (2022), 144–6, 173
  presidency of the Council, 139, 140, 141, 149
  Rule of Law Report, 136
  systemic infringement actions against, 85

INDEX

under Orbán's leadership, 35–9
veto power, 42, 44, 119, 120, 124
withholding EU funding to, 107, 118

'deal theory, 9–10, 15, 67
immanent critique, 68–71, 84, 117
immigration, 147, 163
infringement actions, 70, 84–6
Intergovernmental Conference of the European Union (1996), 24
'invisible hand' metaphor, 147
Israel, 31
Italy, 6, 24, 57

Jaraczewski, Jakub, 107
Jourová, Věra, 47, 51, 52, 53, 54, 168
Juncker Commission, 48, 51
Juncker, Jean-Claude, 47, 49, 53, 56

Karácsony, Gergely, 171
Kennan, George F., 128
Kirshner, Alexander, 185–7
Klestil, Thomas, 32
Klima, Viktor, 30
Kochenov, Dimitry, 84
Kuciak, Ján, 163
Kurz, Sebastian, 34
Kušnírová, Martina, 163

Latvian Parliament, 131
Law and Justice Party (PiS), 6, 7, 8, 10, 39–42, 148
  judiciary control, 40
Le Pen, Marine, 7, 63, 145, 148
Leeden, Michael, 162
legal containment, 129–30, 132–43
Lepora, Chiara, 102, 107

Lipset, Seymour M., 164
Lisbon Treaty, 23, 26, 28, 72
Loewenstein, Karl, 183, 185, 195

Maastricht Treaty, 24–5, 27
Mahler, Gustav, 158
Majone, Giandomenico, 159
Malta, 167–8, 176
Meijers Committee, 140–1
Meloni, Giorgia, 57, 148
membership fatalism, 12, 16, 19, 21–2, 23–8, 35–44, 66, 95
Merkel, Angela, 119
Metsola, Roberta, 146
Michel, Charles, 145–6, 150
Milei, Javier, 147
militant democracy, 99, 181–5
  existential threat and necessity conditions, 185–8, 190–1
  justifications for, 185–90
  term, 183–4
Mishustin, Mikhail, 163
Mitten, Richard, 33
modernization theory, 164
Monnet, Jean, 112
Mouffe, Chantal, 159–60
MSZP (Hungarian Socialist Party), 36, 113
Müller, Jan-Werner, 132, 191
Multiannual Financial Framework, 14, 120
Muscat, Joseph, 167
Muscat, Michelle, 167
'muzzle law', 40

nationalism, 147
Nazi Party, regime, 24, 29
the Netherlands, 3, 119
NextGenEU funds, 123, 124, 170
Nice, Treaty of, 25, 28, 29, 33, 43
Nicomachean Ethics (Aristotle), 142
non-governmental organizations (NGOs), 37

INDEX

non-ideal (theory), 10, 15–6, 67–8, 131, 157
Norman, Ludvig, 90
normative political theory, 66–7, 68–9
Nuti, Alasia, 187

Orbán, Viktor, 36–8, 46, 63, 113, 114, 115, 124, 163
   2022 re-election and congratulations, 145–6, 149
Oreja, Marcelino, 33
Organization for Security and Co-operation in Europe (OSCE), 40–1, 173
ÖVP-BZÖ coalition, 34

Panyi, Szabolcs, 163
Partit Laburista, 167, 176
Party of European Socialists (PES), 176
Pech, Laurent, 135, 137
Pegasus Project, 146
Pellegrini, Peter, 163
pluralist democracy, 15–16, 49, 59–63, 95–9
   See also autocracy, containing; EU complicity, correcting
pluralist democracy, cultivating, 98–9, 151–78
   to counteract injustice externalities, 168–71
   counterargument to, 155, 173
   democratic pluralism, 60
   objection from illegitimate partisanship, 172–6
   partisans of, 161–2
   pluralist democratic ideal, 155–61
   political pluralism, 158–9
   reasons for, 153, 161–71
   to repair the harms of democratic backsliding, 166–8
   for supporting pro-democratic actors, 162–6
   value pluralism, 158
Poland, 6, 8, 10, 12, 14, 23, 24, 39–42, 47, 57, 100, 107, 117, 121, 122, 123, 161, 179
   Article 7 proceedings, 12, 39, 41, 43, 57, 73, 74, 113
   budget conditionality, 44
   cohesion funds, 118, 124
   COVID-19 recovery funding, 119, 192
   EU funds, 118 GDP, 118
   general elections (2023), 3
   judiciary violations, 123
   media freedom, 40–1, 54
   NextGenEU funds, 123, 124
   veto power, 42, 44, 119, 120
Polish People's Party (PSL), 39
political containment. *See* autocracy, containing
political parties, deregistration of, 70, 87–90
political pluralism. *See* pluralist democracy, cultivating
populist radical right (PRR), 6, 22, 35, 57
Portugal, 24, 31–2, 35
practice-dependent political theory, 9–11, 13, 67–8
Putin, Vladimir, 145

radical right-wing populists, 147–8
Rafaela, Samira, 140–1
Rassemblement National, 7, 148
Raz, Joseph, 68
Recovery and Resilience Plan, 42, 44, 123
recovery funds, 118–20, 170
Reding, Viviane, 114
redress, 99, 106–8, 122–5, 166
Reflection Group, 24, 27, 28

INDEX

reparations, 106–8, 166
Reynders, Didier, 48, 51
Riess Passer, Susanne, 32
right-wing populism, 21
Rijpkema, Bastiaan, 185–6
Rot-blaue Koalition, 29
Rule of Law and Fundamental Rights, 51
Rule of Law Conditionality Regulation/Instrument (2020), 13, 14, 42, 44, 58, 70, 84, 86–7, 91, 107, 111–2, 117–22, 123, 130, 169, 170, 180
'rule of law conditionality', 86–7
'Rule of Law Framework' (2014), 111, 115, 133, 137
'Rule of Law Mechanism' (2019), 11, 111, 134–5
'Rule of Law Report', 11, 58, 111, 134–6
Rule of Law Review Cycle, 134–5, 137
Russia, aggression against Ukraine, 6, 52, 53, 107
Rutte, Mark, 192, 196

Sadurski, Wojciech, 28, 82–3
Salvini, Matteo, 145
sanctions mechanisms, 21, 22–3, 27, 28–35, 60, 74, 116
Scheppele, Kim Lane, 39, 84, 123
Schuman, Robert, 24
Schüssel, Wolfgang, 32
Sedelmeier, Ulrich, 133, 135
Slovakia, 24, 174, 197
    Slovak election, 163
Slovenia, 54
Smer party, 163, 176, 197
Smith, Adam, 147
Social Democratic Party (SPÖ), 29, 30, 34
solidarity tax, 170

Solidarna Polska (United Poland), 8
Spain, 24, 147
strategic lawsuits against public participation (SLAPPs), 145, 166–8
Sweden Democrats, 148
Sweden, 23
SZDSZ (Alliance of Free Democrats), 36
Szijjártó, Péter, 163

Timmermans, Frans, 38, 47, 51, 56
Treaty on European Union (TEU), 28
    Article 2, 11, 13, 25–6, 71–2, 74, 80, 81, 86, 88, 89, 96, 116, 123, 133, 143, 175, 195
    Article 4, 172
    Article 4.2, 155
    Article 7, 4, 12, 13, 38–9, 43, 47, 57–8, 65–6, 70, 72–8, 79–80, 84, 90, 91, 95, 111, 116, 131, 132–4, 137, 141, 142, 179, 180, 197
    Article 7.2, 73–4, 83, 116, 133
    Article 7.3, 76–7, 82, 132, 133, 191
    Article 9, 195
    Article 10, 72, 116, 131, 195
    Article 10.3, 11, 72
    Article 15, 120
    Article 16.9, 139–41
    Article 17, 110, 175
    Article 17.5, 141
    Article 20, 198
    Article 50, 16, 195
Treaty on the Functioning of the European Union (TFEU)
    Article 235.b, 141
    Article 236.b, 140

INDEX

Articles 258–60, 13, 14, 70, 84–6, 110–11, 122–3
Article 326–34, 197
Trump, Donald, 147
TVP (broadcaster), 41

Ukraine
 EU accession talks, 147, 170
 EU funding for, 124
 invasion of, 6, 52, 53, 107
United Kingdom, 156
United Right (ZP) alliance, 39
US foreign policy, 128
USSR, 128

value pluralism. *See* pluralist democracy, cultivating
van den Brink, Martijn, 141–2
Várhelyi, Olivér, 48, 54

V-Dem Liberal Democracy Index, 136
Vlaams Blok (now Vlaams Belang), 35
von der Leyen, Ursula, 47, 49, 52–3, 54, 55, 56, 145, 146
Vox party, 6–7
Vučic, Aleksandar, 147

Wagrandl, Ulrich, 132, 190
Weimar Germany, 183
West Germany, 24
Wilde, Pieter de, 62
Wilders, Geert, 3, 147
Wolkenstein, F., 104
World Justice Project Rule of Law Index, 136

Ziobro, Zbigniew, 8